SHEBA REVEALED

Also by Nigel Groom

Frankincense and Myrrh: A Study of the Arabian Incense Trade
London, Longman, and Beirut, Librairie du Liban, 1981

A Dictionary of Arabic Topography and Placenames
London, Longman, and Beirut, Librairie du Liban, 1983

The Perfume Handbook
London, Chapman and Hall, 1992

The New Perfume Handbook
London, Blackie Academic and Professional, 1997

The Perfume Companion
London, Apple/Quintet, 1999

SHEBA REVEALED
A Posting to Bayhan in the Yemen

Nigel Groom

LCAS

The London Centre of Arab Studies

Sheba Revealed
A Posting to Bayhan in the Yemen

© Nigel Groom 2002

Produced and published in 2002 by the London Centre of Arab Studies Ltd,
63 Great Cumberland Place, London W1H 7LJ
www.lcas.co.uk

Edited by William Facey
Designed by Marsha Lebon

A catalogue record for this book is available from the British Library

ISBN 1 900404 31 1

Typesetting and digital artwork by Falcon Electronic Imaging, Cambridge, UK
Printed and bound in the UK by Creative Print & Design (Wales), Ebbw Vale

To my wife
Lorna
with love

and to the memory of
Sharif Salih bin Nassir al-Habili
than whom I could not have had a better friend in difficult times

Contents

Illustrations

Maps

Photographs

All photographs were taken by the author.

Between pages 64 and 65:

1. Sharif Hussain bin Ahmad al-Habili, regent of Bayhan on behalf of his son, Amir Salih bin Hussain.
2. The rooftops of Asaylan, looking south over Wadi Bayhan.
3. Bayhan al-Qasab seen from Sharif Hussain's *dar*.
4. Sharif Hussain's white stuccoed *dar* at Bayhan al-Qasab.
5. Jabal Raydan towers over the Political Officer's *dar* at Bayhan al-Qasab.
6. Bayhan al-Qasab: looking north from the Political Officer's *dar*.
7. A Bal Harith salt caravan arrives at Bayhan al-Qasab.
8. Sharif Awadh bin Ahmad al-Habili, elder brother of Sharif Hussain.
9. Shaykh Qassim bin Ahmad.
10. Sharif Salih bin Nassir al-Habili, a cousin of Sharif Hussain, with two of his sons (Haydar on the right).
11. Sharif Abdullah bin Salih, a cousin of Sharif Hussain.
12. Amir Salih bin Hussain (right), with Sharif Awadh bin Ahmad (centre) and Shaykh Nassir bin Hussain of the Bal Harith.
13. Sharif Salih bin Abdullah, one of Sharif Hussain's Wakils.
14. Said bin Ali al-Harithi, a shaykh of the Bal Harith.

15. Shaykh Ali bin Munassir al-Harithi with his son Abdullah al-Bahri at his right hand, and two of his younger sons.
16. A group of Bal Harith tribesmen, led by their *aqil*.
17. Shaykhs assemble in Bayhan al-Qasab for the first meeting of the *Majlis al-Uqal* (Council of Shaykhs).
18. Sayyid Muhammad Aatiq al-Bakri, Qadhi of Bayhan.

Between pages 256 and 257:

19. Wadi Bayhan, looking east from the walls of Hayd Kuhlan, ancient Tumna: a camel-draw well irrigates fields overlooked by the ruins of a Qatabanian temple.
20. Remains of the main temple of Tumna (Hayd Kuhlan).
21. Alabaster carvings and an iron anklet from Qatabanian tombs near Tumna (Hayd Kuhlan). (Now in the Cambridge Museum of Archaeology.)
22. Inscription R 3688 of c.160 BC in Shaab Labakh recording rights given to the Labakh people by the Qatabanian king to collect rents in Dathina. A corner of inscription R 3689 can be seen at top right.
23. The paved Qatabanian camel road, over the Mablaqa pass between Bayhan and Ayn.
24. The giant "pebble" near the summit of Jabal Raydan.
25. Ruins of the main temple at Hajar Hinnu az-Zurir, ancient Haribat, in Wadi Harib.
26. Shaykh Qassim bin Ahmad stands by a section of the imposing masonry of Hajar Hinnu az-Zurir, Wadi Harib.
27. Part of an ancient necropolis on the slope of Jabal Dhahat Shaqir, in the Ayn district.
28. Husn al-Aatabar, in Wadi Ayn, belonging to the Amr tribe.
29. A *husn* or stronghold in Wadi Bayhan.
30. A *ghayl* in the upper reaches of Wadi Bayhan.
31. Oxen being used to amass an earth dam.
32. The fort at Najd al-Mizr, the Government Guard outpost in upper Wadi Bayhan, in Arifi territory.
33. Arifi tribesmen painted with indigo.
34. Gipsy dancing girls, or *shahadh*, with their troupe of musicians.
35. Indigo vats and indigo cloth hanging up to dry in Suq Abdullah, Bayhan al-Qasab.
36. Jews in al-Haraja, upper Wadi Bayhan, weaving one of the typical Bayhan rugs.
37. The village of al-Haraja, in upper Wadi Bayhan, nestling among acres of eroded ancient Qatabanian fields.

Preface

This is an account, drawn from diaries of fifty-odd years ago but written while the memories were still clear, about one small area of what is now Yemen in one brief period long ago. It seeks to provide a picture of an extraordinary people and a fascinating land in closer detail than is normally found in books about Arabia, which mostly portray wide landscapes on broad canvases. It is intended to be didactic, because the past of the people of Arabia is a key to understanding their present outlooks and values, and it describes a way of life which is fast disappearing and will soon be forgotten altogether if it is not recorded. But I hope my tale will be found entertaining, for that has been my purpose too.

My fascination with the pre-Islamic history of my area, which may once have been ruled by the Queen of Sheba herself if one believes the ancient story, needs no explanation. In Bayhan I was surrounded by ancient sites and inscriptions, most of which had never been reported before. I hope that my description of these, and my account of the coming of the first archaeological expedition to excavate them, will interest both the travellers and the archaeologists who visit them today.

There was a secondary object in writing this story, which was to provide, through my personal experiences, a description of the life young men of the Colonial Administrative Service lived, albeit in my case in perhaps the roughest land to administer anywhere in the British Empire. In telling something of the responsibilities we shouldered, the difficulties we faced, the feelings we felt, I hoped to demonstrate that, while respecting their traditions, we were deeply concerned to assist the people of our territories to face the modern world, and this despite the fact that, immediately post-war, there was very little money available to improve their lot. If this book removes some fraction of the current misconceptions about "colonialism" then the writing of it will have been well justified.

I have had to face the usual difficulties over transliteration of Arabic names and place-names. In the 1940s in South Arabia we had no formal system and either followed old precedents, where they existed, or invented spellings which best conformed with the sounds. As the subsequent compiler of a dictionary which sets out how Arabic place-names should now properly be transliterated (under the internationally recognised PGN/PCGN system when used with the English language) I felt obliged to practise what I had preached. My place-names are therefore written in accordance with that system, modified under the accepted convention that, in informal works such as this, where exactitude is not important, the diacritics, and what Arabists know as *hamza* and *'ayn*, can be dropped. But diacritics (principally lines above vowels to indicate their prolongation and dots below consonants to show Arabic consonants for which there are no real equivalents) are sometimes important indicators of how a word should be pronounced, so that without them the system does not always work very satisfactorily. Accordingly, I have provided a phonetic rendering of the pronunciations in brackets on the first occurrence of some of the more significant place-names, and, while spelling most of the personal names and other words under the same system, have written some of them in a more phonetic form. This in itself creates some difficulties. The Arabic letter "j", pronounced as in "jam" and "jump" in most parts of the Arab world, is pronounced as a hard "g" (as in "gun" and "gag") in most of South-west Arabia. I have retained it as a "j" in the transliteration here for the sake of consistency with what is found in other books and maps, but readers will have to bear in mind that, for example, the word *jabal* (a mountain) is pronounced "gabal" in SW Arabia. I have also used the spelling "Hussain" rather than "Husayn" because that is the conventional and widely recognised spelling for this personal name in the West. While avoiding all diacritics in the main text I have however introduced the line above a vowel, signifying prolongation, where relevant in the Glossary to assist in pronunciation. This may all sound very complicated, but it should only worry people who take their Arabic and their Arabian geography very seriously!

The system for referencing inscriptions (and their translations) has developed in a very haphazard way over the years. The principal corpus of recorded inscriptions used to be the *Répertoire d'épigraphie sémitique* (RES) and the *Corpus Inscriptionum Semiticarum, Inscriptiones Sabaeas et Himyariticas Continens* (CIH), published in large tomes in many volumes. Most of the important inscriptions discovered up to around the Second World War are to be found in these and are recorded as RES (sometimes abbreviated to R) or CIH respectively, followed by a serial number (e.g. RES 3689).

Subsequently, while some recording in RES continued and a computerised French corpus, *Corpus des inscriptions et antiquités sud-arabes* (CIAS), was founded in 1977 by Dr Jacqueline Pirenne, most inscriptions have been published in academic books, papers and journals, many being referenced by the name of the discoverer or translator with his own serial number. Thus many of the inscriptions I found in Bayhan, which were sent by the Aden Director of Antiquities to Professor Gonzague Ryckmans in Louvain, were published in the Louvain journal *Le Muséon*, where Ryckmans recorded them as Groom 1, Groom 2 etc., but these are also and more usually referred to by the number of the paragraph in his paper in *Le Muséon* in which he discussed them. Hence the Mablaqa inscription Groom 12 is also Ryckmans 389, but an inadequate copy had previously been obtained by Glaser and is recorded as RES 3550. Most of the leading epigraphists have recorded very many inscriptions with their own names and serial numbers in this way, and these are frequently abbreviated, so that, for example, Glaser becomes Gl (e.g. Gl 1604), Ryckmans becomes Ryck and Jamme becomes J or Ja. Museums may have their own reference numbers for inscriptions in their collections. There are many complications. Inscriptions frequently have to be published more than once to allow a revision of the text; for instance a photograph may enable corrections to be made to a text previously known only by a hand-written copy (as with my photographs of the Labakh inscriptions), or a significant new meaning of a word or phrase may have been established, or scholars may differ over the meaning of a text, or there may even be inadvertent duplication. Hence, for example, Gl 731 = RES 4814 = Ja 2840 (a Sabaean inscription near Marib). With thousands of ESA inscriptions now recorded and translated in a large number of books and journals in different languages by scholars of many different nationalities, it can be extremely difficult to ascertain where a particular inscription is to be found even when a reference number is known.

Professor Kenneth Kitchen's monumental work on the major inscriptions, which is still in progress (see the Bibliography), should greatly help to ease this situation. In this book I have tried, at my publisher's behest, to give a reference number to identify all the inscriptions mentioned, but it would be too complicated for the needs of the book to define more exactly where they have been published.

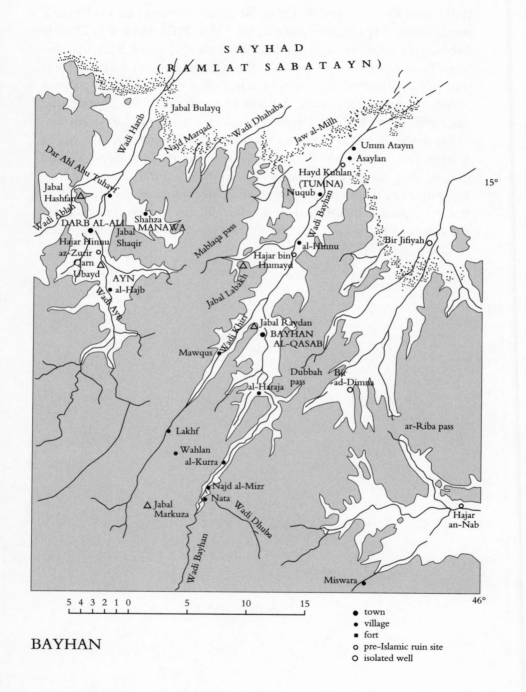

SAYHAD
(RAMLAT SABATAYN)

Jabal Bulayq

Wadi Harib

Najd Marqad

Wadi Dhahaba

Jaw al-Milh

Umm Ataym
Asaylan

Dar Ahl Abu Tuhayf

15°

Hayd Kuhlan
(TUMNA)
Nuqub

Wadi Bayhan

Jabal
Hashfan

Wadi Ablah

Shahza

DARB AL-ALI   MANAWA

Jabal
Shaqir

Mablaqa pass

al-Hinnu

Bir Jifiyah

Hajar Hinnu
az-Zurir
Qarn
Ubayd

Hajar bin
Humayd

AYN
al-Hajb

Jabal Labakh

Wadi Ayn

Wadi Khirr

Jabal Raydan
BAYHAN
AL-QASAB

Mawqus

Dubbah
pass

Bir
ad-Dimna

al-Haraja

ar-Riba pass

Lakhf

Wahlan
al-Kurra

Najd al-Mizr
Nata

Jabal
Markuza

Wadi Dhuba

Wadi Bayhan

Hajar
an-Nab

Miswara

5 4 3 2 1 0   5   10   15

46°

● town
● village
■ fort
○ pre-Islamic ruin site
○ isolated well

BAYHAN

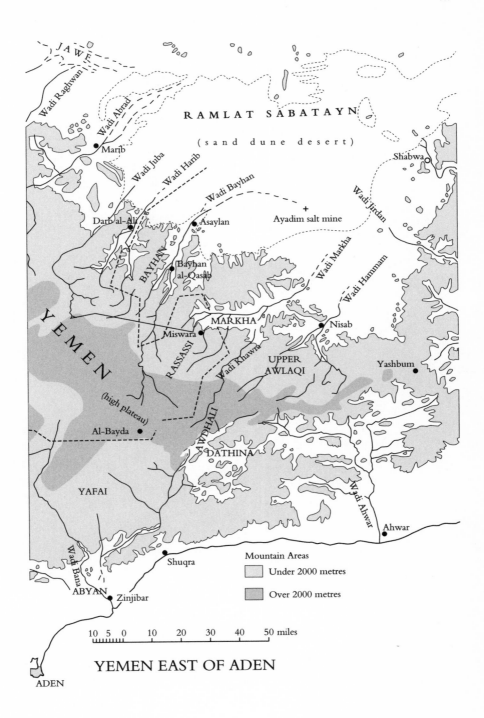

JAWF

Wadi Raghwan

Wadi Abrad

Marib

Wadi Juba

Wadi Harib

RAMLAT SABATAYN

(s a n d d u n e d e s e r t)

Shabwa

Wadi Bayhan

Ayadim salt mine
+

Wadi Jirdan

Darb al-Ali

Asaylan

BAYHAN

Bayhan
al-Qasab

Wadi Markha

Wadi Hammam

Y E M E N

MARKHA

Miswara

Nisab

RASSASSI

UPPER
AWLAQI

Yashbum

Wadi Khawra

(high plateau)

AWDHALI

Al-Bayda

DATHINA

YAFAI

Wadi Ahwar

Ahwar

Wadi Bana

Shuqra

Mountain Areas

Under 2000 metres

Over 2000 metres

ABYAN

Zinjibar

10 5 0   10   20   30   40   50 miles

YEMEN EAST OF ADEN

ADEN

1

The Bombing of the Bal Harith

Somebody shouted: "There they are! Look! They are coming!", and the call was taken up by soldiers and tribesmen on the flat roof-tops of the village.

We peered into the void. Arabs have very long sight and acute ears. I could neither see nor hear a thing.

To the south of us, flanked by rocky hills, was a wide, sandy wadi valley. Its water channel, recently flooded, meandered down the middle like a damp ribbon. It was still early morning, and lingering shadows picked out precipitous mountain slopes and the pale brown walls of distant villages. As the sun climbed higher, the shadows would fade away, the villages disappear and the hills merge together, leaving the view flat and without perspective. The distance had already vanished into heat haze under the cloudless sky.

"Over there!" Sharif Awadh called out, pointing excitedly. We squinted into the glare. Three black specks hovered above the wadi, growing larger, and a faint noise of engines began to swell. Quickly the specks turned into fighter planes of flashing silver, hurtling towards us and suddenly streaking over our heads with a roar.

Abdullah Hassan, glancing at his watch, said: "Exactly on time. Almost to a second." It was nine o'clock.

The three Tempests of No. 8 Squadron, Khormaksar, circled twice together and then peeled off to make their run, one behind the other, over Umm Ataym village, a mile to the north of us.

From the leading plane two dark shapes dropped diagonally, shimmering in the sunlight as they fell towards the empty houses. Two balls of black smoke turned into swirling brown columns, which spurted high above the roof-tops, and were followed an instant later by a tremendous bang. From the second plane, a pair of 500-pound bombs landed on dry fields at the front of the village, hurling up a huge blanket of dust. The bombs of the third Tempest hit the buildings, and the whole village disappeared under a cloud of dirt and debris. The noise deafened us, and beneath us the roof-tops trembled. Gaining height, the Tempests grouped together, circled over us once more, and then disappeared at speed into the haze over the Yemeni mountains, back to base in Aden. Abdullah Hassan said: "They are only allowed five minutes here, otherwise they will run out of fuel on the way home."

The departure of the planes left an eerie silence. We peered at Umm Ataym village, expecting to see a heap of rubble, but, as the curtain of dust thinned and settled, its walls emerged almost unchanged. A voice of disbelief exclaimed in Arabic, "It is still there!"

On the roof of the guest-room, alongside the terrace where we stood, Sharif Awadh had positioned a group of his Tribal Guards, wild-looking men in a variety of dress, their red turbans, above shoulder-length, tousled hair, the only concession to a uniform. They were manning an old Italian machine-gun, and its stumpy barrel pointed eastwards towards the huge sand-dunes which piled up against the northernmost mountain spurs like an angry sea. "Last year the Bal Harith shot at the planes from the sand-dunes," Awadh said to me. "Then they fired on us in Asaylan." He smiled grimly at the recollection and added: "This year I don't think they will want to come quite so close!"

One of the Tribal Guards started to gesticulate and the others followed his gaze. Tribesmen on a nearby roof were shouting: "*Mashallah*! Heavens above! Look at that!" Abdullah Hassan clutched my arm and, pointing back southwards over the wadi, said: "It's one of the Lincolns." Nobody there had seen an aeroplane of such size before, for the squadron of Lincoln bombers had been flown to Aden from their base in East Anglia especially for this operation. As the great, four-engined machine cleared the haze, rumbling and droning above our heads, a voice among the onlookers called out: "*Wallah*! That must be the father and mother of aeroplanes!" It disappeared over the desert reaches to the north, then returned, circled round us unhurriedly, and released a stick of three large bombs. We watched them fall until they exploded on the edge of Umm Ataym with a shattering roar. Once again the village vanished in dust. "*Mashallah!*" the tribesmen repeated.

I thought: "What the hell am I doing here?"

I had only reached Bayhan six days before, on 19 February 1948, flying up in an Anson of the Royal Air Force with Abdullah Hassan and some Arab soldiers. I had been in Arabia for about five weeks, starting as a guest of the Governor in the august surroundings of Government House. "I am posting you to the Western Aden Protectorate," he told me when I arrived. Later, in the Protectorate's headquarters office in Aden (known as the WAP Office), my posting was explained in more detail. "The Protectorate has a wide coastal plain, with a range of mountains north of that stretching eastwards from the Yemeni plateau. On the far side of the mountains the wadis flow north into the central Arabian desert. Your parish is all the area beyond the mountains. We call it the North Eastern Area, so you will be Political Officer North Eastern Area, or PONEA. Your base will be in Bayhan, which is at present the only part we control, and as there are no roads over the mountains you can only get there by plane." Asaylan village was in the northernmost part of my area, some two hundred miles north-east of Aden, on the edge of the sand-dune desert called the Ramlat Sabatayn.

My briefing before leaving Aden had been sketchy and spasmodic. "Just get to grips with the Bal Harith problem," I was told. In the WAP Office a fellow Political Officer, Kenneth Bell, had explained something of the background, but he had never been to Bayhan. I had read through thick files and taken copious notes. Then I had spent eight hours in a lorry, bumping and slithering over tracks washed away by flash floods, to visit John Allen, ninety miles to the north in Dhala. Allen, a tall, thin man with tousled grey hair and wild eyes, who had recently arrived from the orderly administration of Tanganyika, was the Protectorate's second-in-command and was currently standing in as PONA – Political Officer Northern Area. From him I was to receive guidance on the role of a Political Officer. We discussed the strange Protectorate set-up of feudal barons and

uncontrollable tribes. In Dhala the Amir, a deranged and brutal
tyrant, had just been ousted after a last-ditch stand in a remote mountain stronghold, and was now trying to foment a rebellion from his
sanctuary on the other side of the border with the Yemen. All over
the Protectorate lawlessness abounded. "It helps to be mad", Allen
had said.

"Bayhan has two main tribes: the Musabayn, who live in the
mountains and the upper reaches of the wadis, and the Bal Harith,
who own the delta area of Wadi Bayhan, where it flows into the
desert sands," I was told. In pronouncing "Bal Harith" the stress was
on the "Har", to rhyme with "bar", while Bayhan was pronounced
"Bay-harn". "The Bal Harith have a few villages in the wadi and
grow crops of millet and Indian corn in fields irrigated from the flood
waters. But during the dry season, or when there are no floods, they
simply pack up their few belongings on the backs of camels and move
out into the desert sands, pitching black goat-hair tents wherever
they can find grazing for their herds and flocks. They have always
been very independent, and they have not taken kindly to being
governed by the Sharif these last two years. Recently they refused
to pay their taxes, or even to discuss their grievances, and now they
have said they will no longer accept the Sharif as their ruler. If they
get away with that, then the Musabayn will rebel as well and the
regime will collapse. We've only just pulled the country out of total
anarchy and we can't allow it to revert back again. The Yemenis
are intriguing in the background, of course, and the Sharif has been
very high-handed, but his authority simply has to be restored. We've
given the Bal Harith every chance, but they have refused to listen.
Now there is nothing open to us but the time-honoured process of
air action. There are strict rules for conducting that which everybody understands, the golden one being to avoid at all cost any loss
of life."

Some days before my arrival an ultimatum had been dropped by
air on the main Bal Harith stronghold, but they ignored it, and had
left their lands and villages in the wadi for the desert. A second ultimatum followed, warning them that, if they did not come in to
discuss a settlement, their buildings would be bombed, commencing at a stated place and hour. "That is the routine procedure," I was

told, "and it gives them plenty of time to evacuate everything. But this time there is an important new feature in the operation. Never before have we been able to carry out a bombing operation at this distance from Aden which could be pressed home, because no aircraft has ever had sufficient range. As a result, the desert tribes have come to believe that if they stay out in the sands of the Empty Quarter they cannot be reached. But now the war is over we've been able to call on the Lincolns. They are very long-range aeroplanes. We can keep one droning over the desert dunes, anywhere where people could be hiding, for hours on end. That should have a devastating effect on the morale of the Bal Harith and anyone else with rebellion in his mind who regards the desert as a sanctuary."

We discussed the role of the Political Officer.

"You must be ready, with Abdullah Hassan, to negotiate with the Bal Harith when they seek terms, as they are bound to do eventually. Until then you must go on trying to persuade them to surrender. You will have to provide information and direction for the RAF, and be prepared to go out with a rescue party should any plane have to make a forced landing. Asaylan is the Sharif's administrative centre for the area, and it is on the very edge of Bal Harith country, so it is the obvious place for you to be. Don't worry! You can leave everything to Abdullah Hassan. He'll know just what to do."

On the journey up, Abdullah Hassan had confided: "Asaylan may not be a very safe place for us. We could come under attack from the Bal Harith, because the village is in rifle range from the sand-dunes. Worse still, the planes might get the wrong target." His long experience had taught him how difficult navigation could be over these unmapped territories, their features blurred in the pallid heat haze, especially for air crews only just arrived from England.

The operation demanded swift communications. For my contact with the WAP Office in Aden I had a small morse transmitter, running off an accumulator and operated by an Arab. More sophisticated equipment was needed to talk to the bombers, and this was provided by the RAF, who had sent up a corporal with his own radio. With him came a corporal medical orderly, ready to help if we had to send out a rescue party. The two corporals had arrived in Bayhan after me, travelling up from the landing-ground at Bayhan al-Qasab, the

Sharif's capital, on donkeys with a small escort. Saddle-sore and sun-burned, they were now installed, with their boxes of equipment, crates of service rations and a stretcher, in a tiny room on the fifth floor of the high central tower, or *husn*, of the village; in normal times this was the home of the Sharif's Wakil (pronounced "wakeel"), or local governor, a cousin called Sharif Abdullah, but his family had moved elsewhere until hostilities were over.

"Are you going to be all right up there?" I asked the corporals shortly after their arrival.

"We'll be OK, Sir," one of them said, and then, after a pause, added: "Have you seen the bog yet, Sir? Christ! It's really terrible! You have to go down on all fours to get through the bloody door. It's like a little cupboard inside, with nothing but a bloody hole in the floor. You can see daylight underneath, and a six-foot pile of the stuff, and simply millions of flies. I shan't go there in a hurry!"

It was a discomfort we all shared.

My guest-room, on a first floor, was at the foot of Sharif Abdullah's *husn* – a room with a lofty ceiling, newly white-washed, with a heavy wooden door and tiny shuttered windows. Purple carpets, woven locally from goat-hair, covered the mud floor, and at one end a raised platform had been built to provide a hard bed. My W/T set was in a small room next door, complete with its noisy petrol engine which charged the accumulators. The veranda outside, where we stood to watch the bombing, had lime-cemented corners with drain-away holes in the floor, over which I could wash and shave from a canvas camping basin. It was all a little spartan.

Throughout the morning the Lincoln rumbled overhead, occasionally disappearing to drop a bomb on a far-away mud-brick *dar* with a noise of distant thunder and sometimes sweeping low to strafe a nearby building with its cannons. Abdullah Hassan and I busied ourselves with an endless stream of visitors and problems, while next door the W/T set chattered away in morse. With Sharif Awadh, whose small army of tribesmen included many Musabayn shaykhs whom it was hoped to impress with this evidence of air power, we discussed the disposition of our forces and the likely whereabouts of the nearest Bal Harith. Discussion was slow, because I had so many questions to ask and as yet knew little Arabic.

The flat delta plain to our north was dotted with shrubs and *ilb* trees. The Bal Harith villages in it, constructed of bricks made from pale, yellow-brown sun-dried delta mud, had the colour of their surroundings and were sometimes difficult to see. The sides of the delta were lined by the sand-dunes of the Ramlat Sabatayn, interpreted by some as "the sands of the two Shebas", by others as "the sands it takes two weeks to cross", an off-shoot of the Empty Quarter. They were sands of a rich golden hue, stretching beyond the haze of the horizon in an ocean of immense, wind-rippled chains up to two hundred feet high.

The previous day, shortly after our arrival, Abdullah Hassan had pointed out a small, square, stone-built tower a short distance away. "That building belongs to the Bal Harith," he said. "It is called Dar Ahl Ali bin Ahmad – 'the fort of the family of Ali son of Ahmad'." It looked uncomfortably close should the Bal Harith decide to re-occupy it. "Doesn't the Operation Order list that as one of the first targets for the Lincolns?" I asked. "Yes," he replied.

I had not spent three wartime years as a soldier in India and Burma without learning something about the risks of high explosives. "It looks dangerously close," I said. "We had better signal Aden immediately to find out the danger radius of a thousand-pound bomb." The reply from Aden was swift and terse: "One thousand yards repeat one thousand yards."

"We will have to send out a patrol as soon as the sun goes down," I told Sharif Awadh. "They can make sure the *dar* is empty, but more importantly they must pace the distance back."

That evening six Government Guards, uniformed in khaki with black turbans, had moved stealthily towards the fort and, after assuring themselves that there was nobody in it, returned over the fields directly back to Asaylan counting their steps: 660 paces, or about 550 yards.

"Essential exclude Dar Ahl Ali bin Ahmad from the Lincoln target list" read my signal, and I added: "To mark our own position clearly to aircraft we are laying out a cross of black carpet strips on the flat roof of the mosque. Please ensure all crews informed."

At noon the Lincoln came back from a distant sortie and its crew, probably a little bored by now, decided to give us a grand finale before

going home for lunch. I heard it swooping low over our heads and
there was a sudden chatter from its cannons. "They are shooting at
Dar Ahl Ali bin Ahmad," Abdullah Hassan called out as I hurried
on to the terrace to watch. The great aeroplane circled round until
it was over our heads again, and this time we gazed in frozen horror as a 1,000-pound bomb dropped from its belly and plunged with
a whistle towards the ground. It landed in a field between Dar Ahl
Ali bin Ahmad and ourselves. There was a tremendous explosion
which battered against our ear drums. The buildings we stood on
shuddered, some of the walls cracked with small puffs of dust, and a
great hail of stone and shrapnel poured down on us out of the
swirling cloud of dirt, smoke, sand and debris.

I dashed up the steep steps of the tower, half expecting it to
crumble. The RAF corporals were looking pale and apprehensive,
one of them clutching his earphones tightly to his head. I dug him
in the ribs to attract his attention and grasped his headpiece.

"That was far too close!" I shouted into the microphone. "You
nearly hit us!"

"Too close?" said a calm, laconic voice from the ether. "Are we?
Where are you?"

"In Asaylan village," I replied impatiently. "We've marked it out
with a black cross."

"Oh! The black cross!" said the voice with mild surprise. "Really?
Good grief! We are starting a run against that one at the moment."

In the afternoon the Tempests returned with rockets and cannons
to renew the attack on Umm Ataym. Buildings were now beginning to fall, although it continued to cause bewildered astonishment
that so many walls remained standing. Only houses receiving a direct
hit disintegrated under the blast. There seemed to be an elasticity in
those mud bricks which held them together, despite the repeated
close explosions of bombs of a type which had, over the previous
few years, successfully demolished most of the brick, steel and con-
crete installations of Nazi Germany.

After the Tempests had made their quick raid, a second Lincoln
replaced them and circled at a great height dropping occasional sticks
of bombs. "Be warned. It will be unsafe for any of you to return
into your wadi at night," we had told the Bal Harith in the last

ultimatum, and to demonstrate this the Operation Order laid down
that delayed action bombs would be dropped as well. Umm Ataym
was chosen as the repository for three such missiles. Unfortunately
they missed their target and landed with heavy thuds in the fields
midway between that village and Asaylan. The Bal Harith heeded
the warning, but for us in Asaylan the night was one of tense apprehension, since we knew that at unpredictable times, we would be
jerked into wakefulness by the thumps of the more distant detona-
tions, and blasted into deafness by the thunder of three gigantic
explosions close at hand. The bombs went off in the small hours.
The walls of Asaylan seemed to withstand this further buffeting as
efficiently as those of Umm Ataym, but sleep that night was quite
out of the question.

Last thing in the evening I had sent Aden a proposal for the next
day's programme of attack. By that time we knew that a redoubtable
old Bayhani, Shaykh Qassim Ahmad, who had gone down to Aden
to give advice during the operation, would be in one of the Lincolns
to make certain that the targets were correctly identified. The distant thuds and plumes of dust coming from well over the northern
horizon had not impressed the Musabayn, who could see nearby
habitations still looking almost unscathed, and they were beginning
to feel that air power was something rather less than devastating, for
all the noise it might make. "Suggest aim achieve maximum effect
on Musabayn onlookers by concentrating on nearby targets," I had
signalled, with some apprehension.

The Tempests started the day on schedule with an attack conducted at tremendous speed on the nearest building of all – Dar Ahl
Ali bin Ahmad. Rockets and cannons were used from a low level.
Some rockets, hitting the ground on an almost horizontal trajectory,
bounced like balls over the hamlet, to explode when they landed on
the other side. Some did not explode. But a direct hit on the central tower disintegrated its top floors in a cloud of rubble. Our
garrison burst into a roar of applause.

For the rest of the morning one of the Lincolns concentrated on
Umm Ataym and began methodically to demolish it. In the afternoon, five Tempests arrived to attend to Bishaa, a small, fortified
hamlet close behind the wreckage of Dar Ahl Ali bin Ahmad. Their

attack was soon over. As rocket after rocket struck home, a fever of excitement gripped our soldiers, and the dour Musabayn tribesmen greeted each hit with a wild cheering, while Sharif Awadh, dignity cast aside, began to hop up and down, arms waving, beard wagging, shouting: "Bishaa *khloos*! Bishaa *khloos*! Bishaa is finished!"

From the moment the operation commenced, there had been no time to relax. Muhammad Ahmad, my wireless operator, had hardly left his set, passing and receiving a stream of signals in stuttering morse. Aden had to be told in detail how the bombing was proceeding; there were questions to answer and suggestions for new targets to put; intelligence reaching us about Bal Harith reactions had to be assessed and summarised; between us and Bayhan al-Qasab a relay of messengers kept the ruler, Sharif Hussain, informed of progress and gave us his views to pass on to Aden. In addition we had to deal with the complaints and requests of local tribesmen and villagers, for whom normal life had been abruptly halted, and with all the logistical problems of a small army in the field.

Our messages to Aden went to Basil Seager, the British Agent for the Western Aden Protectorate, who maintained a tight control. That evening an Immediate telegram arrived from Seager. "I have decided," he said, "to call off the air attack for three days to give the Bal Harith a further chance to submit. They should be so informed at once and warned that if the bombing has to be renewed it will be very severe." In the same message he asked us to consider an entirely new suggestion – that we should invite Kuhlani, Amil of Harib, who was the local Governor of the province of Yemen which bordered Bayhan, to come over to mediate. I convened a small conference to discuss this development: Sharif Awadh, Hussain's elder brother and expert on tribal matters, who was in command of our tribal forces; Amir Salih, Hussain's seventeen-year-old son and heir apparent; and Abdullah Hassan Jaffer.

I was totally reliant on Abdullah Hassan Jaffer; not only was he my interpreter, but his knowledge of Bayhan was vital. A Persian in origin, he was an Anglicised government officer, able to take a level, detached view of Protectorate politics and, being a man of some private wealth, he was above the corruption which often played so significant a part in those politics. He was a widely experienced

Assistant Political Officer, with a better knowledge of Bayhan than anyone else still in the Political Service. He had been seconded especially for this operation from his own area, Dathina, which had only just been brought under control and was going through a critical phase. In Dathina, too, peace had only just been created out of anarchy, but he had established there something unique in the Protectorate at that time, a state run by a council of shaykhs rather than by an autocratic tribal ruler. "My little republic," he called it.

Awadh pondered over Seager's message for a while and said: "We can't possibly stop the bombing yet. It's only been going on for two days. If we bring it to an end now the Bal Harith will say the *hakuma* is weak."

"We should give them a chance!" Abdullah Hassan responded. "What they have seen already may be enough to turn their minds."

"*Wallah!*" said Awadh. "It will need more than that to convince them. They are tough, these Bal Harith. Tough and very obstinate, like all the bedu of the desert."

Abdullah Hassan applied gentle persuasion, and together we drew up a letter addressed to the Bal Harith shaykhs on the lines Seager had suggested.

"As for asking Kuhlani here," Awadh said, "he interferes enough in the affairs of Bayhan already. Only my brother can invite him here. Out of respect for Seager I will write and ask my brother, but I do not think he will ever agree."

Overnight it poured with rain, drenching Asaylan and driving the sleeping garrison off the roof-tops into the dark, airless rooms below. There had been distant thunder and with a clouded dawn we learnt that a great *sayl*, or flash flood, had poured down the wadi, reaching far past Asaylan into the depths of Bal Harith territory. The flood was enough to irrigate most of their lands for the first time in three years. Surely now they would submit in order to start ploughing and sowing? But we were over-optimistic. At the end of a day which was eerily quiet after the jarring clamour of engines and explosions, our messenger returned from the Bal Harith camps. "We are the friends and servants of the British Government, the *hakuma*," they wrote, "But if you insist that we remain subjects of Sharif Hussain then we will stay for ever in our tents, for that we can never agree to. We can never talk to you while you make such a demand." Almost at the same time a letter reached us from Sharif Hussain. "How can anybody suggest we ask Kuhlani to mediate!" he wrote angrily. "He is dishonest and insincere. He is an intriguer. He cannot be trusted." I prepared signals for Aden with this news and awaited developments while we searched our minds for some further way of overcoming Bal Harith intransigence.

We had known all along that there was Yemeni encouragement behind the Bal Harith rebellion, probably engineered by, among others, Kuhlani himself. The Bal Harith had a pro-Yemeni faction centred on two young tribesmen, Abdullah al-Bahri and Alawi bin Ali Ghurayba. These two men, both the sons of leading tribal shaykhs and both in their twenties, held extremist views which seemed unlikely to be shared by some of the older shaykhs, who in the past had always been allies of the Sharif. The Bal Harith, moreover, were men of such individual temperament that none of their eleven sub-tribes would admit inferiority to any other, and hence they refused to accept any shaykh as paramount. There was no overall leader, but instead eleven shaykhs, also known as *Aqils*, who deliberated together on matters affecting the tribe as a whole and would not always act in concert. The sub-tribes varied in size and wealth; sometimes the weaker might have to submit to pressure from the stronger, but notionally each could go its own way. "There must be something in all this that we can exploit," I said to Awadh and Abdullah Hassan. "If the flooding of their land is a strong inducement to return, let us play on it. Can we reach one or two of the more moderate *aqils* and persuade them to lead in their sections? Perhaps others would then follow and the rebellion would collapse."

With much deliberation, we composed a letter to be sent personally to each of the *aqils*. It was a long letter and it had to be written out twelve times – eleven copies for the *aqils* and one for us. We assembled a group of scribes – the Sharif's clerk, my wireless operator, one of the Musabayn leaders, the officer in charge of my Government Guards, Abdullah Hassan and Amir Salih himself. Each letter was addressed individually to an *aqil*.

We were about to seal up the completed copies of this letter when a further signal arrived from Aden. Seager now proposed new terms for the Bal Harith. Our original demands had included the payment of a ransom of fifty rifles and one hundred camel loads of salt. The Bal Harith traded in salt, which they dug from a mine in the desert some thirty miles north-east of Asaylan, and which gave them a modest though by no means lucrative income. Seager now proposed to release them from this fine and in addition to offer them a Political Officer to examine their affairs for at least six months – an appointment which I visualised would fall on me. We composed a second set of letters containing this offer, one to each *aqil*, and our runners set out.

"Where do these messengers come from who are prepared to put their lives at risk to the Bal Harith?" I asked innocently.

"They are *ryot*," Abdullah Hassan replied. "Peasants, not tribesmen. They are labourers who work for the tribesmen. Nobody kills the *ryot*."

"Where do they live?"

Abdullah looked at Sharif Awadh. Awadh said: "In the villages around. Most of them are Bal Harith *ryot* and come from Umm Ataym."

"So we are destroying their houses?"

"Yes. It is true. We cannot ask the aeroplanes to pick out only the houses of tribesmen. But have no worry. They live only in shacks made of mud brick and wattle or huts made of sticks and straw. It is not difficult to build another."

In planning the operation against the Bal Harith the existence of these unfortunates had been overlooked. They were not a political factor and they did not count. It was a disturbing discovery, because, unlike the tribesmen, the *ryot* did not possess tents and could not live out in the sand-dunes. Most of them were now refugees in Asaylan and other villages further up the wadi. But the *ryot* themselves took their plight philosophically enough and I soon discovered that they were used to far more drastic treatment at the hands of extortionate local merchants and their Bal Harith overlords than this temporary deprivation of their homes, homes which in any case needed rebuilding almost every year. We paid them well for their service as messengers and there was no shortage of volunteers.

We knew from our returning messengers that the Bal Harith tents

were now clustered around the few available watering places out in
the sands, at points between ten and thirty miles away. It could thus
be two days before any reply requiring tribal consultation would
reach us. Replies to earlier messages were still coming in and I was
already becoming familiar with the simple, dignified but uncompromising phraseology of the Bal Harith *aqils*. They wrote
laboriously, the few who could write at all, with pointed sticks and
black dye in scrawling Arabic on tattered sheets of crumpled paper.
Abdullah Hassan would translate their letters into English for me as
he read them out and I would copy the translation down in my notebook. Very soon I was able to tell exactly what was coming next.
The theme was always the same. "We will submit to the *hakuma* at
any time, but to the Sharif, never."

On 28 February, a Saturday, the truce ended and planes came over
again. I had suggested that, to impress the Musabayn tribesmen, the
Tempests should concentrate on the final obliteration of Dar Ahl Ali
bin Ahmad and this they proceeded to do, completing the job with
another attack in the afternoon. All day long Lincoln bombers
droned in wide circles above us, disappearing for periods over the
northern horizon, dropping their loads of destruction almost with
lackadaisical nonchalance and returning home with a farewell flip of
the wings for drinks in the Mess at Khormaksar. On Sunday they
were back again.

There had been more rain overnight and the continual blasting of
high explosive so near to us, coupled with the softening effect of the
rain on mud walls and roofs, were beginning to take effect. Some of
the walls of Asaylan's houses cracked ominously and, while I was
talking to the two RAF corporals in their eyrie at the top of the
tower, a sudden roaring turned our gazes downwards to see a house
abruptly disintegrate into rubble and dust. Nobody was hurt, but the
lesson was clear. If the Bal Harith were still sticking it out, we in
Asaylan had already had enough. I sent an immediate signal to Aden
asking that in future the bombs should be dropped well away from
us. From then on we could not see any of the bombing at all; only
occasional thuds coming from the northern and eastern horizons,
and now and then a sparkle of sunlight on fuselage or wings,
reminded us that the operation was still in progress.

On the same day, Sunday, the first replies to our circular letter reached us from some of the *aqils*. It was apparent that there had been some tribal consultation, because six of the replies were markedly similar, with firm refusals even to consider surrender. But the seventh, from one of the minor *aqils*, gave us more hope. "There is water flowing strongly in the wadi," he said, "and my people would be happy if they could open the sluices to flood our fields. But I am not strong in the tribe and my words count for little. I cannot come in without the others, for we are all one people." Abdullah Hassan composed a new letter encouraging him to lead in his men, but we could not feel very optimistic.

The time had now come for Abdullah Hassan to leave. "You won't be able to keep him for very long," I had been warned in Aden. "He is needed in his own area, Dathina. He has just set up a new constitution there, for rule by a council of shaykhs, and it is running into difficulties. It is also time to collect the first grain tax, and if he isn't there to supervise that, there will be misappropriation." Though we were beginning to develop democratic-styled constitutions in the Protectorate, we had barely begun to solve the problems of graft and corruption. "You seem to be very impatient to go back to Dathina," I had told Abdullah one evening. "Yes," he said. "I am very worried about what will happen in my little republic while I'm away. Before you have been here much longer you will have discovered for yourself that nobody in this country can be trusted when there's a chance to make money."

Abdullah's planned relief was another Assistant Political Officer, a younger and considerably less experienced man, but in the event trouble elsewhere in the Protectorate kept him back and on the Monday I was left on my own, with my wireless operator, Muhammad Ahmad, acting as a temporary interpreter and translator of simple phrases. The removal of Abdullah Hassan's cheerful, tactful guidance marked, in a way, my graduation as a fully-fledged Political Officer. But I was promised that, if the Bal Harith sought to negotiate, Abdullah Hassan would return.

Shortly after Abdullah Hassan's departure, a frightened messenger reached us from one of the Bal Harith *aqils* with another blunt refusal to submit to the Sharif. Sharif Awadh said: "He refuses to answer

my questions, because he is afraid the Bal Harith would call him a
spy and kill him, but he has heard something very interesting. There
are old feuds between the Bal Harith sections and one of these has
broken out again. Two of the sections are fighting and one man has
already been killed."

This was not a development we had anticipated, but it was an
encouraging sign that the unity of the tribe in its rebellion might
be cracking. I composed another long letter asking this shaykh to
be wiser than the others and sent it off with the same messenger,
abjuring him to return with more news of the feud.

But in Aden that day Seager had obtained the Governor's approval
to more drastic action. A Bal Harith desert well, Bir Jifiyah, was cau-
tiously strafed and a few sheep and camels were killed. A signal that
evening announced this and instructed me to send letters at once to
the Bal Harith saying that this was only a foretaste of the wrath to
come. If they did not hasten their submission, more of their animals
might be killed and their wells destroyed. The beduin Arab places
his camels next to God and the threat of such destruction, with the
evidence of Bir Jifiyah to prove that it could really happen, must have
been an appalling realisation to the rebels.

Heavy cloud blanketed us next day, shrouding the hilltops. I was
glad of it; it meant that the RAF could not operate and we were not
under any sense of obligation to maintain pressure with further
attacks while the Bal Harith deliberated. In fact we had found their
Achilles heel. With unexpected speed their reply arrived that
evening. Gone was the familiar language of rejection. "We would
like to meet you, *ya* Groom, to discuss our submission. We cannot
resist the power of the *hakuma*. We request you to tell the aeroplanes
to stop bombing us so that we can come to meet you." There was
no mention of submission to the Sharif, but saving face is of enormous importance in the beduin mind and we could see that this was
implied although not stated. I passed the welcome news back to
Seager and a three-day truce was agreed.

Abdullah Hassan came back to Bayhan on the following day and
sent me a message that he would spend the night in Bayhan al-Qasab
and ride up to Asaylan next morning. With his letter came two from
Sharif Hussain. One was a personal warning to me. "Be on your

guard," he said, "The Bal Harith are treacherous. They will probably try some subterfuge." The other was more surprising. "Before the plane which brought Abdullah Hassan here landed," he wrote, "it flew on a reconnaissance over the lower wadi." We had indeed seen the Anson circle over the hills east of Asaylan. "The pilot told us that at the edge of the desert a few miles from Asaylan he spotted more than a hundred men on a hillside. They are wearing white clothes and that must mean that they were Bal Harith. We suspect that they intend to do some harm. Perhaps they are planning to attack you or one of the Ashraf villages." The villages of the Sharifs (or Ashraf in the Arabic plural) were grouped together a few miles south of Asaylan, and it seemed quite possible that the Bal Harith might seek to show their defiance by a hit-and-run attack against one of them.

We had not been preparing for an attack from the south. Sharif Awadh immediately sprang into action. Runners sped to all the neighbouring villages to warn them of the danger, and scouts were sent off to spy out the area where the raiding party had been seen. In Asaylan we prepared for an assault, doubling our sentries and holding a practice stand-to on the signal of a Very light.

Late that night Sharif Awadh came to my door with a curious look in his eyes.

"The scouts have returned, *ya* Groom."

"Did they see the raiders?" I asked.

"They found the party described by the RAF," he said deviously.

"What were they doing?"

"Nothing."

"What do you mean, 'nothing'?"

"There was only one man there."

"I thought there were over a hundred!"

"That is so. But it was no army they saw from the aeroplane." His face began to wrinkle into an embarrassed grin.

"There was just a shepherd. The rest were his sheep."

At long last we had a day in which to relax – Thursday 4 March, just ten days after the first bombs had dropped. In all that time I had had barely a moment to myself. The wireless set next door had been chattering from early morning until late at night with a continuous

flow of reports, instructions and routine administrative messages. I
had used up several message pads.

In those days, to obtain some degree of security in our radio
communications, in particular against the chance that the Yemenis
might be listening in and the greater possibility of our own wireless
operators selling the information they were handling, we used the
Government Telegraph Code. This was a heavy black-bound volume, like an old family bible, containing hundreds of five-letter
group cyphers for all the more common words and phrases.
Sometimes this helped to shorten the signal text, because a long
phrase like "reference your message sent last night" could be contained in five letters, but more often it would lengthen it, especially
when it was necessary to spell out some Arabic name not included
in the key. "AZFIV" was the cypher, but hardly an abbreviation, for
"and". To shorten the process of encoding and decoding, and at the
same time to make the message more difficult for any local spies to
understand, we would use a great deal of cryptic *en clair* language in
the form of slang, or puns, or literary allusions. These strange phrases
were combined with the cyphers of the Government Telegraph
Code. The art lay in so wording the *en clair* passages that they read
as if they referred to some entirely different and quite innocuous
matter. Seager was a past master at this form of communication and
the unravelling of his messages was like solving a crossword puzzle.
It was amusing, but it all took a very long time.

When I was not wrestling with the Government Telegraph Code
there were always other matters to attend to and my room was usually full of people until late at night, excepting when meals arrived,
for then it was a local politeness for everybody to leave. I had brought
up with me a Yemeni, trained in European households in Aden, to
cook and look after my personal wants. Ahmad was a tall, thin youth
with the wan complexion of so many Yemenis resulting from the
habit of chewing *qat*. He had a quiet, unassuming nature, always
anxious to please, and produced meals with a patient regularity from
some hidden kitchen which, knowing the origin of the flies, I dared
not inspect. His meals were conjured out of my supply of tins,
supplemented with minute eggs from the local chickens, and eaten
hurriedly while people queued up at the door. Nor was there time

to think about personal comfort. A quick wash and shave at dawn during the call to prayer, a splash of hands and face at night, were the best that could be offered to the god of cleanliness. But with the lull one became more conscious of the faults and inadequacies of the surroundings. In particular the flies began to force recognition of their presence.

I had not appreciated the importance of insecticide until I found that Ahmad had used up my entire supply of Flit trying to stem the invasion of his kitchen. The rain had greatly increased the fly population and now they began to attack in huge cohorts, crawling over one's face in a black mass, settling by the score on clothes and arms and legs, entirely refusing to take fright at the threat of rolled-up paper clubs. The Arabs, children especially, seemed inured to this discomfort, and paid no heed as whole phalanxes of flies crawled over their faces in search of sweat, tear and saliva. My own nerves could not emulate such blissful torpor, and the persistence of the Asaylan flies was agonising torture.

Worse was to come. If I had seen flies by the hundred in my room, I was to learn that they were but a tiny force in relation to the great armies outside. That day we were invited to lunch by Sharif Awadh. He was quartered in a large, carpeted room reached through a maze of minute alleys and dark passages and up a final, low flight of mud steps. The walls were hung with flat dishes made of basketware. Two large "hubble-bubble" pipes, decorated with tassels and silver filigree, were placed in the middle of the room and their snake-like tubes passed from mouth to mouth around the fifteen persons present. Then the food was brought in.

For Abdullah Hassan and myself special delicacies had been put to one side – a bowl of rice and a plate containing the choicest pieces of the sheep slaughtered for the occasion – liver, heart and kidney. The other guests fed from a communal pudding of heavy dough, known as *masub* ("masoob"), and the carcass of mutton was then carried in on a great basketware platter. On their entry both *masub* and mutton were so covered with flies that they were completely black. Awadh, wielding his silver-hilted dagger, locally called a *jambya*, like a wood-chopper, flailed away at the flies and started to cut up the meat into chunks, which he then tossed to his guests. On later occasions, when the company was more numerous, I was often to see meat being passed from hand to hand till it reached the person for whom it was destined, for each guest received a portion commensurate with his social status. The meat was eaten rapidly in a silence punctuated by sucking noises, regurgitations and murmurs of "Praise be to God". Bones were clean-picked, cracked with a *jambya* so that the marrow could be sucked out, and then thrown through the open doorway on to the veranda outside, where further clouds of flies descended on them and completely covered them from view. Without more ado most of the guests then left. We stayed for a little while to sip gingered coffee while Sharif Awadh finished up the leavings, for the host does not eat until his guests are replete. But in the end the flies won the day and I retreated to the only place where I could escape them, under the mosquito-net on my camp bed. By that stage much of my office work was being done from my bed.

Seager had signalled his intention to be present at our meeting with the Bal Harith provided he could use the landing-ground next to the main Ashraf village of Nuqub, for the journey up from Bayhan al-Qasab was time-consuming and tiring. A few months before, the RAF had condemned this landing-strip as being too soft, but Awadh and his cousin Abdullah, the Wakil of Asaylan, a tall, awkward man with a black beard and hawk-beak nose, were indignant at this and insisted that we should inspect it again. I was glad of the opportunity to get out of Asaylan and rode over on horseback with Sharif Abdullah and one of his henchmen, a slave, both armed to the teeth, to look at the site. The journey was a gentle canter over low sand-dunes and long stretches of flat wadi bed, now empty of water again. The surface of the strip seemed no softer than that at Bayhan al-Qasab and it was difficult to understand the RAF's objections, but my signalled assurance that it was usable did not convince them and Seager was unable to come.

As we were returning from Nuqub we saw in the distance, weaving over the sand-dunes out of the empty Bal Harith lands, a group of eight men on riding camels. Our sentries in Asaylan had spotted them too and the soldiers and tribesmen of our garrison were manning the walls and covering them with their guns. They approached us slowly, white-robed figures, each with a rifle, and waited near the ruins of Dar Ahl Ali bin Ahmad. Sharif Abdullah said: "They are not Bal Harith," and sent his slave off to make enquiries. Presently the slave led them to the gateway of the village and they dismounted.

They were tall men who walked with great dignity. Some of them were old and had white beards.

"Mishqas," Sharif Abdullah said to me, using a word which loosely defined almost any tribesmen from the far eastern deserts.

As they advanced towards us each fired his rifle in the air in salute. A number of people had joined us outside the village walls and we formed up in a line facing them. The strangers then moved slowly down the length of our rank touching hands and making a kissing noise with every person in it. This was the traditional greeting of the desert tribes. After they had all filed past, Sharif Abdullah led them into the village.

"We are of the Ahl Misfar section of the Kurab," one of them explained once we were settled down in the Sharif's courtroom and the prolonged formal greetings were over. "We come from near Shabwa. We had brought our camels west for the grazing when aeroplanes came and dropped bombs on us. Two of our camels were killed. There was no warning given to us and we were nowhere near the Bal Harith camps. We have come to seek compensation from the *hakuma*."

A glint of avarice in his eyes suggested that they were hoping to receive far more than the camels were worth.

Sharif Abdullah turned to me with relief. "It is a matter between the Kurab and the *hakuma*," he said, shrugging his shoulders. I had no idea what was expected of me. Sharif Awadh would have been of more help, but unfortunately he was away. "Leave it to me," I heard the welcome voice of Abdullah Hassan saying from behind me, and he started to address the Kurab in a soothing voice.

"Two years ago," he said, fixing his eye on the Kurab spokesman, "did not the Political Officer Peter Davey come to your territory?"

"*Aywa*, he certainly did that."

"And did you not refuse permission for him to pass through?"

"He sought our permission to travel through our land."

"Yes. But you would only let him pass on payment of three hundred dollars." Abdullah Hassan was referring to the big silver Maria

Theresa dollars which were the only currency in those desert regions. "He paid you that money because otherwise you would not let him go any further."

"He was willing to pay."

"He paid because it was important for him to continue his journey quickly. You extorted the money from Davey. It was a shameful thing to do. You should return the three hundred dollars to the government. If you do that now, then perhaps the government will compensate you with two hundred dollars for the loss of your camels – they cannot have been worth more than that."

The grave faces of our visitors pondered on this statement impassively for a while and then wrinkled into embarrassed smiles. The subject was not mentioned again. For about an hour we talked amicably of other matters. Then, abruptly, they rose, walked out of the village gateway, mounted their camels, and departed towards the sand-dunes in stately silence. They did not look back.

Sharif Abdullah said: "They have the courage of lions, those Kurabis. They are at feud with the Bal Harith and they have travelled without a protector. If they meet any Harithis on the way back, they could be killed."

If we had cause to be suspicious of the Bal Harith, they for their part were taking no chances either. "They are frightened that we may imprison their delegates to stop them bargaining for terms," Awadh said. Seager had joined in the warnings about Bal Harith treachery and insisted that we choose our meeting-place carefully and ensure that we were covered by the machine-gun. A few hundred yards north of Asaylan, about midway between the ruins of Dar Ahl Ali bin Ahmad and Umm Ataym, was a graveyard where the outstretched branches of two large trees provided an area of shade. We directed the Bal Harith to come there at dawn on Saturday. They protested in a sequence of letters demanding that they be allowed to choose the venue, and the scheduled time came and went without sight of them. At last, at about nine o'clock, we saw a little procession of robed figures winding their way through the fields and bushes to the trees in the graveyard.

It would have been a political mistake to use the Sharif's men as our guard at this meeting-place. A small group of Government

Guards, the soldiers of the *hakuma*, was waiting there for the Bal Harith to arrive, while the Bayhan Tribal Guards and the Musabayn irregulars were kept back in Asaylan. This arrangement helped to save the faces of the Bal Harith, who had been so insistent that they would submit only to the Government and not to the Sharif. Face-saving was always a major factor in South Arabian politics and the word *sharaf*, meaning respect, loomed large at all times. Any act which caused a *kassar sharaf*, meaning a "breakage of respect", was an insult demanding remedy or revenge. It was *sharaf* as much as any other factor which had motivated the Bal Harith once they had come out in rebellion, for to submit without a fight after the decision to revolt had become irrevocable would have been unmanly. By subjecting them to a bigger bombing operation than any tribe had ever had to endure previously we had, in effect, saved their faces and made it excusable for them to submit.

We watched the Bal Harith leaders sit down on the sand beneath the trees and then left the protective walls of Asaylan to meet them. Little Shaykh Qassim Ahmad, who had been advising Seager and had latterly been guiding the bomber crews, had come up from Aden with Abdullah Hassan and was one of our delegation. Sharif Awadh represented his brother Hussain. Awadh had always been held in high respect by the Bal Harith. He was himself a man of the desert, married into a leading family of the Kurab tribe whose shaykhs had sought compensation two days earlier. Shortly before the Second World War, when the Imam of Yemen had tried to disrupt the "Ingrams peace" in the Hadramawt, Awadh had distinguished himself by helping Hamilton (later Lord Belhaven) to raise an army of tribesmen against Yemeni forces investing Shabwa. Subsequently he had done much to settle feuds and disputes in the area. In consequence his reputation went beyond Bayhan and Seager had jocularly (and quite inaccurately) dubbed him "The King of the Empty Quarter", a title which always afforded him great pride.

As agreed, our total delegation numbered twelve, to match the twelve of the Bal Harith who rose to greet us. Abdullah Hassan introduced me to each in turn in a friendly way and they replied with quiet smiles which masked an underlying nervous apprehension. They were tall men, bearded, with white robes falling to below the knee, *jambya*s and belts of ammunition at their waists, rifles in hand. They looked tired and anxious. Foremost were the two most powerful shaykhs of the tribe, Ali bin Munassir and Nassir bin Hussain. Behind these two were the young renegades whose influence in the rebellion had been so strong: Abdullah al-Bahri ("Abdullah the Sailor"), who was Ali bin Munassir's son, a tough, barrel-chested man, and his cousin Alawi bin Ali Ghurayba, slighter of build, with glinting eyes above a bushy, black beard.

We sat down cross-legged on the sandy ground, facing each other in two long lines. The morning sun, piercing the foliage of our tamarisk tree shelter, flecked us with patches of bright light. A mild breeze gusted hot air and occasionally whipped up miniature whirlwinds of sand and dust. The sky was cloudless and pallid, portending the coming heat of day.

I realised at that point that I was the only unarmed man on either side, for even Abdullah Hassan had conjured up a revolver. The Bal Harith had their rifles pointed towards us and the barrels of our own rifles similarly faced the Bal Harith. Each person had paired off with his opposite number and was surreptitiously sizing up his chances of getting off the first shot if any shooting began. My "partner" in this was Abdullah al-Bahri, who, with a look of bad-tempered misgiving, pointed a modern Lee-Enfield rifle at me, loaded and cocked, with the safety catch forward and his finger nervously stroking the trigger. The Government Guards sat to one side, trying to look indifferent, with their rifles at the ready. As an extra precaution they had brought a Bren machine-gun with them, which now covered the Bal Harith at a range of about thirty feet. Behind us, crowding the rooftops of Asaylan, were the tribal irregulars and the Tribal Guards with their Italian machine-gun. Behind the Bal Harith, lining the foremost ridges of the sand-dunes which edged the plain, was a large fighting force of Bal Harith tribesmen ready to join battle with an assortment of weapons if anything went wrong. It was an unnerving commencement to a discussion about peace.

The principal spokesman for the Bal Harith was the youthful Abdullah al-Bahri, who became more and more loquacious as time went on. He and his cousin bore no resemblance to the young nationalists of later days. Their protest was of an entirely different nature – a tribal expression of youthful objection to the lack of tangible benefit from the Sharif's rule. They voiced a feeling of *kassar sharaf* at having to pay taxes without seeing anything come back to them in return. The flames of discontent, with others lurking furtively in the Bal Harith minds, had been fanned by Yemeni encouragement and cash. There was some justification in their attitude, for the Sharif had never forgiven them for an earlier rebellion and relations with his administration had remained sour. But Abdullah al-Bahri, as he sat in front of us toying with his rifle, occasionally working himself up into a state of vociferous and heated indignation, knew as well as the elder shaykhs beside him that they now had no option but to submit: their tribesmen were fed up and anxious to start ploughing in the eight days left before the moisture from the floodwaters disappeared, while the feud which had broken out had ended their tribal unity.

Throughout the meeting some of the minor *aqils* remained studiously quiet. "It looks," Abdullah Hassan whispered to me, "as if our letters to them have had some influence." But for two hours the more obstreperous leaders haggled over the terms of settlement. "It's all done for *sharaf*," Abdullah Hassan said. "That and a vague hope that they'll extract more concessions from us. But in their hearts they know that we are being quite fair." Slowly the heat went out of the argument, until one after the other agreed on complete submission. Suddenly the atmosphere of the meeting changed completely. Jokes were made, hands shaken, shoulders clasped, and I watched with some relief as al-Bahri pulled the safety-catch of his rifle back and slung the heavy weapon nonchalantly back over his shoulder. The minor *aqils*, looking immensely relieved, began to join in the banter and gathered in small groups to commence whispered conversations among themselves. We threaded our way back to Asaylan. "You can dismantle the machine-gun," Awadh called out to his men pointedly.

We had arranged that the Bal Harith would provide eleven hostages, one member from the family of each of the *aqils*, to be held in Bayhan al-Qasab. This was a normal and traditional feature of such settlements. Until the hostages were formally handed over we were to keep four of the *aqils* from the delegation. Two wizened old men with white beards accordingly accompanied us to Asaylan, but we permitted the other two to return to their tents to prepare themselves before rejoining us in the afternoon. "Hostages have quite a pleasant life," Abdullah Hassan explained to me. "They will be under guard, and at first that had better be two Government Guards, but they are allowed to move around fairly freely both inside and outside the village and their friends can call. What is more, it is the custom to honour them with a feast when they first arrive, and with another feast, a suit of new clothes and a few gifts when they are released. They'll be well treated and perfectly happy."

The fine of one hundred camel loads of salt and fifty rifles demanded in our ultimatum had been discussed at great length. We had not imposed a time limit on the payment of the salt fine, and knowing that Seager was prepared ultimately to drop the demand for rifles, we had been vague in specifying who was to produce them. I composed a long signal telling Seager the outcome, and then chatted to Abdullah Hassan and Shaykh Qassim, sipping orange juice, while the muezzin of the Asaylan mosque called out from the mosque roof in his high-pitched, wailing chant, that peace was declared and the people of the village could return to their fields in safety. We felt elated by a sense of achievement.

Seager was not so easily contented. His reply arrived before I had left Abdullah's room. He was dissatisfied with the terms. Abdullah's face fell. He had exhausted himself in the hours of intense haggling, bearing with Shaykh Qassim the brunt of the arguments, straining to make his points in the face of beduin obtuseness, patiently explaining, good-humouredly exhorting, quietly interpreting to me. Now he had no alternative but to call at once for a horse to be saddled for a fifteen-mile gallop to the landing ground through the heat of the day. Qassim said: "I shall come with you. It is best that we see Seager together." Almost at once they were gone.

In the evening another long signal was flashed from Aden in stuttering morse. "I have seen Abdullah Hassan and Qassim," Seager said. "I am now satisfied with the terms. But you should give the Bal Harith a time limit of twenty days to pay their salt fines and tell them that, as a sign of our goodwill, we will forego the fine of rifles." We set to on the now familiar, late-night process of composing and writing out copies of a letter to each of the Bal Harith shaykhs.

Next morning, a Sunday, the two RAF corporals returned on donkey-back to Bayhan al-Qasab for a plane back to Aden. They had lived uncomfortably without complaint and one of them showed signs of dysentery. That night, while I was typing out my report, my own stomach gave in. In the face of the flies, which continued to swarm around us in their thousands, it had done well to last out so long. I took to my bed, feeling utterly wretched, and drank nothing but liver salts for forty-eight hours, for no other medicines were available. The attack subsided as abruptly as it had begun, and on the Tuesday morning I was greeted by a smiling Sharif Abdullah, bearing with him a priceless gift from Sharif Hussain. "Look, *ya* Groom!" he said. "I have brought you a new tin of Flit."

If the ending of the operation against the Bal Harith had produced a feeling of satisfaction and well-being, it was as nothing compared with the elation and utter relief brought about by my personal, single-handed victory that day over the Asaylan flies.

2

A Stranger in the Land

There was still work to do in Asaylan and I could not yet return to
Bayhan al-Qasab, which, from this desert outpost, began to assume
the allure of a great metropolis. I longed for the spacious coolness of
the Political Officer's *dar* there, for the comfort of its rickety *charpoy*
bed, for the chance of a proper wash, for the cleaner, sweeter water
– the Asaylan water had a brackish taste –, for some respite from the
flies, and, more than anything else, for a few hours completely to
myself. In Asaylan, ever since the operation had commenced, my
room was the administrative office, battle headquarters and social
club combined. Even when I was ill there was a constant flow of
callers. Privacy existed only during the hours of sleep, all too short
after exhausting days. In the brief period of wakefulness after climbing into my creaking camp bed I would reflect on my strange
situation, transported so abruptly into this other world with little
preparation for its manners and customs and almost no knowledge
of its language. Luckily it was Arab courtesy to be indulgent to this
newly arrived, twenty-three-year-old Political Officer – the *thābat
as-siassa*. In Arabia a man is proved by his actions, which need time
to reveal themselves. Besides, the inexperience of a new officer in
no way diminished the potency of the *hakuma* behind him.

No dream was fulfilled nor ambition attained by my arrival in
Bayhan. Arabia had always fascinated me, but circumstances brought
me to Bayhan in a way which could not have been foreseen. Like
many soldiers on their way out to India and Burma, I had first
glimpsed Aden through the porthole of a troopship on a sweating,
airless morning. We were not allowed ashore. While our converted

cargo boat, with its great canvas awnings funnelling air down through the hatches into the crowded troop-decks in the holds, was taking on fuel, oil and water, I had glanced across the flat calm of the harbour at the legendary "barren rocks". Whitewashed buildings with arched verandas and green shutters clustered diminutively at the foot of the bare, brown mountains. Lines of oil tanks and warehouses obtruded to the water's edge. The sun was merciless. There was nothing to appeal in that view seen under such circumstances. I had hardly given Aden a moment's further thought. After the war, successfully seeking a career in the Colonial Service, I had attended a training course in Cambridge and London prior to being posted to Palestine; but the Palestine mandate fell through and suddenly it was a posting to Aden instead, with three weeks left of the year of training in which to learn something about my new territory.

Considerately, the Colonial Office provided a pamphlet for every officer entering the Colonial Service which gave "information as to the conditions and cost of living" in the country to which he was posted. The pamphlet dealing with Aden covered both the Colony and the Protectorate and was only five pages long. By the time I received it I was aware that the Colony consisted of no more than those eighty square miles of sand and barren rock in a horse-shoe shape round the harbour which I had dismissed from mind four years before, while the Protectorate was a large stretch of hinterland with partly undefined borders, containing a population of about eight hundred thousand people and administered quite separately by direct grants of money from the British Treasury. The pamphlet supplemented this meagre knowledge, but not in the most reassuring way. It started with a list of the tropical diseases which might be caught there and ended with a paragraph, headed "General Remarks", which commenced: "Conditions in some parts of the Protectorate are primitive. An officer should be prepared for an arduous though interesting life. If he looks after his health there is no reason why he should not remain fit and healthy." Sandwiched between was advice on the climate, communications, housing, the cost of living, income tax, household requirements, staff and other subjects.

I did not know whether I would be serving in Aden Colony or in the Western or Eastern Protectorate. I was replacing an officer

murdered in the Western Protectorate, but it was left to the Governor
how to post his officers. Certainly in terms of climate the Colony
was not made to sound very attractive. "It is such," said my pamphlet, "that prolonged residence causes gradual but definite
deterioration of health and efficiency." At least there was climatic
variety in the Western Protectorate, but it hardly seemed alluring.
"The maritime plains are damp and hot in summer and are subject
to sandstorms and high winds. Living is trying and can be uncomfortable... Malaria, sand-fly fever, mild intestinal trouble and prickly
heat occur in the summer, although fevers generally and stomachic
ailments are commoner in the winter... Malaria is prevalent throughout." Perhaps the Eastern Protectorate would be a better alternative.
The position here was more simply stated. On the coast "from
October to April, the weather is consistently pleasant. The maximum temperature is 106°." But wherever the Governor might enjoin
me to go I was not unduly concerned. I had barely lost that bright
yellow complexion, common to all British soldiers in the wartime
Far East, caused by a heavy consumption of mepachrine anti-malar-
ial tablets. Furthermore, a year of training with Colonial Service
cadets destined for the most part to go to territories in Africa, coupled with a visit to the Museum of Tropical Diseases as a part of our
course, had made familiar the names and symptoms of numerous
frightening and revolting ailments which it was encouraging to find
had no mention at all in the Aden list.

On other matters the pamphlet had surprisingly little to say.
"Transport in the Protectorate," I learned, "is still mostly by camel."
As far as kit was concerned, if I was posted to the Protectorate, I
would need "a camp bed with mosquito net, folding table and chair,
canvas wash-basin and bath"; I should buy "tin plates or mugs" rather
than glass or china and would find a pressure lamp "useful". Finally
there was the question of servants. "A household staff in the Colony,"
the pamphlet averred, "usually consists of a Cook (about 60 rupees
a month), a Head Boy (about 50), a Second Boy (about 35), a
Sweeper (about 30) and a Dhobi (about 20)." The rupee at that time
was worth one shilling and sixpence. Servants, it explained, were
usually Arabs or Somalis, Arabs being preferable up-country, and the
Dhobi (the laundryman) would be shared with other families. And

the pamphlet added mysteriously: "It is not possible for a bachelor to do without a second boy."

This was the basis of advice on which I had prepared for my posting. But my demobilisation gratuity had been used up on living expenses during the training course and the "outfit allowance" covered only a small part of the equipment we were advised to buy. When I arrived in Bayhan I brought with me a camp bed and chair, a pressure lamp, a tin wash-basin, a small amount of clothing, a substantial quantity of tinned food, a few cherished books, an office typewriter, and a heavy sack of Maria Theresa silver dollars, drawn from the vaults of the Aden Treasury whilst on my way to the airport, to meet my official expenses. My staff consisted solely of Ahmad, who was to cook and carry and manage my domestic affairs during all my time in Bayhan.

In the evening Ahmad pumped up my Tilley lamp and carried it into my room, which became the brightest lit in the village, for elsewhere there were only Hurricane lanterns and primitive local oil lamps. The light and the radio, which Sharif Hussain had sent up from Bayhan al-Qasab for me, attracted others in Asaylan like moths to a candle. Radios were still a rarity in the Protectorate and in Bayhan only the Sharif himself possessed such a thing. They required in those days to be run off accumulators – the dry battery transistor set belonging to a much later day – and the only charging engine available was the one provided for my communication wireless. While we allowed the Sharif to charge his accumulators on this petrol-driven engine, we could not extend the privilege, because of the engine's limited capacity. Consequently the wireless in my room was an exciting novelty. People came to Asaylan from long distances just to sit in the courtyard outside and listen to it, and my room of an evening would be crowded with more privileged persons, sitting cross-legged on the floor, waiting to hear the Arabic news. There was no radio station in Aden and the huge transmitters of Radio Cairo, with their virulently anti-British "Voice of the Arabs" broadcasts, had not yet opened up. We listened to the BBC Arabic service from London and the crackling voices of Radio Sanaa, the Yemeni station which had just commenced broadcasting. All ears, as well as all eyes, were on the Yemen. Two days before I arrived in Bayhan the old Imam Yahya, who had been reigning for forty-four years, had been assassinated.

The assassination marked an attempt by other members of the royal family to pull the country out of its medieval despotism. The *coup d'état* plunged the Yemen into turmoil. Communications were completely disrupted and wild rumours replaced news. On my way up to Bayhan, our Anson aircraft had diverted slightly from the normal route so that a reassuring message could be dropped over Bayda, the provincial capital, where the Amil – or Governor – was well-known to Seager. Our message, contained in a tin attached to a long red cloth streamer, told him what little we knew of events and assured him that the Aden Government did not intend to intervene.

Thus night after night it was news of the Yemen that my visitors most hoped to hear from my atmospheric radio. They would listen tensely to the vague accounts of the day's fighting and political developments. Soon it was apparent that the liberal new regime was having great difficulty in establishing itself. Kuhlani, the Amil of Harib, whom the Sharif had refused to trust as a mediator, suddenly arrived in Bayhan as a refugee, not knowing which way to turn while the situation remained so uncertain. His whole province was said to be in revolt and he knew that if he backed the wrong side he could quite literally lose his head. His decision to flee was a wise one, because in due course the old Imam's immensely cruel son Ahmad won the day and settled down to a further reign of tyranny. Scores of persons, including some of the new Imam's brothers, were decapitated by the sword and their heads mounted on poles over the main gateway of Sanaa.

But we had more to do than just listen to the radio, however fascinated my audience was by these momentous events.

"Tomorrow," I said to Thabit Qassim, the Rais (or "captain") commanding my Government Guards detachment, "we must go out into Bal Harith country to inspect the damage and locate the unexploded bombs."

"It will be dangerous," he responded. "There may be tribesmen who are resentful and will try to do harm."

Sharif Awadh added his concurrence. "You must have a large escort. Your Government Guards will not be enough. My Tribal

Guards shall go with you."

I doubted the necessity of Awadh's offer, made, I suspected, to rub into the Bal Harith that they had submitted to the Sharif as well as to the *hakuma* rather than because of the danger, but there was no point in refusing. Then Awadh added: "I will come with you." It was a courageous offer, because if the Bal Harith were to shoot at anyone it would be the representative of the Sharif. We set out on foot a little after dawn.

Our route crossed over newly ploughed fields bordered by low mud banks which had been scraped up to retain the flood water. The fields were spattered with *ilb* trees, growing in wildly twisted shapes, with a profusion of angular branches and tiny leaves. Sharif Awadh decided to educate me. "This, *ya* Groom, is the most important tree in Bayhan. You won't find date palms in this part of the wadi; they have to be near a well where they can be watered regularly. But the *ilb* grows roots that go down and down to reach water deep underground. The roots are bigger than the tree itself. Look at the branches! They are very strong. They are the wood we use for building, the beams for our houses. And the leaves. We use those to feed our animals. They are the best of fodder. Now look at the *dawm*!" From the foliage of a tree we were passing he plucked a number of small berries, looking like cherry-stones covered with a wrinkled skin but no flesh. "They taste sweet and they last for many weeks. The Bal Harith carry little bags full of them when they go out into the desert. With the *dawm* fruit and camels' milk they can live in the sands for weeks. Yes. It really is a very important tree, the *ilb*." My bodyguard were darting from tree to tree to pick the *dawm*, like small children eating blackberries on an English heath.

The destruction of the Bal Harith settlements had been more thorough than appeared from a distance. The few walls of Dar Ahl Ali bin Ahmad and Bishaa which still stood erect were cracked and crumbling and likely to collapse with the next shower of rain. Umm Ataym was so flattened that there was nothing left but a heap of rubble. In a field on the edge of Umm Ataym were seven large bomb craters; growing right up to the rims of these craters, a healthy harvest of wheat, irrigated from a well, was now being reaped.

Everywhere Bal Harith tribesmen and their *ryot* were hard at work trying to catch up on lost time. Their ploughing was primitive. A shaft of *ilb* branches, bound together and tipped with some jagged piece of metal to make a ploughshare, was dragged across the soil by an unhurrying camel or sometimes by a pair of oxen, leaving a shallow furrow. A child led the camel, the plough itself was controlled by an adult man and another child followed sowing the seed. The more ingenious had developed their tool a stage further by connecting a hollowed-out branch to the plough just behind the share, into which the ploughman fed handfuls of seed from a bag tied round his waist.

In spite of the bitterness of the rebellion I was greeted affably wherever I went and small boys ran around excitedly, pointing out the unexploded bombs. Of these there were all too many. To the Bal Harith they were a tempting prize, because they contained explosive which it was thought could be used to refill spent cartridges. Ammunition was about the most important and expensive purchase a tribesman would make after his rifle, and the dud bombs offered the prospect of considerable wealth to anyone who could extract the powder safely from them. There was no fear of explosion, for that would be Allah's pre-ordained will.

At one place I heard a loud hammering noise, and we rounded an eroded irrigation dyke to see an old man sitting in the shade of the earth bank flailing away at something with a small boulder.

"What are you doing there, old man?" someone called out.

"I am trying to open up this bomb. I have been trying hard all morning. Perhaps you can help me."

He was astride an unexploded rocket head, attempting vainly to knock off the fuse with his piece of rock. He had already chipped off a fair-sized chunk of the metal casing.

"Come sit beside me," the old man went on. "Maybe you can tell me what I am doing wrong."

"You will blow yourself into small pieces if you go on doing that. It is most dangerous."

"God is merciful," the old man said, and gave the rocket head another resounding thwack.

It was hard to make the local instinct for self-preservation overcome the conviction of predestination. When we got back I issued another letter to all the Bal Harith chiefs, this time asking them to warn all their people about the dire consequences of tampering with these dangerous relics. Then I sent off a signal to the WAP Office: "Essential you arrange as soon as possible for the RAF to send up an armaments officer to destroy unexploded missiles before there is loss of life."

A few miles north-west of Asaylan, surrounded by the golden sand-dunes of the Ramlat Sabatayn, there is an unusual physical feature: the sand-dunes dip down into a hollow nearly a mile long and six hundred yards wide, the surface of which is hard and absolutely flat. The sands of the desert are always moving. Enormous quantities are hurled great distances during heavy sand-storms, but there is a more gentle movement all the time as the breeze whips up a light plume of sand grains to a foot or two above the surface, brushes it up the slope of the dune and tumbles it over the other side in a smoky spray. By this means, with some reversal of movement when the prevailing wind gives way to winds from other directions, the dunes march forward slowly but irresistibly. Yet here, in the hollow on the plain known as Jaw al-Milah ("the salty valley") the sand-dunes never rested. By some freak of nature the wind swept the sand straight across it from the huge dunes on one side to those on the other. Such places existed elsewhere too. "There is a hollow near Shabwa," I was once told by a Hammami from the country east of Bayhan, "where you can still see the tracks of the motor-car which Abdullah Philby used when he came to our lands. The marks of the tyres are still quite clear." Philby had passed that way twelve years before.

Jaw al-Milah was a natural landing ground and had been marked out for this purpose with white-painted kerosene tins, but in 1945 a Royal Air Force Dakota had crashed in flames on taking off, its crew being killed, and since then it had never been used. Towards the end of March, making a second visit to Asaylan, I rode over to Jaw al-Milah with Shaykh Qassim Ahmad in the cool of the early morning to see if it were still fit for planes to land on. We brought with us camels carrying water in goatskin bags and a supply of lime whitewash. The rebellious Bal Harith had done their best to destroy the markings and we spent some hours with my posse of Government Guards retrieving the battered tins, painting them white

again and putting them back in position as markers. After we had
finished and galloped back to Asaylan I sent a message by horseman
to Bayhan al-Qasab, where my radio was reinstalled, to say the landing-ground at Jaw al-Milah was serviceable again. Two days later we
returned to it, this time with camels carrying brushwood and
kerosene, for there was no wind-sock and the wind direction had to
be indicated by smoke from a bonfire. After a long wait in the shimmering heat an RAF Anson landed with Squadron-Leader
Blaymires, the RAF's Intelligence Officer, and Flight-Lieutenant
Cobbe, the Armaments Officer. Over the next few days further
explosions thudded over the Bal Harith fields as Cobbe dug out and
destroyed some fifteen bombs and rockets.

The role of the RAF in the pacification of the Aden Protectorate
is well known, but the significance of their contribution to the more
ordinary needs of transport and communication is not generally
appreciated. At that time, 1948, it was literally true that there were
no proper roads at all anywhere in the Western Protectorate. From
the moment when the pole at the customs post on the border of the
Colony was pulled to one side, one was on sand, following whatever appeared to be the flattest and smoothest of the tyre marks left
by previous lorries, struggling in bottom gear where the ground was
soft and rushing the low dunes in order to surmount them by sheer
momentum before becoming stuck. There had once been a tarmac
road over the short distance to Lahej, but sand-dunes had covered
almost the whole of it. Eastwards to the important cotton-growing
area in Abyan, then being developed, the only route was over the
beach when the tide was low. As one drove further inland and
reached the mountains, the routes twisted up the courses of the wadis
over broken rocks and jagged outcrops, through patches of deep dust,
up and down banks and dykes, along pot-holed, heavily-rutted tracks
which could be washed out by a sudden flood. The journey to Dhala,
only ninety miles north of Aden, took anything from five to ten
hours of extremely uncomfortable and bruising travel. To many
places just accessible over these savage paths the journey was one of
days. To the more distant parts there were no motorable routes at all.
The mountains were high and the *kawr*, a huge cliff marking an off-
shoot of the Rift Valley formation of which the main extension is

the Red Sea, was impossible to climb over most of its length. Most remote of all was Bayhan, for it lay on the far side not only of the mountain range, but also of territory as yet uncontrolled and still hostile, the tribal area of the Awlaqis.

Because the roads were so bad, if not non-existent, we used the aeroplane. All over the Protectorate small landing strips had been smoothed and scraped out in rocky valleys in the mountains or marked out with white-washed boulders or old kerosene tins on some firm stretch of desert like that at Jaw al-Milah. The Royal Air Force provided the Political Officers with their taxi service and their groceries and mail deliveries; they ferried agricultural pumps and barrels of locust poison; they brought in reliefs of Government Guards, with their ammunition and supplies; they took away the sick for hospital treatment in Aden, or elderly shaykhs seeking to present grievances to the British Agent, or veiled women, with mysterious reasons for calling on relatives in town, who could not hope to cover the long journey by camel. The Vickers Vincent and then the Albacore had been used for these purposes and in my time it was the Anson – a rugged and extraordinarily reliable little two-engined air-craft carrying about eight passengers. The Anson merits an honoured place in the history of the development of South-west Arabia.

I had been expecting Cobbe, with his fuses and detonators, but nobody had mentioned Blaymires. "I've been asked to look at Ayadim," he said. Then I knew what it was all about.

Shortly after the Bal Harith submitted, a young Harithi tribesman had come in to ask if I had medicine for a bad leg ulcer. I did what little I could to help. "I was near Ayadim when the aeroplanes attacked it," he told me in the course of conversation. Then he added: "One bomb dropped right inside one of the saltpits – a very big bomb it was – and there was much smoke. Now there is a black liquid coming out of the rock in that pit; it smells like kerosene and if you soak it up in a rag and put a match to it it burns."

The salt domes which show themselves here and there in the geological structure of Arabia are regarded as good indicators of oil-bearing strata and the Harithi's story clearly suggested oil at Ayadim. In later years the Aden Protectorate was traversed by teams of oil prospectors, but no oil company had shown any enthusiasm for our terrain at that time and we were anxious to attract one. I feigned disinterest to my visitor, lest tribal cupidity be aroused, but reported the matter to Aden, telling them I was sending another Harithi, said to be reliable and discreet, off to the mine secretly to collect some specimens. When the samples arrived a few days later they were very disappointing – no more than ordinary rock salt and a bottle of discoloured water – and he brought the information that the liquid flow was drying up. It seemed improbable we had located more than a foetid puddle left behind by the recent rain. But Aden was immensely excited by the rumoured oil strike and nobody there would wait for my confirmation. Blaymires had been despatched post haste to examine the phenomenon, bringing a letter for me from Seager asking me to arrange an expedition forthwith.

"I am afraid it is not as easy as that," I told Blaymires once we had reached the shade of my room in Asaylan. "We cannot yet be confident of our security in Bal Harith country. If we are to go to Ayadim we shall need a sizeable escort."

We went over the logistics of such an expedition with Sharif Abdullah and Rais Thabit Qassim.

"It is a day-and-a-half on a camel and there is no water and no shade anywhere," Abdullah said. "You will have to take Bal Harith guides, who can be your *rafiq* ("rafeek") to guarantee your protection against other Bal Harith."

Thabit Qassim did some sums with his fingers. "With the soldiers and baggage and water supplies we shall need at least fifty camels."

"Remember that the Bal Harith are still at feud among themselves," Abdullah went on. "Dissident Bal Harith might attack you."

"Why should they do that?"

"Because such a big party would be a temptation, and because they would gain *sharaf* from shooting at you. They would fire a few shots and then they would run."

"But if we had Bal Harith *rafiq* surely other Bal Harith would not fire on us?"

"That depends. It might even be arranged beforehand that the *rafiq* would desert you just before the attack. Those Bal Harith are very cunning, *ya* Groom."

Thabit Qassim, a Qutaybi from the lawless mountains north of

Aden but experienced in other battles in the desert, nodded his head in agreement. "That is true. Yes, indeed, that is true. It would be dangerous to go until the Bal Harith are properly under control again." Thabit Qassim was not one to endure discomfort if he could avoid it.

I had sensed already that Sharif Abdullah wanted to keep us out of Ayadim, perhaps because our intentions smacked of an encroachment by the *hakuma* on the *sharaf* of the Sharif. He had never been very sympathetic towards the Bal Harith, who hardly seemed likely to want to expose themselves to further punishment in the way he was suggesting. But his warnings could not be ignored, especially when my Government Guard Rais supported them. In any event I was tired out after the long, wearying days of the operation and secretly grateful to him for his discouragement. Nor did I have enough dollars left to hire such a large number of camels, for our expenses were tightly restricted. With some relief I told Blaymires we would have to postpone the journey until a later day. Instead I took him to Tumna.

The ruin-field called Hayd Kuhlan is about two miles south-west of Asaylan on the far side of the wadi. We had ridden past it on our way up to Asaylan, when I had seen tumbled stones littering the side of the mound, and the remains of a great building in the wadi bed to one side of it. Even to a casual visitor it was an impressive place. In Palestine, fifteen acres would be a fair-sized archaeological site and thirty acres a large one. Hayd Kuhlan was at least fifty acres, a plateau of fallen stone and rubble, of small mounds, broken walls and over-lying sand. The layout of some of its buildings and streets was still apparent, but at that time most of it remained intriguingly buried beneath the invading dunes.

At the south end were signs of a main gateway, with a wall of huge stones covered with inscriptions in the neat, square lettering of the pre-Islamic South Arabian alphabet. Beyond it, past many tumbled ruins projecting tantalisingly through the sand, four feet of the top of an inscribed obelisk (RES 4337) stood in the centre of a sandy plain which was once the central market-place. On a later visit, Sharif Awadh described to me how my predecessor in Bayhan, Peter Davey, had put men to work to dig down to the bottom of this obelisk:

"*Wallah!*" he said, waving his arms with a flourish, "They dug down eight, ten, twelve feet and the sand kept sliding in again and still they had not reached the bottom of that stone." I passed this information in due course to the American archaeologists who came to Bayhan to excavate Tumna and they started to dig a huge pit around the obelisk, some ten yards square, in order to ensure they reached its base, visualising something on the lines of the Egyptian *stelae* in Karnak. Awadh, however, was prone to a tall story. The base was found to be a mere three feet below the surface of the sand.

Close to the obelisk were the impressive remains of a large central temple, with massive blocks of stone marking its outer walls and the remnants of steps, pillars and alabaster friezes lying in shattered confusion within. Pliny, in his *Natural History* written in about AD 70, described Tumna as a city of sixty-five temples. The whole surface of the site was littered with shards and fragments – pieces of glazed pottery, alabaster and variously coloured stone, lumps of metal and broken earthenware jars. In places it was possible to detect a buried layer of ash, the signs of the holocaust when Tumna was destroyed.

We wandered round the site for nearly an hour trying to work out the plan of streets and buildings, fascinated by this tangible evidence of south Arabia's mysterious past. I sensed a longing to send for a shovel and start to explore the secrets hidden by the sand. The soldiers of my Government Guard escort leaned on their rifles looking bored and indifferent as we poked among the ancient relics. One of them said: "How can you waste time among these broken stones? Why do you marvel at these forgotten ruins? This is an awful place where the heat burns you up and the sand blows into your eyes. Let us take you somewhere more comfortable."

Disinterest in the sites of antiquity was a common feature among south Arabians. There was little lore or legend about their remote ancestors and no concern at all about the history of their country other than that affecting tribal prejudices. Blood feuds were remembered which went back for generations. Disputes over land and water rights would carry on for decades. But the great ruin-fields of Bayhan and its neighbouring wadi, Harib ("Hareeb"), belonged to the "Days of Ignorance" before the Prophet, unworthy to be remembered and therefore best forgotten. The long inscriptions at the main gateway included the name Tumna and so identified Hayd Kuhlan with Pliny's city of sixty-five temples. But when I pointed out the ancient name to my Arab companions on a later visit it aroused no interest at all, even among members of the ruling family. The Bani Himyar, as the Himyarites, the last of the ancient kingdoms, were remembered, were commonly thought to have been giants, since that was the only possible explanation for their evident ability to erect buildings with such enormous blocks of stone. I was frequently told about this ancient race of giants, but nothing else at all about the Himyarites.

The ruin-fields had one value to local minds and that was as a quarry, for the ancient masonry was far superior to the modern. When building a house, no better or cheaper stone could be found than that available, already cut and shaped, in nearby ancient sites. Most of the stone forts of Wadi Bayhan and Wadi Harib showed the unmistakeable work of the skilled masons of two thousand years before, sometimes with a finely carved inscription embedded, upside-down perhaps, in a prominent position in a wall as a sort of talisman. The sites themselves bore tragic witness to this depredation. On a high point of the mound of Tumna was a magnificent house which had recently been constructed for Sharif Awadh out of stone quarried in this way, no doubt disposing of more than one of Pliny's sixty-five temples in the process. In due course it became the residence of the first archaeological expedition to excavate in Bayhan, that of the American Foundation for the Study of Man organised by Wendell Phillips.

There was another value placed on Hayd Kuhlan. For many years rich merchants in Aden had handed out sizeable sums of money to Protectorate Arabs in exchange for the alabaster carvings and other ornamental pieces occasionally found in these ruin sites. Kaiky Muncherjee, one of the wealthier Parsee merchants, had acquired a notable collection of relics in this way, including items of gold jewellery, which he had put on display in a small museum in Steamer Point. While demand for these pieces was limited the harm done was not too serious, although archaeologically it was damaging enough because no record was kept of their provenance. In the

Muncherjee collection there were important statues of kings of Awsan, but the location of the royal tombs they came from has never been discovered. By the time I reached Bayhan, however, growing numbers of Government officials and servicemen in Aden were seeking to acquire these relics and the trade was expanding substantially. The Sharif of Bayhan was himself a prime offender; anxious to please his many official and service visitors, he would present them with alabaster carvings. Government Guards would come up with funds provided by their officers to pay labourers to dig for these souvenirs. Locals living near the sites were starting to go out with spades in the hope of finding something to sell, either alabaster or, if they were particularly lucky, gold.

I had been well tutored about archaeological matters before I came up to Bayhan by Charles Inge, an archaeologist by training who had dug under Sir Leonard Woolley at Ur and who was now working in the Aden Secretariat and held the part-time post of Director of Antiquities. With his backing I struggled to prevent further looting and we managed to persuade Sharif Hussain to stop presenting alabaster carvings to his itinerant visitors and even to pass an edict banning further digging. He was courteous and co-operative about it all, and until I left Bayhan tomb-robbing was brought under control, to the great benefit of the American expedition when it arrived in 1951. But the truce lasted no longer than that. The revelation of what lay buried beneath the sands was too much for the impoverished inhabitants of the wadi and after the Americans left the sites were attacked again with zeal; the Sharif led the way, constructing a splendid new palace for himself at Nuqub with the stones of a magnificent city gateway and related buildings exposed by the American excavators.

Even in 1948 the graveyard of Tumna, adjoining a hill north of the city called Hayd bin Aqil (pronounced "Akeel"), was a sorry sight. The graves were constructed by the Qatabanians in the form of stone chambers, sometimes a dozen or more in one mausoleum, lining either side of a central aisle. The American expedition found that there were often two or three layers of these chambers, but fortunately this was not realised by the local tomb-robbers who would dig down four or five feet and if nothing worthwhile were found would then try elsewhere. Digging deeper was hard work, because the sand kept slipping back into the hole. While this meant that tombs at a lower level stood a chance of being undisturbed, it had also led to the entire surface of the graveyard being churned up. The acres of sandy ground were littered with shattered fragments of alabaster, pottery and uprooted stones and glinted white with a coating formed out of myriads of tiny, brittle pieces of human bone.

On our way back from Hayd Kuhlan to Asaylan we passed a large, isolated building made of stone. A wizened but remarkably agile old man in a loin-cloth who lived nearby had attached himself to our party, and I asked him: "What is that building?"

"It is the tomb of the prophet Shayf", he replied, adding: "He was a giant."

"Can we see inside it?"

"Yes indeed. Come! I will show you."

We picked our way towards the tomb through tufts of low bushes. The old man went on: "Not many years ago a Bayhani who lived near here dreamed that if he dug at this spot he would make a great discovery. He started to dig next day and under the sand he found this huge grave. That is how it was discovered. Shayf lived in the time of the Himyarites. He tried to warn the people of Hayd Kuhlan to turn away from their evil life before they were destroyed." The same story is related of other such prophets in other parts of Arabia.

We entered a dim interior down low steps.

Certainly the tomb was big enough for a giant. It was about twenty feet long. There was a large stone slab at each end, and a wall of mud brick built round it to support a pointed dome. The name Shayf was embossed in Arabic script on to the plaster of the roof. Holes just large enough for an arm to enter pierced the mud wall, leading into a pitch-black cavity under the dome. I peered into this with a match, a little apprehensive of scorpions and snakes, but could see only the smooth mud surface of the grave.

"People often come here to pray for Shayf's help," the old man said.

Maybe the gods of Qataban and Sheba were not totally forgotten.

3

"My House Is Your House"

In the middle of March a signal arrived from Seager saying that he would visit Bayhan in order to talk to the Bal Harith. I had done all I could in Asaylan for the time being and we prepared to return to the capital. The Government Guards looked delighted and there was a sudden hustle and bustle.

A few days later we set out, intending to travel in the early morning cool, but, by the time the last of the cameleers had led in his grumbling animal and the sometimes bitter arguments over loads had been sorted out, and the ponderous burdens hoisted and tied on to unwilling backs, it was nearly noon and the heat was intense. Seeing the delay I demanded something to eat before we departed and Ahmad came up with a heavy *chapatti*, dry, burnt and full of grit, which I chewed while we waited. "You won't feel hungry after that," he said.

Our main caravan had twelve camels and thirteen donkeys. Most of the soldiers accompanied it, guarding not only the baggage, which included ammunition, but also the Bal Harith hostages. I was to follow them a while later with Sharif Abdullah and Rais Thabit Qassim in a second, faster-moving party on horseback. Behind us would come the Bal Harith elders on riding camels, anxious to learn for what reason Seager had summoned them.

In all my travels it was usual to move separately from the baggage caravan, since a pack camel will normally average no more than two-and-a-half miles an hour, which is slower than walking speed. For any lengthy journey one could leave long after the luggage in the knowledge that it would be overtaken on the way. But Ahmad always had to stay with my belongings, zealously ensuring that they came to no harm from clumsy loading or any foolish exacerbation of the camel's irritable temperament.

As soon as we were on our way, struggling to restrain our horses from a wild gallop, since they knew they were going back to the comfort of their own stables, Abdullah said: "First of all I am going to take you to Nuqub. My cousin Awadh is waiting for us there. They are expecting us for lunch." We steered towards the towers of the three Ashraf villages just visible in the far distance. My hasty snack began to weigh heavily inside me.

The Ashraf were not tribesmen, even though in Bayhan they carried arms, but they held a special position through their descent from the Prophet (through his grandson Hassan), which invested them with an aura of sanctified nobility. There were clans of them in Harib and Marib, as well as those in Bayhan, and numerous others elsewhere in Arabia. They were much in demand as mediators and peacemakers and from them, in the wider history of Arabia, have come many ruling families. Sharif Hussain was thus well qualified to be the head of the state we had helped to set up in Bayhan. Throughout the Protectorate there were also many Sayyids, another line of descendants from the Prophet (through his younger grandson Hussain); they too were influential as mediators. In Bayhan most of them lived in their own villages; some of them would not carry arms, but others took a full part in the internecine quarrels which abounded, and went about armed to the teeth.

The Ashraf villages of Bayhan stood directly between the tribal lands of the Bal Harith and the Musabayn; this fact had enhanced the Ashraf reputation as peacemakers, and given them an influence over those two tribes which Hussain's father, Sharif Ahmad, a forceful personality, had skilfully developed. In 1903 he formalised his position by signing a Protectorate Treaty with Her Majesty's Government. The treaty recognised him as ruler of all the tribal territory of Bayhan, something which was by no means established in fact, for the tribesmen were jealous of their tribal independence and the territory was unmapped and undefined. But the "protection" of His Majesty's Government, the *hakuma*, meant that he could expect assistance against any invasion from outside – very significant to anyone on the borders of the Yemen – while as a treaty chief he received an annual stipend of money and, more importantly, rifles and ammunition. To maintain influence by mediation was one thing; to be able to fortify it by distributing arms as *largesse* in a country where a gun was a tribesman's most important possession was quite another. Yet even then the Sharif of Bayhan had never been able to administer his country until we recognised him firmly as the ruler in 1944. By that time the temperamental Bal Harith were more or less behind him, but the more numerous Musabayn, racked by their own inter-sectional disputes, still for the most part disowned him and anarchy prevailed throughout most of the wadi.

Nuqub, then, together with the other two Ashraf villages and some outlying *husn*s (fortified houses), had for long been an island in a wild tribal sea. Until about two years before this, my first visit, the Sharif of Bayhan had based himself there and it was often still regarded as his capital.

The villages were built imposingly on high mounds, walled, fortified, with unusually tall central towers of stone. The mounds were quite clearly what archaeologists term *tell* sites, formed from the debris of centuries of occupation since the distant days of Qataban and Sheba.

Our horses clambered jerkily up the side of the mound to the gateway of Nuqub. "*Ahlan wa sahlan!* Welcome!" Sharif Awadh stood outside his ancestral home – tall, patrician, beaming pleasure with a flash of white teeth above his greying beard. "Meet my uncle," he continued, pushing forward an aged, white-bearded man, the *doyen* of the Nuqub Ashraf. We shook hands warmly and moved forward to greet a dozen other members of the clan, then followed the old man into the village, and up the steep, dark steps of its central tower.

There was a feeling of ease and relaxation in Nuqub which was always missing elsewhere in the country. The Ashraf still had their enemies in the tribal territory. Wherever the Sharif, or his son the Amir or his brothers went, an element of danger still lingered. The bodyguard of slaves, mostly of Abyssinian origin, and the escort of Tribal Guards were not ceremonial soldiers but there for the very necessary purpose of providing physical protection. Moreover, in the capital and during their tours round the sharifate, the Sharif and his family were always on duty: receiving petitions, settling disputes, hearing complaints, ordering and administering and enquiring without cease. It was only in Nuqub that they could relax completely and unwind, untroubled by cares of state and security, surrounded solely by their own kinsmen. This relief of tension showed in Sharif Awadh as he motioned us proudly into the guest room – a room floored with goat-hair carpets and brightly patterned cushions, luxuriantly cool and delightfully restful even after such a brief taste of sun and saddle.

"Would you like to drink?" Two of the young sons of the Nuqub Ashraf stood waiting inside the doorway with large wooden bowls full of cool, clear water. My mouth was already parched and the saliva on lips and tongue had dried up, so that it was difficult to talk. We drank greedily, sucking up the water in great gurgles of appreciation, and the bowls, constantly replenished, were handed round from one to another. Then we sat down stiffly, leaning on the cushions, and gained new strength from cups of bitter, gingered coffee. "*Ahlan wa sahlan,*" the old man kept repeating, "My house is your house. We are honoured."

Cooking had been put in hand when we were first sighted, so the meal was not long in coming. It was a simple one, such as Sharif Awadh had served in Asaylan. First a great dome of wheaten dough, *masub,* soused with sesame oil (*simsim*), into which the right hands of the whole party tunnelled with competitive energy. Then a huge basket platter laden with chunks of boiled sheep, which Sharif Awadh handed out personally. We munched quietly and contentedly until every bone had been picked and, as each of the Nuqub Ashraf finished, belching and praising God for his bounty, they rose and departed. Soon we too were on our way again. The outside glare was blinding after the dark interior.

Sharif Abdullah left us to return to his duties in Asaylan, but Awadh took his place and our escort was increased by a contingent of Tribal Guards on foot, who kept pace almost effortlessly with our fretting horses by sprinting some distance ahead and then walking until we caught them up. We took a path through low sand-dunes covered with *rak* and *hammal* bushes, crossing occasional patches of dry field and the water courses of small tributary wadis. At one point we passed close to a large, flat-topped mound in the centre of the wadi plain, which the main *sayl* bed had eroded on one side into cliffs. "That is Hajar bin Humayd," Awadh said on perceiving my interest. "It is another place where the Bani Himyar used to live. This wadi is full of their traces."

As we got further south the great peak of Jabal Raydan rose higher and higher in the centre of the plain. Wadi Bayhan flows on the east side of a narrow range of which Raydan is the northernmost and dominating mountain. On its west side is a major tributary, Wadi Khirr. The two join together immediately below Raydan. East of the peak at its foot lies the town of Bayhan al-Qasab.

Bayhan al-Qasab began as three separate Musabayn villages of which the main one, Suq Abdullah, was the traditional market. It was built for the most part of square, mud-brick houses, rarely more than two storeys high, with the tiny windows found everywhere in Bayhan which served both to keep the sun at bay and to act, during times of trouble, as loopholes from which a man could fire his rifle with a measure of concealment. Some of the houses had white-washed friezes round the doors and windows, but most were quite undecorated and the general mud colour blended so competely with the surrounding terrain that when seen from a distance in some lights the town almost disappeared into its background. But one building always stood out prominently; this was the five-storey tower where Sharif Hussain lived, made of stone covered with a stucco of white gypsum which gleamed dazzlingly in the sunlight as if it were made of glass. It was sited in a small plain between Suq Abdullah and al-Wusta which was being filled up with new buildings. In front of it was a large courtyard surrounded by administrative buildings, entered by a main gate. Tribal Guards manned the gate.

The guard turned out as we arrived. Their notion of drill was rudimentary. Their commander had been trained by Government Guards, who were themselves under British officers, and the words of command had descended strangely from some ancestral British drill sergeant.

"God! Shin! – Sloob imps! – Prison imps!"

The tousled line shuffled from the "slope arms" to an untidy "present" and the guard commander saluted extravagantly.

"God riddy fin spishin."

I saluted back. The men let their rifles slide down haphazardly to the ground and I inspected them in the fashion of the land — by walking down the line and shaking each one of them warmly by the hand.

Slaves led our horses away as we walked stiffly through the arch of the gate and into the Sharif's public *diwan*, kicking our shoes off at the threshold, for shoes are never worn inside an Arab house. It was the largest room in Bayhan, achieving an abnormal width by dint of a central roof girder of aluminium salvaged from the frame of an RAF Albacore which had crashed at Nuqub some years before. The room was already full of people and Sharif Hussain stood prominently among them, taller than most, holding himself very erect, a handsome man in his early forties with a black beard and a soft, cultured voice. He greeted us with great warmth and, after we had shaken hands all round, led us to cushions at one end of the room, which was carpeted with long, locally made strips of goat-hair rugs woven into black and purple stripes. A white cloth stretching down the centre of the floor was being prepared for our meal and soon, after we had quenched our thirst with orange juice, brought up from Aden in tins, the Sharif was entertaining eighty people to supper. It was a meal much enlivened by the excitement of four small boys among the guests — Bal Harith hostages from the previous summer's operations, who were now to be released. Inwardly I felt a similar excitement, for at long last I would be able to enjoy some privacy in my own *husn*.

The Political Officer's quarter was next door to the Sharif's tower in one corner of a quadrangle contained by the barracks of the Government Guards. It was hardly a luxurious apartment. On the ground floor was a windowless, cavernous and empty storeroom, with a kitchen and a small room for Ahmad to one side. Climbing up a flight of mud steps one reached the main room, which had a mud floor and a high ceiling of rough-hewn branches laid on cross-beams of gnarled *ilb* tree trunks. The walls, plastered with mud, had been whitewashed for my arrival a month earlier. There was no door in the entrance and the three tiny windows, though larger than the conventional loopholes of most houses, had no glass but only crude wooden shutters around which the air and dust blew in freely. The furnishing was meagre in the extreme: a table and a shelf made out of old packing-cases, a small box-wood cupboard, a wooden *charpoy* bed, my folding camp-chair and two locally made goat-hair carpets in purple and black stripes. Above this, reached by a narrower flight of stairs, was a much smaller room, empty when I first moved in, behind an open rooftop terrace screened by a shoulder-high wall; I made this my bedroom, using the terrace as a washplace, sharing a lavatory with the soldiers in another corner of the quadrangle – a deep hole in a dark stable floor. The tower was to be my home and office for a year-and-a-half.

Ahmad had me up next morning at first light. All Bayhan awoke with the dawn. The call to prayer, a plaintive voice from a distant muezzin unaided by the electronic amplifiers of later times, was supplemented by donkeys braying imperiously, couched camels grunting and gurgling, goats bleating and the squeal of unoiled wooden pulleys at the wellheads. In Bayhan al-Qasab another stranger noise soon added itself to this dawn chorus: this was a loud, rhythmic hammering which would go on with mechanical relentlessness until dusk – the indigo dyers beating their cloth as they prepared it for sale.

I had arranged to call on Sharif Hussain, so that we could proceed to the landing ground to await Seager's aeroplane. Once again the guard turned out at the main gate for inspection as I approached. We entered the large room where we had eaten the night before. This time it was rearranged for its primary purpose as a courtroom and office, with a flat-topped desk at one end and an incongruous-looking row of tubular-steel and canvas chairs down one side. Hussain came forward from a throng of people to greet me.

"*Salaam alaykum* – peace be upon you."

"*Wa'alaykum assalaam* – and on you be peace."

We shook hands while the greeting was taken up on all sides.

"*Subah al-khayr* – good morning."

"*Subah an-noor* – and a bright morning to you."

Thus far the conventional Arabic exchanges, but the Sharif had something to say in English too. "You sleep well?" He spoke with a broad smile, showing a flash of white teeth and dark glittering eyes.

"Thank you. Very well," I replied.

Unfortunately at that time his English vocabulary extended no further.

Hussain wore a green *futah* – a length of cotton cloth wrapped round the waist like a long kilt, which was the normal male attire in this part of Arabia – with a shirt and a white cotton coat. Round his waist was a heavy leather belt supporting a large *jambya*, the hilt and scabbard of which were decorated with silver filigree and red cornelian stones. On his head was a bright green and purple Indian-style turban. With his erect stance, he was an imposing figure.

The main theme of my time in Bayhan was to be my relationship with this remarkable man, figuratively a giant among the many colourful personalities of the Protectorate. His face was always full of expression – bright and smiling at that time, but later I was to know it in other moods: showing vexation, anger, even sullenness, or a controlled impassiveness through which nothing was revealed, or the patient, understanding resignation of a schoolmaster towards a dull but earnest pupil, or outbursts of schoolboyish merriment. He could be disarmingly friendly and had a natural warmth and a remarkable ability to put his guests at their ease.

Hussain's son Salih was with him – a quiet, smooth-faced youth with long, black hair and a noticeable squint. When old Sharif Ahmad, Hussain's father, was on his deathbed he had nominated Hussain, because of his obvious talents, as his successor. Awadh, Hussain's elder brother, had accepted this without any apparent signs of jealousy, but the history of Arabia is full of appalling tales of intrigue and parricide and Hussain was astute enough to take no chances. Accordingly, the year before, he had suddenly announced his abdication in favour of his son Salih, who was to be called the Amir (Prince) of Bayhan, and nominated himself as Regent during Salih's minority. Salih was now just of an age when he could take over some of the responsibilities of government, but this was not the Sharif's idea at all – with a father of such dominant personality there was little part for Salih to play for many years to come. Salih was a friendly, intelligent boy with whom I was able to establish a good *rapport*, for in age he was much nearer to me than was his father.

We started out at the head of the crowd towards the landing

ground on the far side of the wadi flood-bed. The arrival of the
British Agent was a big day in Bayhan and half the population of the
capital had already lined up on the edge of the strip to greet him.
All the shaykhs and notables of the land were there and with them
were some unusual and colourful additions: Kuhlani, the refugee
Amil of Harib, a small, fat, rather over-dressed man wearing the flat
turban of the Zaydis, the Yemeni ruling classes (more literally the
religious sect to which the Imam's adherents belonged); he was
accompanied by the Qadhi (or religious judge) of Marib, who had
also fled from the Yemeni troubles; they were surrounded by a bodyguard of Yemeni soldiers who had remained loyal to them,
conscripted tribesmen, fierce-looking under their coating of indigo
dye, with light blue shirts, ancient rifles and broad leather bandoliers
heavy with ammunition. Not far from this group was another contingent of Yemenis, a delegation of wild-looking men headed by the
young son of the Rassassi Sultan, a Yemeni subject who had rebelled
against the authority which Kuhlani still claimed to represent.
Hussain whispered to me: "They have come here secretly to seek
arms and ammunition." Separate from the main crowd, their white
robes contrasting with the prominent indigo-blue of the Yemenis
and Musabayn, their faces grim, were the Bal Harith elders, main-
taining the proud bearing of the desert tribesmen.

We waited as the sun grew hotter, but there was no sign of the
plane. Then a slave on one of the Sharif's horses galloped over with
a wireless message for me.

"One of the engines broke down and the plane has not taken off,"
I told the Sharif. "Seager will come tomorrow."

"*Ma feesh khawf. Bukra, Inshallah!* No matter. Tomorrow, if God
wills."

These must be about the most frequently uttered words in Arabia,
where time is so rarely of the essence.

The crowd started to disperse in small groups. As we crossed the
dry sand of the flood bed Hussain said: "Stay with me, *ya* Groom.
We will take a walk around Suq Abdullah."

Two Government Guards detached themselves from the rest to
join the escort accompanying the Sharif and we headed into the Suq.
Visually some of the charm of the town remained once one moved

close in among the buildings, but the smells, the swarming flies and the filth lying on the ground destroyed any trace of the romantic. It had grown quite haphazardly, with no attempt at plan or proper order. The streets were extremely narrow, twisting and turning, with many of the side alleys no more than four feet wide, and were surfaced only with an accumulation of sand, dust and litter. The houses were mostly of mud brick, with tiny windows and low doorways, and from their upper floors projected primitive gutters made from hollowed-out branches, which dropped sullage into muddy channels leading down the centre of the streets to open cess-pits. There was a consequent hazard in walking through the *suq*: one needed to look down on to the ground to avoid the mud, the drainage trenches, the cess-pits and the little heaps of animal excreta, which were collected and used for manuring the fields; but at the same time a wary eye had to kept upwards to dodge the drips from some broken or badly positioned gutter.

For much of the way we moved down the streets in single file, with two large, negro-featured members of the Sharif's bodyguard keeping as close to him as possible and two more attaching themselves similarly to the Amir and his young brother, a seven-year-old boy called Qaid. Everywhere men ran up to shake and sometimes to kiss the hands of the Sharif and the Amir, while small children stared and brushed the flies off their faces. The few women we encountered, veiled though they were, retreated from us or turned their backs until we had passed. Animals abounded: donkeys chewing hay; goats picking at the litter; pack camels sitting in impatient confusion, necks outstretched, with long dribbles of white saliva hanging from their mouths.

The Sharif was an animated guide. "This is one of the presses where they make *simsim* oil," he called out over his shoulder, speaking slowly because of my limited Arabic. In a clearing a camel harnessed to an horizontal pole was plodding an incessant circle round a crude tub in which the sesame seed was ground into oil. "Now I shall take you into a shop." We entered several shops – no more than windowless rooms where goods carried by camels on the three-hundred-mile journey from Aden were on sale. The goods were basic essentials: tins of kerosene, Hurricane lamps, sacks of sugar, aluminium cooking pots, rice, lentils, cigarettes, soap. In comparison with Aden the prices were astonishingly high.

"These merchants try to look poor," the Sharif said inside one shop, "but most of them are very wealthy men. They make a big profit, by God, but they pretend not to. You see, they don't like paying taxes."

"Not true!" the swarthy, indigo-turbanned man squatting among his merchandise replied wryly. "We are indeed poor. How could we be otherwise when so many people take customs duty from us. The Fadhlis, the Yafais, the Awdhalis, the Awlaqis, the Zaydis – whichever way you go they all take money from us. Besides, we have to feed the camels and there are so many other expenses. And then, *ya* Sharif Hussain, you take more customs duty from us when we reach Bayhan. Indeed we are but poor men." Two thousand years before, Pliny had recorded precisely the same complaint from the merchants of Tumna: "All along the route (from Tumna) they keep on paying, at one place for water, at another for fodder, or the charges for lodging at the halts, and the various customs duties, so that expenses amount up to 688 denarii a camel before the Mediterranean is reached; and then again payment is made to the customs officers of our empire." But the cargo on that journey was frankincense.

"We have factories too," the Sharif called out to me. "I want to show you how we make indigo cloth." In an open square a score of men were working at a line of earthenware tubs filled with the dark blue dye, one man to a tub, kneading and pounding the cloth in the tubs with long poles. The dye splashed over and the ground was stained with it for yards around. "We always used to weave our own cloth in Bayhan," the Sharif went on, "like that old man there is doing." He pointed to a far corner, where a primitive loom had been set up, suspended from two wooden posts about twenty feet apart; the old man was laying out strands between the posts from a large ball of cotton thread. "The cotton we grow in Bayhan is not very strong, so now the merchants mostly bring up Americani from Aden instead." The cloth being pounded in the vats had come from bales of American calico. Long strips of it, dripping with the dark blue liquid, were being hung up on clothes-lines to dry in the sun. "One of these days I will show you the plant that the dye comes from. It grows in the fields around here, in Musabayn country. But now you must see what happens to the cloth next." The Sharif led us down an alley to a low building from which the mechanical thumping that dominated the sounds of the town was coming. It took a while for one's eyes to penetrate the gloom. Several men were squatting on the floor, each with a large flat stone in front of him, over which the pieces of cloth were deftly passed and hammered with wooden mallets until they had acquired the smooth sheen required by local fashion. The noise inside the small room was deafening.

Indigo-dyed cloth was used as the main item of dress by several of the Musabayn tribes of Bayhan and by many other tribes around, both in the Protectorate and in the Yemen. Many of these tribesmen also dyed their bodies blue with indigo, claiming that it kept them free from disease and was both warm in winter and cooling in summer. But the dye was by no means fast, and over the months the white-washed walls of the main room in my tower became lined with blue along their whole length, rubbed in by deputations of indigo warriors who came to visit me, piling their shoes at the entrance way, stacking their ancient rifles in a corner, squatting down to sit cross-legged on the floor, and leaning their backs against the wall for support.

Most of the houses in Bayhan, including my own room and the courtroom and private quarters of the Sharif, were furnished with little more than the locally-made carpets. These were woven out of goat-hair by families of Jews. On the day I arrived in Bayhan, the pilot who brought me had come with a substantial order for such carpets on behalf of the Royal Air Force Officers' Mess in Khormaksar. The chief carpet maker, named Shaul, was sent for — a small, untidy man with his hair in long ringlets on either side of his face. For over an hour, while we sipped orange squash, Sharif Hussain and Abdullah Hassan Jaffer had haggled with him good-humouredly over the price. Once the bargain was struck the old man withdrew, wringing his hands, walking backwards and repeatedly bowing to the Sharif until he reached the door. Now the Sharif said: "Let us pay a call on Shaul the carpet-maker."

Shaul's loom was set up in the ground-floor room of his house; the conventional size of the Bayhan carpets, about three feet wide and twelve to fifteen feet long, was probably determined by the shape of such rooms. The old Jew showed us his work with pride. Using bright reds and yellows as well as purple and black, with traditional motifs woven into the stripes, his product was colourful as well as inexpensive. He worked with his three sons, two of them mere boys. "If we work all day like this," he said, "we can complete one carpet in one day."

"How many are you going to make for the RAF?" I asked.

"Five hundred." He seemed quite undisturbed by the daunting nature of his commitment, but then he was probably sub-contracting to his cousins at great profit to himself.

Hussain said: "We have come to eat with you."

The old man looked up from his loom in utter astonishment. In his wildest dreams he could never have imaged such an honour. "*Ahlan wa sahlan! Ahlan wa sahlan!*" he kept repeating, and rushed forward to kiss the Sharif's hand. "This is a most humble house, but everything we have is yours," he said. "You should have warned me, so that we could be ready for you. I will send for a sheep. *Ahlan wa sahlan!* This is *sharaf* indeed!"

"We will do without meat," the Sharif said tersely, "but we would like some tea."

One of the young sons ran upstairs to warn the womenfolk, and a few minutes later our whole party, including the soldiers and slaves, trooped up into the Jew's living-room to await his hospitality. His women had retreated to a kitchen on the roof.

Hussain had evidently deduced that this was an opportune moment to demonstrate political enlightenment; his was a gesture calculated to be noticed by me and reported onwards. This was a most sensitive time in Arab-Jewish relations. The Palestine mandate had just ended and the State of Israel had been set up. From the Yemen and the Protectorate numerous small communities of Jews in towns and villages were being rounded up by Israeli agents and brought down to Aden to be flown off to their new homeland. Despite considerable hostility to Jews in most of the Middle East, there was as yet no ill-feeling whatsoever against the Jewish community in Bayhan. To the Bayhanis the Jews were peaceful citizens, non-tribesmen and therefore of no great consequence, likeable in their way, speaking Arabic and living in almost all respects other than religion in the same way as everyone else. As craftsmen they had a vital function. Not only did they make all the Bayhani carpets but, more important still, they provided silversmiths, who melted down the Maria Theresa dollars which were the main currency, and turned them into filigreed jewellery for women and ornamental dagger sheaths for the men. No Arabs could do this work in Bayhan and it was appreciated that, when the Bayhani Jews left, some vital crafts might come to an end. The Sharif had acted to cope with this problem. While truckloads of Jewish families were pouring down into Aden, subjected as time went on to some disgraceful acts of looting and despoliation at many customs barriers they passed through on the way, the Sharif persuaded the Jews of Bayhan to stay until their ancient crafts had been taught to selected local Arabs. Only when the carpet weavers and silversmiths had been "Arabised" could the Jews of Bayhan leave the country, to enjoy the fulfilment of the Old Testament prophesy that they would fly to the Promised Land on the wings of an eagle. Their eagle flew from Aden under charter to the Israeli government and, incongruously in this burning heat, the contract had been secured by the icicle-decorated planes of Alaska Airways.

We sat for over an hour in Shaul's living-room, long enough for the whole of Suq Abdullah to learn where we were, drinking his gingered tea and consuming flat cakes of heavy bread. Our host had relapsed into silence, overwhelmed by the significance of the occasion and the illustriousness of his guests, so that we talked among ourselves. Then the Sharif got up without ceremony and left. We followed him.

As I was saying good-bye outside the white tower, we began to hear a distant sound of men singing excitedly at the top of their voices. We waited as the song grew louder, until five Tribal Guards marched jauntily round the corner in line abreast, hands clasped like children at play, rifles slung over their shoulders, leading a train of camels. They stopped in front of us and fired their rifles into the sky in salute, then came up to speak to Sharif Hussain.

After a while Hussain turned to me. "They have come here with good news," he said. "Very good news. Too many people have been travelling through Bayhan from the Yemen without paying their customs dues, so I have been sending out patrols. This patrol caught a caravan of Awlaqi smugglers passing through Bal Harith country with Yemeni wheat."

"Have they arrested them?" I asked.

"Oh no! They fired at them. The Awlaqis fired back and then fled. One of the camels was killed, but these four were captured. It will be a good lesson to other Awlaqis."

Next morning we reassembled on the ar-Rawna landing strip, and this time Seager's Anson landed punctually.

Up to that time I had seen very little of Seager. He had been so preoccupied with political crises and the visits of Protectorate chiefs while I was preparing to come to Bayhan, that I had missed my formal briefing from him and had instead gone to Dhala to be initiated by John Allen. Seager was tall and thin, very upright in stance, with a sharp nose, tight lips and a precise, rather rasping voice – a man of great energy and forcefulness who commanded immediate respect. He spoke Arabic quickly and fluently, and although the Bayhanis would laugh at his grammar and pronunciation they had no difficulty in understanding what he said. In Aden he did most of his work at home, where he could avoid the constant disturbances of the WAP Office, and would dress for comfort there in nothing but a short *futah*, a bizarre sight to an unsuspecting visitor in the neatly starched white shirt and shorts which were the conventional uniform of both official and commercial man in Aden. But now he was wearing a khaki bush tunic and trousers, with a pink-checked north Arabian *kufiyah*, the beduin head-dress, worn like a scarf round his neck, and holding the double black ring of the *aqal* in his hand like a rosary.

Basil Seager had started his Arabian service in Jiddah, after an earlier life in Turkey, and then became Frontier Officer in the Yemen, travelling the length and breadth of the southern borders of Yemen with his Yemeni counterparts to ensure that the frontier markings, where they existed, were untouched and that peace was preserved in the nebulous undemarcated regions. This had given him a unique background knowledge both of the Western Protectorate and of the Yemen. He had an immense understanding of local problems and a deep but detached feeling for the people of the region. His flair for the devious politics of South-west Arabia was never rivalled. Two years later, while staying with me in Dhala, he was slashed to the bone from cheek to lower ribs by an assassin's dagger. Though he survived, it marked the end of his long career – a grievous loss to the people of the Western Aden Protectorate.

When Seager first became British Agent, he confronted a far more difficult situation than did Ingrams in the Eastern Protectorate, for the entire Western Protectorate was split into tiny tribal factions, racked by bloodfeud, poverty and hatreds, and the terrain was quite uncompromising. We had treaty relations with some of the chiefs, but few of them wielded any significant influence and when they did it was usually for their own benefit rather than that of their subjects. There was no economic wealth to pay for development, like the fortunes remitted to the Eastern Protectorate from the East Indies by rich Hadrami merchants. The war had brought a stand-still to all forms of assistance from the United Kingdom, and the lingering aftermath of financial insolvency in London meant that there was still, two years after the end of hostilities, neither staff nor supplies nor money for any but the most limited steps towards progress. Seager's main task had been to plug holes in an old boat which kept springing leaks; and yet, somehow, he had managed to foster the rudiments of orderly state administration from which federalism could later be developed. His successes in almost impossible conditions were due to a powerful personality which could win friends, inspire confidence and avert bitterness.

This, then, was the man who now stepped out of the little aircraft to a fusillade of rifle fire, a salute capped by my Government Guards with a burst from a Bren gun. Guards of honour were inspected, the boys of the local school sang a song of welcome, and five hundred hands were shaken before we moved to the Sharif's courtroom with a crowd of dignitaries and officials. The mediaeval nature of so much of the Protectorate was always typified in this court of the Sharif, who presided from a plain wooden chair with a wooden box on the floor at his side which he used as a spittoon. Here were wise uncles, powerful brothers, gallants, flatterers and fops, yeomen, serfs and slaves. Their features, moulded by the harshness of their lives, were caricatures of their personalities, like faces in a Brueghel painting.

Seager had little time to spare and the crowd of onlookers was soon shooed out to allow business to commence. The first interview was with Kuhlani, who wanted to discuss the revolution, no doubt hoping Seager would tell him which side to back. There was a glint of cunning intermingled with fear in his small, dark eyes. He left with exaggerated obeisances. Next a place was given to the young son of the Rassassi Sultan; he sat silently on the floor while his mouth-piece, a very holy and extremely dishevelled *sayyid*, tried to inveigle Seager into supporting the Rassassi rebellion against their Zaydi rulers. Finally the Bal Harith delegation entered, looking wary and ill at ease. Seager spoke to them for twenty minutes. He reprimanded them sternly for their behaviour, induced them to admit their errors and explained the attitude of the *hakuma* towards them. This was Seager at his best: commanding yet placatory, injecting severity with good humour, totally convincing. The suspicions and bitterness of the Bal Harith faded away and their sullen faces crinkled into smiles of relief. "You are our Father Seager, *Abu* Seager," old Ali bin Munassir said. "We are your children. You give us the stick like a father to his son." When they stood up to depart, their disgruntlement had disappeared, and even the Sharif, who still found their rebellion hard to forgive, looked pleased. In fact the Bal Harith problems were not at an end, but it was no fault of Seager's that things went wrong again.

We lunched silently on a roof in the Sharif's tower. He had invited some thirty people and there was barely enough space. Hussain's private hospitality was sophisticated by local standards, and the white cloth round which we squatted was laid with small bowls containing delicacies – rice, eggs, pieces of chicken, and cans of tinned peaches – and for European visitors who had not mastered the art of eating rice or peaches with the fingers, he provided spoons. We ate, we washed our hands and faces from a bowl of water held out by a slave at the doorway, and we climbed one floor higher to another room containing a four-poster bed. Brightly coloured cushions were scattered over the bed and round the floor, and the walls were decorated with crudely painted Arabesque patterns. There, while we chatted, we drank small cups of gingered tea and smoked cigarettes from our host's tins of Players Medium Navy Cut. Then we walked back to the airstrip and Seager returned to Aden.

That night there was more feasting. It was now the turn of the Government to demonstrate its good intentions towards the Bal Harith by entertaining their *aqils* and hostages. I drew fifty-six Maria Theresa dollars from my dwindling supply and the Government Guards set to as butchers and cooks. The Sharif and his court attended the meal, mountains of *masub* followed by basket loads of boiled sheep, which our sixty guests rapidly demolished.

As presiding host I was beginning to feel with some satisfaction that the customary regurgitations marked the successful conclusion of a chapter in Bayhan's history when there was some murmuring and exchange of looks between the Bal Harith elders. Presently Shaykh Nassir bin Hussain, always a volatile and difficult man to deal with, reared up and shuffled towards me.

"I seek permission of the *hakuma* for Salih to return with me. I will send you another hostage tomorrow to take his place." He returned and sat down.

Sharif Hussain and Sharif Awadh were beside me and we held a whispered conversation.

"What is the custom when such a request is made?" I asked, for I knew that the selection of hostages had been agreed only with much argument.

"You cannot allow such a thing," Hussain said. "It is far too soon to start changing hostages."

Awadh added: "He is doing it for his own reasons. There is no need for Salih to be exchanged. He wishes to show the Bal Harith his influence over the *hakuma* for the sake of his own prestige."

"They are your hostages," I said to the Sharif. "Will you tell him that we cannot accept his request?"

"That is for you to do, *ya* Groom. This is a matter for the *hakuma*, for it is you who have bombed the Bal Harith and decided the peace terms."

Hussain was clearly avoiding having to announce a decision which he knew would annoy Shaykh Nassir and his faction. I could not argue with him in front of our guests and was left with no option. I turned to the shaykh.

"This would not be in accordance with the custom over giving hostages," I said. "You have agreed in discussion who your hostages should be and for the time being we can make no changes."

I hoped Shaykh Nassir would accept what I said, but instead he started to grumble, and when Awadh took up his challenge he became angry and vituperative. Finally he rose abruptly and stalked out of the room. The other *aqil*s followed him.

"Don't worry," Awadh said. "They are beduin and they behave like children. They were about to leave anyway. I will talk to Shaykh Nassir when he has cooled down and all will be well."

The exchange of Nassir's hostage was not mentioned to me again, but his peculiar fickleness was demonstrated a fortnight later. I had called him in with Shaykh Ali bin Munassir for a general discussion about Bal Harith affairs, but only Shaykh Ali arrived. "He set out," I was told later. "As Shaykh Ali's *dar* was on the way, he called there so that they could travel to you together. But Ali had already left. He thought that meant that Ali intended to gain your ear before he arrived. It made him so angry that he turned round and went straight back home."

Nassir's suspicions of Ali were not without foundation. For Ali's section, which included the powerful Ghurayba family, was the largest, wealthiest and most influential in the tribe. Ali believed that this justified his recognition as the paramount shaykh of the Bal Harith. "If only the other shaykhs would agree to that!" Abdullah Hassan had commented. "How much easier it would be to resolve their problems! But they guard their independence as if nothing else matters." Every few weeks Ali would take me to one side or call on me alone. "Has Seager agreed to my becoming *shaykh min shiyukh*, the shaykh of shaykhs, yet?" he would whisper. I never had the heart to tell him that we saw no chance of it.

When Seager left Bayhan I had been in the country only a month, but so much had happened that the day of my arrival seemed like an episode in the remote past. Events and problems had crowded in, one on top of another, like the whirlwinds which coursed in great spirals of sand and dust down the wadi, picking up leaves, straws and feathers and clutching angrily at the palm tree fronds as they passed. Chance would bring some small problem to notice; to understand it properly, other matters had to be examined, exposing further complications. So the vortices of my whirlwinds grew, and the pace of them quickened, and there was little control over where they would lead. Bal Harith affairs had been the major preoccupation, and their problems had become more complex the more deeply one probed into them. But I had no sooner returned from Asaylan than visitors from other areas began to call. Often they raised only petty matters, and sometimes their real object was clearly to collect the largesse which, with a little luck and some dissimulation, a Political Officer could be expected to hand out. But others came with the most complicated stories, necessitating lengthy discussions with the Sharif before any response was possible.

My first Musabayn visitor was already waiting outside my door on the evening of my return. He was Shaykh Ahmad Alawi of the Fatami section. "The government must help me!" he demanded peremptorily. "Bandits in the Yemen have looted one of my caravans. They have stolen four camels and five thousand dollars' worth of goods." He was sure to have exaggerated, but it was difficult to arrive at the right facts in such a matter and even more difficult to redress the wrong, for the Imam's administration was not responsive to such complaints. Theoretically, at least, relations with the Yemen were my concern rather than the Sharif's, so the Fatami shaykh was correct in coming to me, though I was to discover as time went on that the Sharif had his own channels of communication and some intricate involvements with officials on the far side of his borders about which he told us nothing.

Fortunately there was one man in Bayhan able and willing to give me honest, wise and totally unprejudiced advice. This was Shaykh Qassim Ahmad, who had gone down to Aden to help Seager and the RAF with the bombing operation and had returned there with Abdullah Hassan to explain the peace terms. He had arrived back with Seager, and from then until tragedy struck he was to be my guide and mentor.

In a land such as South-west Arabia, where conditions are extreme and existence is a struggle from birth, if it is survived, until death, which often comes early, only the very toughest in physique and character can stay the course. This is one reason for the intense individualism of its inhabitants. The person who can influence his fellow beings in such circumstances is a personality indeed. A shaykh must be a strong man to maintain authority over his tribe. But from the leaders emerge men with additional qualities which raise them above the rest. I knew three of these men during my time in the Western Protectorate: Sharif Hussain, the most outstanding of the Protectorate chiefs; Sayyid Muhammad ad-Darwish, the great peace-maker of the Dhala area, who eventually fell to an assassin's bullet; and Shaykh Qassim Ahmad.

At first glance Shaykh Qassim was unprepossessing. He was small and slight, with the dark skin of his peasant origin, for he was one of the *ryot* and not a tribesman. His hair was grey and thinning. When he smiled, which was often, he revealed "buck" teeth which looked far too large for his mouth. But his eyes showed a keen vitality, defying his meagre frame. Qassim was over seventy when I first met him, but he still had the strength and vigour of a far younger man: he rode a horse with ease, he could shoot with uncanny accuracy, and he was indefatigable. His beginnings were of the humblest, but he had dragged himself up by strong will and hard work, teaching himself to read and write in the process. His shaykhdom was an honorary title which acknowledged his eminence. On top of an immense courage he possessed a profound wisdom, which was widely recognised, and with it another quality almost unique in these parts – he was incorruptible. "Incorruptibility", he once told me, "is something we all recognise in you British political officers. It brings you great *sharaf* and is one of the reasons why you are always welcome to dispense justice among us. We Arabs are bad people. We always want money for a favour. I try not to be like that. I want the people to trust me in the same way that they trust you."

As a non-tribesman, Qassim had been able to move between the warring factions in the days when all Bayhan was at feud. It was unheard-of for any member of the *ryot* to have a place in tribal politics, but Qassim was a single exception; his advice was sought after and the Ashraf began to use him as a go-between in their efforts at peace-making. In course of time he was appointed Government Agent, with various responsibilities on behalf of the Political Office in Aden: delivering messages, supplying information and advice, making arrangements for the rare visits to Bayhan of the Political

1. Sharif Hussain bin Ahmad al-Habili, regent of Bayhan on behalf of his son, Amir Salih bin Hussain.

2. The rooftops of Asaylan, looking south over Wadi Bayhan.

3. Bayhan al-Qasab seen from Sharif Hussain's *dar*.

4. Sharif Hussain's white stuccoed *dar* at Bayhan al-Qasab.

5. Jabal Raydan towers over the Political Officer's *dar* at Bayhan al-Qasab.

6. Bayhan al-Qasab: looking north from the Political Officer's *dar*.

7. A Bal Harith salt caravan arrives at Bayhan al-Qasab.

8. Sharif Awadh bin Ahmad al-Habili, elder brother of Sharif Hussain.

9. Shaykh Qassim bin Ahmad, a non-tribesman, earned the title of Shaykh for his widely respected integrity and wisdom.

10. Sharif Salih bin Nassir al-Habili, a cousin of Sharif Hussain, with two of his sons (Haydar on the right). Sharif Salih was Wakil of Wadi Ayn, the tributary of Wadi Harib under Bayhani rule. He was posted as Wakil to Asaylan during the latter part of my stay in Bayhan, while Sharif Abdullah bin Salih went to Ayn in his stead.

11. Sharif Abdullah bin Salih, a cousin of Sharif Hussain, was Wakil of Asaylan during the early part of my stay in Bayhan, later changing places with Sharif Salih bin Nassir to become Wakil of Ayn.

12. Amir Salih bin Hussain al–Habili (right), titular ruler of Bayhan for whom his father Sharif Hussain acted as regent, with Sharif Awadh bin Ahmad (centre) and Shaykh Nassir bin Hussain of the Bal Harith.

14. Said bin Ali al-Harithi, a shaykh of the Bal Harith.

13. Sharif Salih bin Abdullah, one of Sharif Hussain's Wakils or local governors.

15. Shaykh Ali bin Munassir al-Harithi with his son Abdullah al-Bahri at his right hand, and two of his younger sons.

16. A group of Bal Harith tribesmen, led by their *aqil*.

17. Shaykhs assemble in Bayhan al-Qasab for the first meeting of the *Majlis al-Uqal* (Council of Shaykhs), established under the new constitution.

18. Sayyid Muhammad Aatiq al-Bakri, the much-respected Qadhi of Bayhan.

Officer or other officials. Lord Belhaven, in his book *The Kingdom of Melchior*, has told of a journey to Bayhan in 1932, when Qassim volunteered to be lowered over the awe-inspiring precipice of Jabal Raydan on a line of knotted well-ropes to explore a cave reputed to contain the treasures of the ancients. This was typical of his courage.

Seager's Anson also brought a new interpreter, Nabih (pronounced Nabee). With no one else apart from my wireless operator speaking a word of English, conversation in my limited, though fast growing, Arabic had been difficult and tiring. From now on I could be more relaxed. Nabih was an Aden clerk, orginating from the Hadramawt, who enjoyed the "perks" of service in the Protectorate even though he grumbled at its discomforts. He was young, fat and jovial, and reached me with a confidential warning: "Keep him in careful check. Otherwise he may start to usurp your functions." Somebody else had evidently had a bitter experience. Nabih was a good interpreter, and as a clown his antics provided great amusement wherever he went, but he was not easy to control and when he was not with me it was a worry that somebody might be trying to suborn him. The Arab assistants in the Protectorate administration were always very vulnerable to tempting offers.

Some time after Seager's visit I rode back from a visit to Asaylan with Shaykh Qassim and two RAF officers who had come to dispose of more unexploded bombs. Qassim insisted that we should stop for lunch at his home about a mile outside Bayhan al-Qasab. He lived in a cool, clean and spacious house which he had designed himself, built in the local style of mud brick, with white-washed edges round the doors and windows. Hard by the house he had uncovered an ancient Himyarite well, which he had dug out and restored, and from it he was now irrigating his fields. We were ahead of the main party, and he took me up to the roof to point out his crops, his goats, his cows munching hay in a thorn-fenced compound, and the new farm building he had started to erect. It was a model of orderly good management and he showed it to me with justified pride.

We sat in an upper room, drinking tea to the buzz of hornet-sized, thread-waisted wasps, which were a constant scourge in Bayhan. When the rest of the party arrived we went downstairs to eat a vast meal, for Qassim had killed a sheep as I crossed the threshold. Both the RAF officers were suffering from "runny tummies" and neither could manage more than a token lunch. "What are we going to do?" one of them said. "We don't want to offend the old man by refusing his food." Nabih said: "Leave it to me", and was as good as his word. As Qassim presented the choicest pieces to his Air Force guests, they were surreptitiously handed on to Nabih, who consumed them on top of his own substantial helping with obvious relish. His gluttony could be useful, but it was not a pleasing trait.

The persistence and lavishness of Arab hospitality was a constant strain, as one could so easily give offence by refusing it. Not only was honour to be gained by entertaining the Political Officer, but it also provided an opportunity to curry his favour as a prelude to some abnormal request or petition. Immediately the sheep or goat had met its ritual death with a sweep of a *jambya* across its tightened neck, often on the threshold so that one stepped over the flowing blood, then one was trapped, for it would be insulting to depart until the meat was cooked and eaten. Like all Political Officers, I would take precautions to avoid being caught, for otherwise there was no time to deal with the business of the moment or to maintain any sort of schedule. Often I would write in advance, or send a messenger ahead, to say that entertainment could not be accepted. "You are honouring me by the invitation itself," I would say. "Another time, *Inshallah*, but today we have pressing business." And on we would go until the protestations died in the distance.

One of the first things Seager ever said to me was: "The primary requisite of any Political Officer is a 'cast-iron' stomach." The day of our lunch with Shaykh Qassim put me in mind of that, for on reaching Bayhan I found there was further feasting to be done. In my absence Rais Thabit Qassim, who commanded my Government Guard contingent, had decided to marry a Bayhani girl. The wedding was fixed for that evening. I could not lower the *sharaf* of my own soldiers by refusing to attend. I loosened my belt, and ensured that Nabih was sitting next to me.

We ate *masub*, followed by boiled sheep. On this occasion the meat was cut up by a bony middle-aged man, naked except for a loin-cloth and a liberal covering of indigo dye. "Who is that?" I asked, and was told: "He's one of Bayhan's biggest merchants. A very wealthy man."

We consumed our meal quickly and silently, and each guest in turn stepped up to give Thabit a wedding present by flinging a silver dollar or two on to a cloth at his feet. Once he had collected his coins, the assembly conducted him in a slow-moving procession towards the bride's house, with much singing, rifle-firing and ribaldry. "You must come with us to inspect the marriage bed," said the Sharif, and led a select group upstairs into the nuptial room, where a mattress and cushions were laid out on the floor. On the far side of the wall the women, with the bride in their midst, broke into rythmic drumming and shrill ululation until we withdrew, leaving Thabit to his pleasure. Until she entered the bedroom that night he had not seen his bride's face, relying solely on the accounts of her passed on by her kinsfolk. In such circumstances one needed good friends!

Nabih was clearly impressed by the ease with which a second wife could be acquired in Bayhan. He had a wife and child in Aden, but they could not accompany him and the bachelor state was not to his liking. Some while later, when I was travelling without him, he sent me a note saying he was about to marry a beautiful Bayhani girl recommended to him by Sharif Awadh. Awadh had a rascally sense of humour and I should perhaps have guessed what was afoot and warned him. When I returned, Nabih was in a most chastened state.

"They are all crooks in Bayhan," Nabih complained bitterly. "You cannot trust anyone. Sharif Awadh swore to me that she was a young and lovely virgin and everyone else who knew the family said the same thing. They said I was marrying the most beautiful girl in Bayhan."

"So what happened?" I enquired.

"She was waiting for me in the bedroom after the feast, with a veil over her face. I was really excited, Sahib. After all, it is a terrible life that we lead here without women. I went forward to embrace her and she pulled the veil off. She was at least seventy years old, Sahib. She started to laugh at me and she had no teeth. She was hideous."

"What are you going to do about it?"

"Oh! I divorced her straight away. They wouldn't unlock the door until next morning, but I said: 'I divorce you' three times and refused to touch her. It was the worst moment of my life."

Nabih never lived down the joke of his arranged marriage, which was enjoyed hugely throughout the land of Qataban.

4

The Incense Country

We know a great deal more now about the early history of Bayhan and the area around it than we did when I was a Political Officer there, and the lists of the monarchs of the past, often vital in working out dates, are now more or less complete. But the most famous monarch ever to rule over Bayhan may never have existed. That was the Queen of Sheba. Sheba, more usually spelt Saba in Arabia, was the first and for long the most extensive of the kingdoms of South Arabia. Its capital, Marib, lay some fifty miles west of Bayhan. The Arabs have always acknowledged the Queen of Sheba and her visit to Solomon, for the Prophet enshrined the story in the Holy Quran. Her name was Bilqis, they say, and the great temple at Marib is still called Mahram Bilqis, the sanctuary of Bilqis. If she made that visit to Solomon it would have been in about 950 BC, but it is hard to believe that she ever did. From the latest archaeological findings the list of Sabaean (or Sheban) kings starts no earlier than about 800 BC and there was never ever a queen among them. Nor is there any trace of trading frankincense and myrrh with Palestine at so early a date.

But the early kings of Sheba, particularly Karibail the Great in the 6th century BC, exercised at least a tenuous control over a considerable area centred on the wadis, like Jawf, Adhana, Harib, Bayhan and Markha, which flowed into the Ramlat Sabatayn desert, where the Bal Harith now roamed. In mediaeval times this desert was called the Sayhad, and the ancient civilisations clustering round its southern and western edges are often now known as the Sayhad culture. All this region as far east as Hadramawt, including what was now my North Eastern Area, had once, in an ill-defined way, been a part of

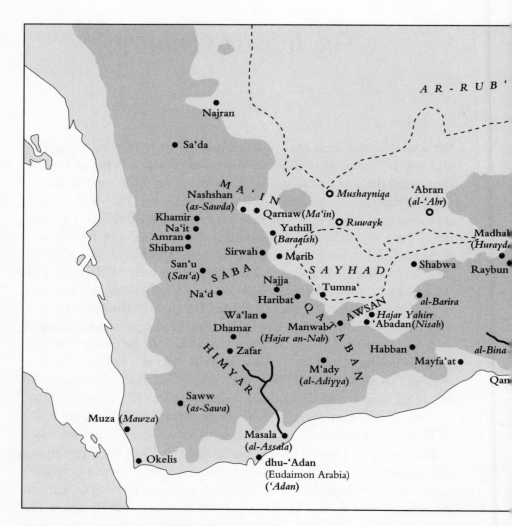

SOUTH-WEST ARABIA BEFORE ISLAM

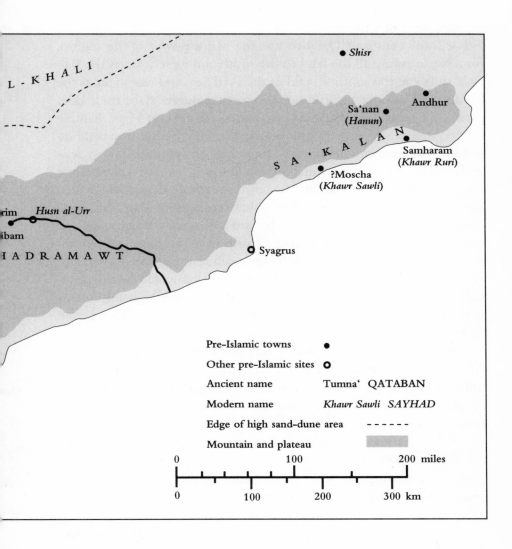

Pre-Islamic towns   ●

Other pre-Islamic sites   ○

Ancient name   Tumna'   QATABAN

Modern name   *Khawr Sawli*   SAYHAD

Edge of high sand-dune area - - - - - -

Mountain and plateau

Saba or Sheba. Then, in around 430 BC, the people of Ma'in, north of Marib, broke away from Saba to form their own kingdom and their merchants, already busy with the incense trade, became Minaean merchants. A century later Bayhan too seceded and set up the kingdom of Qataban.

For some centuries Qataban was the major power of the region, for a while ruling all the land to the south and west as far as the Bab al-Mandab, at the southern end of the Red Sea, and east as far as the borders of Hadramawt, although it never conquered Saba itself. The great ruin heap of the Qatabanian capital, Tumna, at Hayd Kuhlan is exceeded in size only by the sites at Marib, which in my time no outsider was permitted to visit, and Shabwa, another almost legendary city, once the capital of Hadramawt, which lay about a hundred miles to the east in what is now remote desert and which was in my time in uncontrolled tribal territory and so also quite impossible to reach. Qataban, Saba and Hadramawt vied with one another through various fluctuations of power and there were other secessions, such as Awsan, which for a while took over the area of Wadi Markha, but eventually all came to be dominated by the powerful dynasty of the Himyarites, originating in the high mountains of the Yemen, so that all their ancient traces are now usually referred to locally as Himyarite.

Over the extensive period of this pre-Islamic civilisation south Arabia was controlled and administered on a scale unknown again until recent times. Highly developed irrigation systems through canals and dams and sluices tamed the wild seasonal floods; paved roads allowed camel caravans to trade over steep mountain barriers; temples and palaces of finely wrought stonework embellished the towns. Throughout the length and breadth of Bayhan, tumbled stones and eroding silts still give evidence of this golden age, when south Arabia provided myrrh and frankincense for the ancient world along a great caravan highway to Petra and Gaza.

Even the American archaeologists who first excavated Tumna had difficulty in deciding just when Qataban ceased to be. The end of the city appeared to have been sudden, for, even before excavations, a layer of ash could be seen close to the top surface, indicating destruction by fire during the first century AD. This suggested that the city had been sacked and burnt down by the invading forces of Hadramawt. But later studies have revealed that some of its buildings were still being used in the second century AD, while a puzzle remains from the very fact that two magnificent bronze statues of cherubs riding lions were recovered by the Americans from underneath the ashes, where they had fallen during the conflagration. When an ancient city was sacked its metal statues would normally be looted, for the metal itself was valuable and works of art were always trophies of war. At the same time inscriptions exist which show that a puppet king of Qataban had been set up some time after the blaze in a small town at what is now the ruin site called Hajar bin Humayd, a few miles to the south, the last of these probably dating to around AD 150. What happened next is very unclear, for the Himyarites did not leave any inscriptions of their own in Bayhan. By the fifth century AD their own power was beginning to weaken and by that time, too, the great overland trade in frankincense and myrrh had long ago come to an end. The Himyarites fostered trade by sea, helping the merchants of the Roman empire from Egypt to collect incense from south Arabian and Somali ports, but the demand for it rapidly diminished after Rome accepted Christianity. Both Christianity and Judaism had begun to make headway in south Arabia, upsetting the established order. Foreign invaders moved in, first the Abyssinians and then the Persians, in the wake of domestic wars. Finally Islam itself, militant and uncompromising, swept away what was left.

Arabs refer to the days before Islam as the Days of Ignorance. As far as Bayhan is concerned, the period of our greatest ignorance is the thousand years which followed the collapse of the Himyarite civilisation. The early kingdoms left not only fine buildings but also many inscriptions, carved elegantly into the alabaster of memorial stones or hewn almost indelibly onto rock faces. No records survive of the millennium which followed, when Bayhan was a mere backwater. In the Yemen the Persians, who had moved in after the Himyarites, were soon ousted, and the family of the Zaydi Imams, descended from the Prophet's son-in-law Ali, established a dynasty which ruled on and off right through until the twentieth century. At times, as under the seventeenth century Imam Qassim the Great, they achieved immense power and prestige, but at other periods they were weak and almost without influence. Both the Egyptians, in the fourteenth century, and the Turks, in the sixteenth, controlled South-west Arabia for a time, and the Turks returned in force in 1871, when the Imam Yahya rallied support for a war of liberation commenced by his father. Yahya inflicted a crushing military defeat on the Turks in 1904 and recaptured Sanaa in 1911. This was the same Imam Yahya whose assassination had coincided with my arrival in Bayhan.

In outlying areas like Bayhan the ebb and flow of power in the Yemen had little effect. After the Himyarites the trade routes had gone, the irrigation works were neglected, and the land became and remained impoverished. The population, converted at the time of Persian rule at the dawn of Islam to the Sunni sect, had no common cause with the rival Zaydi sect of the Imams and their highland followers. In this vacuum the dominant influence was tribal, for each tribe had to protect its lands and its rights in order to safeguard its very existence. Bayhan and the entire country around it fragmented into independent tribal areas which waxed and waned according to the dictates of various local circumstances.

The British had not entered the South Arabian scene politically until 1839, when Aden was occupied, although there had been earlier trading connections both with Aden and with the Yemeni port of Mukha. With the capture of Aden from the Sultan of Lahej, who had himself wrested it from the Yemeni Imams a century earlier, a treaty was concluded under which the British Government accepted responsibility for certain stipends being paid by the Sultan of Lahej to neighbouring tribal chiefs in order to retain their allegience and keep the trade routes open. This was the basis of all our dealings with the chiefs in what became known as the Aden Protectorate.

Until 1927 the Protectorate was the concern of the Government of India and not of the British Colonial Office. To India the only purpose in dealing with the hinterland was to keep Aden secure as a port of call for coal, water and trade on the sea-route between India and Europe through Suez. Friendly relations with the chiefs and some assurance that no hostile foreign power would get a foothold in their territory were all that was needed to attain this, and no consideration was given to acquiring territory or forcing a Colonial-style government on them. The policy was put into effect by a series of Protectorate Treaties with the Sultans, Amirs, Shaykhs and other local rulers, gradually reaching chiefs far from Aden itself. In 1903 such a treaty was signed with the Sharif of Bayhan.

Had more been known about the political situation in Bayhan at the time, it is improbable that a treaty would have been concluded. The Ashraf, noted already as descendants of the Prophet who owned land and villages dividing the Bal Harith and Musabayn tribes, had no rights as suzerains, and old Sharif Ahmad bin Muhsin's initial efforts were directed towards persuading the tribes that he should represent their interests with the Aden authorities, much like a court advocate.

Treaty or no, Bayhan remained almost unknown to the outside world. In 1904 Wyman Bury, a naturalist who travelled dressed as an Arab under the name of Abdullah Mansur, made a short call on the Sharif at Nuqub on a journey from Nisab, which is recorded in his book *The Land of Uz*. No one else went there until 1931, when the Political Secretary, Colonel Lake, visited it on a carefully planned journey designed to make contact with tribal leaders and study their problems at first hand. At that time Aden had just been made an Air Command and a new emphasis was being placed on keeping the main trade routes throughout the Protectorate secure with RAF assistance.

The machinations of the Imam Yahya had caused trouble in all the border region as he sought to recover areas that he considered were historically part of the Imamate. In 1928 a Yemeni force had been driven out of the Dhala and Radfan areas, north of Aden, but the Awdhali plateau was still occupied, and in 1930 the valleys of Ayn and Manawa, which belonged to Musabayn tribes and were hence Bayhani territory, had been invaded, while some of the Musabayn shaykhs had declared for the Imam. Lake therefore had plenty to discuss with the Sharif, but there was little he could do in such remote parts. Lake took with him to Bayhan a newly arrived army officer from the Aden Protectorate Levies, Hamilton, later to become Lord Belhaven, who described the journey in his book *The Kingdom of Melchior*, but there were no government officers with full-time responsibilities for the Protectorate at that time apart from Lake and Champion, then the Secretary for the Protectorate, who later, as Sir Reginald Champion, became Governor of Aden.

If the Imam was to be restrained, it would have to be achieved by negotiation, and attempts at this led to the signing in 1934 of an Anglo-Yemeni treaty containing agreement to preserve the *status quo* on the borders. But the word used for "borders" had different inter-pretations: to the British it signified defined frontier lines; to the Imam it encompassed complete tribal areas; consequently the treaty was ineffective. The frontier between Yemen and Bayhan had in any case never been defined. Thereafter any action taken anywhere in the Protectorate which was not acceptable to the Imam would be declared by him to be in breach of the *status quo* agreement.

Seager had arrived from Jiddah shortly before the Treaty of Sanaa was signed; he was appointed Frontier Officer and based in Sanaa. In the Protectorate, following Champion's posting to Jordan, Lake became Secretary for the Protectorate and Hamilton was made Political Officer, while a new post was created and Harold Ingrams arrived to become Political Officer for the Hadramawt. This was the modest beginning of new policies for the Protectorate.

Bayhan now began to receive more attention. The Imam arrested his Amil (Governor) in Harib for peculation, and the disgraced offi-cial's brother, al-Jardai, assassinated the successor and fled to Bayhan, where a Musabayn shaykh, Alawi bin Ahmad, gave him refuge. Both Seager and Hamilton visited Bayhan to resolve the resultant crisis. Three years later a Yemeni army occupied Shabwa in order to dis-rupt our attempts to control Hadramawt and the lands to the west of it. Hamilton enlisted the aid of Sharif Awadh to organise a tribal force which compelled the invaders to withdraw without a battle, grasping the opportunity of his stay in Shabwa to excavate one of its ancient ruined buildings.

By the start of the Second World War the pace of political devel-opment in the Protectorate was quickening. The "Ingrams Peace" was bringing benefits to Hadramawt which all could see, and tribes between Hadramawt and Bayhan were beginning to consider the possibility of a wider truce. But the war ended the momentum, further political effort was confined to consolidation, and the tribes of Jirdan, Hadhina and Awlaqi relapsed into anarchy. Hamilton, ill and disillusioned, left. In Bayhan, however, a new Political Officer had arrived in 1939 to begin a new chapter in its history. His name was Peter Davey.

Peter Davey was the officer whose death in 1947 created the vacancy in establishment which I filled. He was shot by a *qat*-crazed minor *aqil* in Dhala whom he was trying to arrest for a murder, and as he had become a Muslim he was buried in an unmarked grave in a Muslim cemetery in Dhala. He spoke Arabic with an extraordinary fluency – "*Wallah!*" Sharif Awadh said to me once, "if you heard Davey talking and did not see him you would suppose he was a Bayhani" – and no other officer in the Aden Protectorate better understood the vagaries of its people, or knew so much about them. When I reached Bayhan there were no files, no office papers whatsoever, but the Sharif handed me a small, thick notebook in a flimsy and rather tattered yellow cover. "You will need this," he said. "It is what Davey has written about Bayhan." In Davey's neat and scholarly handwriting were notes concerning every aspect of the country likely to concern a Political Officer: there were lists of all the tribes and sub-sections, with the names of their shaykhs and *aqils* and the numbers of their fighting men; there were shrewd personality notes on the influential and the notorious; there were lists of villages, wells and populations and notes on habits and customs; there was information about crop yields and taxes, irrigation rights, feuds and truces, tribal boundaries, grazing rights and local lore. This notebook was my only written source of reference and frequently provided urgently needed information which could otherwise have taken weeks to elicit. With Shaykh Qassim Ahmad at my shoulder and Davey's notebook in my pocket I was, despite my lack of office records, well provided for.

When Davey first reached Bayhan, he faced an appalling security situation. The Bal Harith were allied with the Sharif, but inter-sectional feuding complicated the relationship. The more numerous Musabayn were in a state of anarchy. The word Musabayn probably signifies "the two tribes from Saba – (or Sheba)" and the Musabayn had developed into a confederation of several tribes, prepared to act together in matters of great moment but otherwise each retaining considerable independence. Within the main group were sub-divisions linked by common borders or a common ancestry. The three most important sections, the Ahl Salih, Ahl Alawi and Ahl Sahaqi, were known collectively as the Ahl Abdullah, leading to the place-name Suq Abdullah. But the Ahl Salih were intermittently at feud with the Ahl Alawi, so that even within the Ahl Abdullah there was no unity. Other powerful Musabayn sections included the Ahl Naim and the Ahl Arif, who lived in the southern mountains and painted themselves from head to foot with indigo. Some of the more distant sections, like the Ahl Shurayf who flanked the desert in Wadi Harib, had little or no contact with the bulk of their tribe, while others were hardly Musabayn at all, like the Ahl Kuhayl who lived in Wadi Haraja and had formerly owed allegience to the Rassassi Sultan.

The feuds between the Ahl Salih and the Ahl Alawi were the most serious hindrance to peace. Alawi bin Ahmad, the Alawi shaikh, and Ahmad bin Sayf, who headed the Salihis, lived close together in the collection of villages which was to become Bayhan al-Qasab. Not only were their two sections fighting each other, but their own sub-sections fought among themselves. Alawi bin Ahmad's influence had been reduced following his part in the Jardai affair and he sought to increase it by murdering his rival. He was himself killed in revenge. By this time in the villages, where each tribesman's home was a fortified tower, men hardly dared venture out by daylight for fear of being shot by a neighbour. Section fought against section, families fired on families. To maintain a living from the parched earth, men dug crawl trenches outwards from their *dars* to their fields. In some of the bigger *dars* tunnels were excavated to reach the well-shafts outside in safety. At night men crept out to poison the roots of their neighbours' palms with tins of kerosene. The feuding went on far and wide. Amir Salih once brought a young boy, of about eight years old, to meet me. "He is from Wadi Ayn," said Salih. "He is the shaykh of his tribe." The shaykh?" I queried. "He is very young to be the shaykh!" "Indeed so," said Salih, "but there is no one else. His father, his uncles, all the men in his tribe have been killed in the feuding, and their sons are no more. All have gone. In the whole tribe he is now the only male left."

It was government policy not to interfere in the administration of the Protectorate states, and little or nothing which could remotely be termed an administrative machine existed. If we are criticised for the inadequacies of the governmental services in the post-war Protectorate, it is as well to ponder over the meagre foundations on which they were built. Until 1942 not a single organised Sharia (Quranic) or Urfi (Common Law) court existed in the Western Protectorate outside of Lahej, close to Aden. Up to the end of 1943 there were only two primary schools, one in Lahej and one in Dhala, and even by the end of 1946 there were only eleven. Until the war there had been no doctor anywhere, the only medical services available being in Aden or from fifteen "dispensers", who had received three months training in the Church of Scotland Mission Hospital in Aden at government expense before returning to practise in their tribal areas. Of other services there were, until after the war, none.

Development began to gain speed once the war ended, but it was a slow process. By 1947 the approved establishment of Political Officers in the Western Protectorate had gone up to seven, though not all had been appointed. It was now recognised that the British Government had an obligation to improve the lot of the people, but the people were innately conservative and distrustful of anything new, while rulers who possessed neither the money nor the inclination to establish their own social services were deeply suspicious of any attempt by the government to impose such things on them. Money had to be most carefully controlled or it would rapidly disappear in peculation, and there was in any case little available after the bankrupting cost of the war. Looked at against this background, the proposals formulated in the early 1950s to set up a modern style of federal constitution for the Protectorate states can be seen as unrealistically premature. Much vital spadework remained undone.

Certainly a *hakuma* composed of all the Protectorate chiefs would have seemed a wild fantasy to the Musabayn of 1939, and they would have been quite unable to understand the concept. Their thoughts did not stretch further than their own wadis. Economically they were better off than the Bal Harith, because the flood waters always reached their fields provided the rains did not fail completely. This and the geographical differences of their tribal areas, mountain and valley as opposed to the open desert of the Bal Harith country, had moulded them differently from the Bal Harith. The ethnic origin of the two main tribes was also different, for the Musabayn seemed to have Sabaean forefathers, while the Bal Harith had traditionally emigrated from more northern regions. The Bal Harith were passionate, fiery tempered when aroused, open about their grievances. The Musabayn had no need of the desert dweller's intricate code of chivalry and little interest in tradition; they were unscrupulous and more cunning.

The Imam and his Amils in the border provinces played on Musabayn suspicions that Davey's arrival portended the loss of their independence, and by 1942 most of the Musabayn shaykhs were receiving regular salaries from the Yemen in exchange for statements of loyalty to the Imam. Visits by Davey and the Sharif, travelling from Nuqub with strong escorts, to persuade them to accept a truce and peace under the Sharif's rule were greeted with obstinate rejections and a defiant flying of Yemeni flags from the battlements. They were won back section by section, slowly and painstakingly, by the political skill of the Sharif supported by the threat of military action, despite the paramount need to avoid taking human life, which might have extended the feuding. The Ahl Salih section led the return.

In 1948 Shaykh Naji bin Nassir as-Sahaqi, who for years had been one of the most persistent opponents of all efforts to establish an administration in Bayhan, was showing me proudly round his farm, started up with a loan from the new Protectorate Agricultural Department. "When I think about the old days," he said, "I see I was a fool. If only we had believed that the intentions of the *hakuma* were honest! We thought our lands would be taken from us. We thought the Imam understood us better than the *hakuma*. How blind we were!" But not all the Musabayn were yet so loyal. Shaykh Qassim once voiced the same feelings to me. "We could never have established peace here without the *hakuma*," he said. "Everybody knows that. Your *sharaf* is very high now. Soon you must send a Political Officer to Markha and Awlaqi to bring peace and a proper administration there as well. It's what the people there want now they have seen the *hakuma*'s good intentions here."

At the beginning of 1948 our complement of Political Officers was well below the establishment. Seager had a Deputy British

Agent, John Allen, but he had been sent up to Dhala to deal with the serious troubles which had been recurring ever since Davey's death. Ernest Kennedy, with a long experience in the Eastern Protectorate under Ingrams, was Political Officer, Southern Area, where a major cotton-growing irrigation scheme was under development in Abyan. Kenneth Bell, who had been in Dhala (the Northern Area) went on leave as soon as I arrived and returned months later to relieve Kennedy. Alistair McIntosh was expected back from leave, when he would relieve Allen in the Northern Area. There was about the same number of Arab Assistant Political Officers, of whom Abdullah Hassan Jaffer and Ahmad Hassan Mudhaffar were the senior and most experienced. The latter, a man of quiet and competent efficiency, was looking after the WAP Office with a small staff of Arab and Indian clerks and an English woman, the wife of a commercial agent, who was Confidential Secretary. A constant stream of letters and signals was fed out to Seager in his house at Khormaksar.

Nobody could blame Seager for steering clear of his office. It was tucked away in a corner of Crater, the crowded "old town" of Aden built, as its name implies, in the bowl of what was once a volcano. The building was a rambling house of white-washed stone, single-storeyed except for one central upper room over which flew the Union Jack. It had a wide pillared veranda, walled in with green-painted lattice to provide extra working space, and could claim the historical distinction of being the original residence of Captain Haines. In 1838 Haines had tried to purchase Aden for the Bombay Government from the Sultan of Lahej and a year later, after an agreement about the sale had been dishonoured by the Sultan and the town occupied by the Royal Navy with a small force of Indian and British troops, he became its first Political Agent. The house was consequently a fitting place for our headquarters, but it was hardly well suited for the purpose. The interior, dark in contrast to the blinding glare outside, was worn and dingy. Officers and clerks, secretaries and messengers, vied noisily with local scroungers and visiting delegations of up-country tribesmen for room and attention in an entirely inadequate floor-space. Eddies of dust blew in through the open windows, doorways and latticed ventilation ports, the wind tugging at papers anchored under weights against the internal draughts of electric ceiling fans. It was difficult to work effectively in such a place, even on the rare occasion when there was no crisis demanding attention.

I tried to consult the records about Bayhan during a short visit to Aden made with the main purpose of resting and replenishing supplies, but there was nowhere to take them away from the bedlam. The clammy heat of the coast was enervating after the dry breezes of the mountain hinterland and I was not sorry to return to the North Eastern Area, although the aircraft bumped and swayed sickeningly as we pushed through heavy clouds. I brought back with me three chairs and a small wooden filing cabinet. My sitting-room was now a furnished office.

It had rained when I first arrived in Bayhan and on the night of my return it rained again, and another flood roared down the wadi bed. Water dripped steadily through the mud roof of my *dar* into the top-floor bedroom, and trickled through the roof balcony into the living-room below when I sought refuge there. Sleep was impossible. Next morning Shaykh Qassim said: "No one sleeps when there is heavy rain. There is not a roof in Bayhan which does not leak. Besides, we are all rejoicing and praising Allah for his bounty."

The following day I set out on horseback with Amir Salih, Shaykh Qassim and Nabih, escorted by mounted soldiers and slaves, to pay a visit to Wadi Ayn. Before I went to Aden the Sharif had been most emphatic: "It is very important that you should see my stolen lands in Ayn as soon as possible. The Yemenis still occupy some Musabayn villages and we still need the help of the *hakuma* to recover them. You must find out the facts for yourself, and then you can explain my case to Seager. I will arrange for you to go there as soon as you return."

We moved out of Bayhan al-Qasab northwards in almost pitch black darkness, while the baggage was still being sorted into loads for the camels. Packs of pariah dogs, the sentinels of South Arabian settlements, pursued us from a safe distance, barking. The Sharif had allocated for me a fine, powerful grey stallion of the wildest temperament, called Tunis, but his locally made saddle had unadjustable stirrups far too long for me. Tunis would have taken advantage of this handicap in a flash, and I exchanged him for a more steady steed to forestall the *kassar sharaf* of being thrown. A ride on Tunis, and I was to have many, was always an adventure.

As dawn picked out the black silhouettes of the mountains flanking the wadi we headed over soft sand towards a spur called Jabal Labakh which marked the entrance to a side-stream named Wadi Mablaqa. Behind this was a rocky gorge called Shaab Labakh. Some time later, on a similar journey, Shaykh Qassim said: "They say there is ancient writing on the rocks in Labakh" and we persuaded an old shepherd we had encountered to show us the site. There were two Qatabanian inscriptions high on the rock face (RES 3689) and I climbed up to photograph them. A translation* published in 1971 by Professor Beeston of St John's College, Oxford, showed Labakh as the name of the valley then as now, a survival of more than two thousand years. They recorded the granting to the families living there by the King of Qataban of special rights to collect tithes in Dathina – another surviving place name, for it was to Dathina that Abdullah Hassan Jaffer had gone to worry about his grain tithes. The ancient past was always close to one in Bayhan.

Wadi Mablaqa was strewn with stones and boulders and covered with a thick growth of small thorn bushes and scraggy weeds. Occasional patches of field, squared off with low stone walls and for the most part seemingly abandoned, indicated attempts to farm this unpromising terrain. We moved due west up the watercourse for over an hour while the sun grew higher and hotter, the horses picking a slow, tortuous, stumbling route with short canters over brief stretches of sand.

"We are in good time," Amir Salih said to me, "and I would like to visit the Musabayn who live up that *shaab*. They are a very small section of beduin." He pointed to a narrow opening in the mountain wall to our north, adding: "It will not take long."

We were soon forced into single file, climbing a track up a steep, twisting stream bed over jagged rocks. After about a mile the valley widened a little and we came across two beduin tending an enormous flock of goats which dotted the steep mountain slopes on either

---

* A. F. L. Beeston, *Qahtan – Studies in Old South Arabian Epigraphy*. Fascicule 2. London, Luzac, 1971.

side. We sat in the shade of a large overhanging rock while one of the shepherds ran further up the valley to warn his kinsmen of our arrival. Presently other members of the clan approached in twos and threes, firing their rifles in salute and kissing the Amir's hand. The gunfire echoed off the hillsides like the noise of battle. Goat's milk was brought in a bent and blackened metal bowl and handed round from mouth to mouth. There was no water. We drank and I was just preparing to move on when the shaykh, a grey-haired, wrinkled old man wearing a loin-cloth, announced with pride: "I have slaughtered two goats in your honour." It was early still for breakfast but we were trapped.

"*Ahlan wa sahlan!*" the old shaykh continued. "Please follow me. It is only a short distance."

We led our horses for what seemed a very long distance along the narrow path until the gorge opened out again. The black goat-hair tents of the tribe had been dismantled from their family plots and re-pitched on one of the few level patches of ground to make a marquee-sized roof under which we could find shade. To one side two goats sizzled in a vast cooking pot under the watchful gaze of an old woman, helped by two wide-eyed little girls who pushed branches into the fire. The two womenfolk and girls of the tribe studied us from a safe distance.

"*Ahlan wa sahlan.* Your meal will be ready *baad dajijatain* – in a couple of minutes. Please excuse me for a moment." The old shaykh withdrew to converse in whispers with his men, who had grouped round the fringes of the tent to stare at us. Then he went off to attend to the cooking, while the men disappeared.

We talked among ourselves. The old man reappeared from time to time, calling out: "*Baad dajijatain.*"

Presently the men could be seen joining the small boys high up the mountain-side, shepherding their flocks with stones and sticks and strange shouts.

"What are they doing with their goats?" I asked the Amir. Salih looked puzzled.

"*Ya* shaykh," he called out to the old man. "Tell me, what is all the shouting about?"

"It is nothing. It is nothing."

We could see that hundreds of animals feeding on the sparse pastures among the towering peaks above us were being reluctantly rounded up and driven away. Every man in the tribe apart from the old shaykh himself was now scampering after them over the steep mountain slopes.

"Why do you drive your flocks away?" the Amir asked.

"Because we have killed two of their brothers," the old man said. "If they see their two brothers being eaten then you know what will happen."

"What will happen?"

"They will all die, of course. Surely you know that? Every one that sees his brother being consumed will die. By God, we cannot allow that to happen. We are taking them over the mountain to the next valley. Don't worry! It will only take two minutes!"

It was some hours before we finally escaped the hospitality of these superstitious mountain beduin.

There was the excitement of exploration in this journey up Wadi Mablaqa, because I knew that no "foreigner" other than Peter Davey had travelled this way before. Despite his copious notes Davey had never left a map, sharing the Arab inclination to dispense with such a thing, and nobody had any real idea of the geography beyond these mountains. Moreover, Davey had possessed little interest in Bayhan's antiquities and paid little attention to them. Nothing was known of the ancient sites which were said to exist in Ayn and Harib.

The mountain-sides which hemmed the wadi in became higher and closer together as we moved up the *sayl* bed. The gradient steepened, and soon we started to climb the pass and it was no longer possible to ride. As we wound through huge, tumbled boulders I noticed that our pathway was crossing broken patches of an old paved road, about twelve feet wide, which zig-zagged upwards bordered by a low wall. "That is the work of the Himyarites," Shaykh Qassim called out to me. "*Wallah!* They knew how to build roads." The higher we climbed the better the state of preservation of this ancient camel way. Making full use of the natural slopes, the road twisted and turned to provide an easy, stepped bridle path, often supported on artificial stone embankments ten to fifteen feet high which had survived the heat and torrents of centuries with surprisingly few

points of collapse. It was a remarkable example of ancient engineering skill. Climbing several hundred feet, the road eventually became
a series of sharp hairpin bends leading to the pass itself, which was
a chasm over a hundred feet long and up to fifty feet deep. The marks
of primitive cutting tools showed on the walls; the chasm had been
cut through solid rock. Even with explosives and machinery the construction of the pass would have been a difficult project, but to make
it by hand labour alone was an extraordinary accomplishment.

We sat down in the welcome shade provided by this artificial slit
in the mountain. At such a height the air was cool and there was a
stiff, refreshing breeze. Looking down we could see the camel caravan with our baggage and my faithful cook, Ahmad. We had passed
them long before and they were now diminutive specks below us
climbing slowly. Nearer, but still far down the mountain face, Nabih
was struggling to catch up, breathless after his goat-meat breakfast.
On the other side of the pass the same snake-like track zig-zagged
downwards into a long, narrow valley; far below, shimmering in the
heat haze, was the plain of Ayn and beyond it the mountains of Harib.
At this point, as we sat to recover breath, the ancient history of the
land assumed an intense reality. I was a Minaean merchant on the
way to Sheba. Behind me the grunting camels struggling up the steep
pathway were laden with frankincense and myrrh. In front of me
Marib beckoned from misty hills on the far horizon. In seventy days'
time I would be reaching Gaza and the Mediterranean. It must have
happened like that many thousands of times.

The descent was more difficult. For some reason the pathway had
not survived the two thousand years of its life so well on the western side of the mountains and we had to tread warily to avoid
stumbling over loose boulders. But we were soon on gentler slopes
and, where the construction work had ended, or perhaps where it
had begun, Qassim took me round to the side of a very large boulder. "Look! The writings of the Himyarites." On the flat face of the
rock was a long, finely carved inscription. It was translated later by
Professor Ryckmans of Louvain University: "Aswamm, son of
Yasurram, son of Madhim, servant of Sahr, king of Qataban, directed
and carried out all the work and building and paving of the road of
the mountain of Mablaqat and all the work and restoration of the

house of Waddum and Atirat and the palace of the king at Qullay, on the order of his lord Yadaab." (RES 3550)

As I copied the words of the inscription, meaningless to me at that time except for the single phrase "king of Qataban", Qassim said: "In Bayhan we have heard from our grandfathers that the Mablaqa pass was built on the Bayhan side by a woman and on this side by her son. I do not know their names. Perhaps the Himyarite writing will tell you. But there are powerful jinns here and we have to be careful. When we go back we will all throw stones on to the heap at the bottom, otherwise they may do us harm." I had noticed a mound of stones and pebbles on the roadside where we began our climb. From then on I dutifully cast my stone every time I passed it.

Ayn was a fertile wadi, always noticeably greener than Bayhan. At the point where it took on the name Harib, the mountains on either side closed in and the gap was narrowed further by a huge dome of rock called Qarn Ubayd, which jutted up in the middle of the plain. The underlying strata at this point seemed to act as an underground dam, holding back the sub-surface water of Ayn, so that the water table was high and the wells never ran dry. There were always irrigated crops in Ayn, and plush green grass grew on the banks of the water channels. As we cantered down the sandy bed of the watercourse from Mablaqa, we saw wild flowers, birds and brilliantly hued butterflies.

We reached a well and a small boy watering his goats there held out his waterskin. Amir Salih proffered the skin to me. "*Sharab, ya* Groom! Drink! It is good water." The water was a slimy green and I demurred. Qassim said: "The Amir is right. It is excellent water. Do not be misled by the colour!" Holding the spout of the goatskin above their mouths, my companions poured the green fluid down their throats lustily. Then we moved on, veering eastwards past several small hamlets towards a larger village marked by a tall tower. This was the village of al-Hajb. We were not the first that day to reach al-Hajb. The Sharif had despatched Tribal Guards ahead of us, for the better security of his son the Amir, and they now came out with the local garrison to meet us. We saw them moving towards us in a line of red turbans, arms round each others' waists, singing a loud greeting song. As soon as we were near they fired a salute and turned to escort us to the village, where the Sharif's local governor, the Wakil of Ayn, stood in front of the gate with the shaykhs and elders of the valley. There was more rifle fire, always a disconcerting occurence when one was riding an excitable Arab pony, and then we dismounted for the ceremony of shaking hands.

This was my first encounter with Sharif Salih bin Nassir, the Sharif's cousin and the Wakil or Nayb (pronounced "nibe") of Ayn. Of all the Ashraf he was the man to whom I was to become closest, ultimately becoming the only person to whom I could bare my thoughts. He was short and stocky, with a gentle manner, a soft voice and a ready smile which revealed dazzling white teeth above his bushy black beard. Salih was a family man and although, of course, I never met his wife, he was immensely proud of his five sons and several daughters. He was probably about thirty-five years old at that time, but the beard and the simple dignity made him appear much older. Strangely, in this land where the Quranic schools taught a good proportion of boys to read and write and recite the Quran, even though they were taught nothing else, Salih was completely illiterate and his eldest son, Abdullah, was always by his side to read and write for him. Characteristically of the illiterate he made up for the handicap by a considerable memory. He was a man of charm and sincerity, devout and completely honest. "Salih bin Nassir is the most loved of all the Ashraf," Shaykh Qassim had told me. "He is the friend of everyone. Everybody trusts him. He is wise and just. He can be firm, but he is never unfair. And he is full of courage. *Wallah! Huwa asad!* By God, he is a lion among men!"

We moved into Salih's tower, the tallest building in Ayn. As usual, most of the Wakil's own living quarters had been vacated to give us accommodation. We quenched a great thirst from large wooden bowls of water, drank gingered tea, and then feasted on *masub* and boiled mutton. That evening we were visited by the dancing girls.

The dancing girls of southern Arabia are gypsies, or *shahadh* (the word really means "beggars"), who wander round in family groups earning their living as entertainers. Their origin is lost in the mists of time but, like the Romanies, they have a language and customs of their own. Their women do not wear the veil and converse quite openly and unabashed with strange men, a complete contrast at that time with the rest of the female population.

The troupe which now performed for us at Ayn comprised four dancing girls and their orchestra, the male members of the family: one man who beat out complicated rythms on a drum and another who played a pipe very like the chanter of a bag-pipe. The piper created his effect by tying a rag round his cheeks and contriving to keep a continuous pressure of air in his mouth, so that he never paused to draw breath – in effect his mouth became the bag of a bag-pipe. The music, a sequence of cadences and trills, was repeated over and over again, with progressive variations of note and rhythm, much like the changes in church bell-ringing, the whole thing resulting in weird but strangely haunting tunes.

The girls dance one at a time with a male partner drawn from the onlookers, or occasionally two girls would dance together to attract an audience. They wore brightly coloured bodices and long, full skirts down to the ankle, with heavy silver bracelets and anklets and wide silver girdles hung with Maria Theresa dollars which clinked in time with their movements. Their faces were heavily made up, with strong blue and red colouring round the eyes, and their hair was usually a mass of long plaits. They were of all ages, mothers taking turns with their daughters in the ring. One of the girls in this group, Fatima, was spoken of all over Bayhan when the *shahadh* were discussed; she was in her prime, seventeen or eighteen years old at the most, unusually pretty and possessing a sparkling personality and a remarkably quick tongue; Sharif Hussain once asked the dancing girls to the upstairs room in his *husn* following a lunch there, and Fatima, with her lively repartee, was the pivot of the conversation during the whole hour I was present.

The actual dance of the *shahadh* was dull – a gentle "two steps and a skip" shuffle on the dusty square of sand, the man moving impassively, the girl anticipating his movements a foot or two away from him, sometimes edging close to him, circling him, spinning provocatively in front of him, but never allowing any contact between their bodies. As soon as she tired another girl would take her place. When the man gave up another volunteer eagerly took over. Once started the dancing would go on without a break until the call to prayer brought everything to a halt.

The *shahadh* provided almost the only entertainment available in the Protectorate. Usually they were troupes of dancing girls, but occasionally there were bands with other acts. On one occasion two bearded clowns turned up who staged a mock fight with sharp axes; they wielded these dangerous weapons with zest, aiming alternately at each other's head with most forceful blows which were arrested just as it seemed the head would be split open. The ghoulish sight was made more horrific by a loud clacking together of stones at the moment of apparent impact. There were no snake charmers, although I did once come across a small boy with a pair of snakes which he thrust down his throat head first, like a sword swallower. But the most nerve-racking performance I witnessed was given by two Yemeni gypsies who entertained us in a village one evening by the glare of pressure lamps when I called there with Sharif Hussain. They used *jambya*s taken from the belts of members of the audience and therefore with razor-sharp blades. At first they danced like the dancing girls, but from time to time pretending to attack each other with the daggers. Then, still dancing, each man held his dagger above his head, the curved blade pointing downward, and lowered it until the point was, as one saw it, resting on the eye; the supporting hand was then withdrawn, leaving the dancer with a heavy blade seemingly balanced by its point on his eyeball. It was a horrifying sight. The performers were well rewarded with Maria Theresa dollars, but it was appalling to contemplate that men would put themselves so close to terrible injury, if not death, for what must in less august company have been mere pittances.

One disadvantage of being a European in a place where none has been seen before is that one becomes a curiosity. This was frequently my misfortune and it happened on my first morning in Wadi Ayn, when I woke up surrounded by a crowd of onlookers who insisted on watching intently as I washed and shaved. I had been given the Wakil's courtroom as a bedroom and the spectators evidently felt that they still had every right of access to it. But the crowd disappeared when bread and omelettes arrived for breakfast and after that Shaykh Qassim took me in hand. Our horses were saddled and, with Nabih and a small mounted escort, we cantered off for a quick tour of Wadi Ayn. The Amir, who had come partly to show me his principality and partly to make arrangements for the marriage of a young uncle of his, seemed to have dallied too long with the *shahadh* the night before and was still fast asleep when we left.

Shaykh Qassim was always an admirable guide, knowing exactly what one would want to see and wasting no time. We travelled to the southern end of the plain, where the hills closed into a narrow gorge from which the stream of Wadi Ayn issued, and then northwards again, stopping periodically while I noted down the names of villages and mountain peaks. Then we passed the great dome of Qarn Ubayd rising abruptly in the centre of the plain and galloped along a sandy path, twisting through thorn bushes. Ahead of me I could see a cluster of square mud and stone towers, the Yemeni town of Harib, known as Darb al-Ali. We were rapidly drawing closer to it.

"*Ya* Qassim! Where are we going? Are you taking me to call on Kuhlani?" The little Yemeni Amil of Harib was now forgiven and back in office.

Qassim looked back at me over his shoulder. "Don't worry, *ya* Groom! We are still in Bayhan." He pointed from one side of the wadi to the other with a broad sweep of his arm. "This is all Musabayn territory. But I have something special to show you."

Some way on our horses slithered and heaved their way up a steep slope to the summit of a high flat-topped mound. It was littered with the remains of ancient buildings.

"The ruins of the Himyarites," Qassim said. "It is called Hajar Hinnu az-Zurir."

This was a more exciting site to look at than Tumna/Hayd Kuhlan, because, although it was much smaller, the sand had barely encroached on it and all the broken walls were exposed to view. At the south-west end, next to what seemed to have been the main gateway, were the remains of a very large building made of immense and beautifully cut blocks of stone, now draped in a heap of rubble. I photographed Qassim standing on the wide steps at the tumbled entrance to this magnificent building and copied two inscriptions on its walls, together with a relief carving showing two ibex.

"This must have been a temple in the days of Qataban," I said.

Qassim looked puzzled. "No. It belonged to the Bani Himyar." He had never heard of Qataban.

Nearby was another fine building of immense cut stones, its walls standing several feet above ground level. There was no trace of either doors or windows in those walls and it looked like an impregnable stronghold. "That,"Qassim said, "was the bank." The south Arabian uses the English word, though pronouncing it "bunk". The inscriptions I had found named the site as the Qatabanian town of Haribat; since the mint-name shown on some of the few Qatabanian coins which have come to light is "Haribat", Qassim's suggestion may not have been far from the truth.

The surface of Hajar Hinnu az-Zurir, some three hundred yards long and nearly as wide, showed the lower surviving courses of its buildings so clearly that it would not have been difficult to make a ground plan of the whole site. No building surpassed the magnificence of the temple in the south-west corner and most had been much more modestly constructed. The site had been used as a quarry for centuries and much of the masonry had gone, though fortunately the heavy blocks of the temple were far too large for a camel to carry away and this was perhaps why they had survived.

While we walked round the site looking for other inscriptions, Nabih, despite his education, remained with the escort watching us with patient disinterest from a hillock at the side of the mound.

"Why don't you come and see this place with us," I shouted.

"Please excuse me," he called back, "but I would rather stay here. There are jinns among those ruins and we don't want to take any risks."

We had completed our circuit of the outside walls when Qassim called me over excitedly to a large stone at the bottom of the slope, almost hidden among the tumbled masonry by coarse weeds. "I have found more writing for you." The stone bore a long, weather-worn inscription (Ryckmans 391). We cleared the foliage away with our hands and I photographed it and tried to copy it down in my notebook, a difficult task as it had fallen upside down and the glare of the sun, now high overhead, made the faint letters most indistinct and difficult to read.

We returned to al-Hajb at a furious gallop. Nabih said: "If you fall off your horse it will be because of the jinns. The Nayb of the Tribal Guards is quite sure they will do you some harm today."

The next morning we aimed to leave very early in order to cover the journey while it was still cool. The Political Officer's enthusiasm for ancient ruins and writings was now common knowledge and Amir Salih had found someone who knew of another inscription and would guide me to it. Qassim and I left with him at four o'clock, while it was still dark, and threaded our way by the light of the stars through shadowy bushes and irrigation channels to the far side of the wadi opposite Hajar Hinnu az-Zurir. Here, at the foot of the mountains, we dismounted and clambered some forty feet up the rocky slope. On a flat rock surface facing into the side of the hill were two long inscriptions (Ryckmans 387) which I copied down with the aid of an electric torch. Then we moved on to pick up the main party, who had left much later, on the track to Mablaqa and crossed over the mountain range through King Sahr's pass. We were back in Bayhan al-Qasab shortly after midday.

In due course I passed the details of my archaeological findings to Charles Inge, who sent them on to Professor Ryckmans in Louvain, one of the few persons able to unravel the ancient language of Qataban. It was always a hope that one would find previously unknown inscriptions with exciting new historical information about the old civilisation, but as often as not they had already been copied and catalogued. During the nineteenth century three intrepid Europeans – Arnaud (1843), Halévy (1869) and Glaser (1882-8) – had visited the Yemen and made brief visits to Marib. None of them had been to Bayhan or Harib, but they had collected inscriptions brought to them and Glaser had even trained Arabs to search for and copy them. Several of the inscriptions I found during my stay in Bayhan, sometimes remembered only by old men from the days of their youth, who would lead me to perilous positions on steep slopes, were already recorded by Glaser. My consolation prize was to be able to produce photographs and more accurate transcripts of them so that the epigraphists could clarify obscurities and errors.

But nobody had previously described either Mablaqa or Hajar Hinnu az-Zurir.

5

Invaders and Raiders

When we arrived back from Ayn on 11 April, I had hoped for a quiet ending to a long day, but that afternoon Ahmad came up to my room to announce: "There is a man at the gate who wishes to see you. The Government Guard sentry says he claims to have very important business and wants to speak to you urgently."

"Who is he?"

"The Qadhi of Marib."

I had seen Sayyid Ahmad Aatiq before, when he stood with Kuhlani to greet Basil Seager at the landing ground, but I had not spoken to him. He was the brother of the Qadhi (or religious judge) of Bayhan, a worthy man, but the two had little in common. Sayyid Ahmad was a flamboyant and voluble person. He dressed in the dark, heavy, voluminous robes of the Yemeni uplands, with a huge silver *jambya* at his waist, and he carried a Mauser rifle. His face was long and pinched, with wild eyes and a small pointed beard. In both appearance and demeanour he resembled an archetypal conspirator of the Guy Fawkes sort. As a senior official with good connections in the Imamic court, he had access to political gossip of possible interest, and, when he fled to Bayhan after the Imam's assassination, he had claimed he had important matters to reveal to the British Agent. Seager had asked me to get him down to Aden on the first available plane. Now he had made his peace with the new Imam and was on his way home.

While I was in Aden, Seager had told me of the arrangement made with the Qadhi of Marib. It was all very "cloak and dagger". "He is going to send me reports about political developments in Sanaa,"

Seager said. "He is well in with some important political figures, so he may produce quite useful stuff, but I suspect he will also be offering the new Imam what he will describe as important information about the affairs of Aden. We can but see what comes of it."

"How can I help?" I asked.

"You will have to look after his communications. He has undertaken to send me letters in a disguised hand. They will be addressed to you, but on the covers he will put a discreet cross as a sign that they are really intended for me. They will be delivered personally to you by trusted messengers, and will be made to look like ordinary run-of-the-mill correspondence. Don't open them, but get them down to me under seal in your next bag of office mail. I want the whole business to be as circumspect as possible, and it would appear better if you have no direct dealings with the Qadhi himself."

Now that the Qadhi was standing so inadvisably in the public gaze outside my door, I could not refuse him admission without giving him cause for umbrage. Besides, he might have some difficulty to discuss over his new role as a spy. I asked Ahmad to show him up to my room.

"I am just calling to tell you that I am on my way to Sanaa," the Qadhi said breezily, after we had exchanged the customary greetings, adding in a low voice: "Seager will have told you about me, no doubt. Please tell him I am on my way to Sanaa."

"Yes. I will do that."

"I shall send you letters for him," he whispered.

"Yes," I said. "I will pass them on."

He leaned towards me until his mouth was about two inches from my ear. "My letters will have news of great importance. I have been told to mark them with a cross. You will be able to tell them from other letters by the cross. They will need to be sent on to Seager immediately."

"Yes," I said. "I will look out for them."

We talked about other things for a while, and then, as he stood up to go, he said: "I would like you to come and have lunch with me tomorrow before I depart."

I could not possibly accept such an invitation if the clandestine arrangement was to have any meaning at all. I shook my head. "I am very sorry, but I already have other engagements."

He did not pursue the matter. Instead, as he reached the head of my stairway, he said: "You say you have just come from Wadi Harib. Perhaps one day you will visit me in Marib. It is not much further."

"It would be the greatest honour. I have much interest in the remains of the Himyarites and a chance to see those in Marib would be welcome indeed." The chance was, I knew, a negligible one. Marib was still forbidden to visitors from outside.

"Definitely you must come to Marib. I will show you everything. I will show you the palace of Bilqis, the Queen of Sheba. There is such a lot to see." He paused and then added: "When I get to Marib this time on my way to Sanaa I will send you some of the ancient statues of alabaster we have found. That is a promise. I will send you two camel loads of statues. I will attend to it the moment I get there and you can expect them next week."

It would have been a sensational gift, but I did not allow myself to feel too optimistic. The statues did not arrive.

The Qadhi of Marib's new career as a secret agent was hardly a successful one. He did not understand the rules of the game and had no notion of discretion. A stream of notes and sealed envelopes started to arrive at my gate, usually handed over to the guard with an ostentatious flourish by an over-dressed Yemeni known the length and breadth of the land as the Qadhi of Marib's servant. They included several invitations to lunch when he was next in Bayhan and all of them were marked with a mass of conspicuous black crosses, like a child's kisses at the end of a letter. Sometimes, playing melodrama to the full, he would come to Bayhan in person and send an oral message through his servant after darkness had fallen demanding a secret parley with my intermediary. I would summon Nabih, who would be led off furtively into the night protesting: "My God! Somebody may be lying in wait to kill me." On the outskirts of the town the Qadhi would emerge from behind a bush, pass over another heavily crossed envelope, and ask Nabih to relay to me a request for a substantial advance on the stipend Seager had agreed to pay him. The whole arrangement became a farce.

Fortunately the information the Qadhi provided was practically valueless, so that his espionage career was short-lived. But the affair had one serious effect. Sharif Hussain of Bayhan, who ran the best intelligence service in the whole of the Protectorate and who could hardly avoid discovering what was happening, was not made privy to the arrangement and bitterly resented that it was kept from him. Because of this the Sharif began to distrust me.

My rejection of the Qadhi of Marib's invitation to lunch obliged me to refuse other invitations. In the hope of creating the impression to the by-standers (who would pass it on) that the Qadhi had simply made a courtesy call, I escorted him to the gate, where we said goodbye. Before he was out of earshot the Salihi shaykh, who had just emerged from a meeting with the Sharif, rushed up to me calling out: "*Ya* Groom. I was just coming to see you. I wished to honour the *hakuma* by asking you to lunch with me tomorrow."

"I am sorry," I said loudly, so that the Qadhi could hear, "but it will not be possible."

Fast behind the Salihi shaykh was his rival, the Alawi shaykh. "I too wish to honour the *hakuma*," he said rather breathlessly. "Will you eat with me tomorrow evening?"

The Salihi shaykh, ignoring my refusal, interjected: "I will come and collect you tomorrow for lunch."

"And I will come for you tomorrow evening," said the Alawi shaykh, not to be outdone.

"No. It cannot be," I replied to both of them. In desperation I seized on a sudden thought. "I shall not be in Bayhan al-Qasab. I have to go to Asaylan."

It was true that there was some business to attend to in Asaylan. So I summoned Nabih and the Mulazim (Lieutenant) of the Government Guards, who was in command for a while because his senior, the Rais, had returned to Aden, and we made swift arrangements for an early departure. A messenger went off in the night to warn Sharif Abdullah. All of the Sharif's horses had been sent back to Ayn. Rather than suffer the delays of assembling donkeys or camels, I chose to walk, much to the indignation of my companions, leaving Ahmad to follow with the baggage caravan. I set out with Nabih, the Mulazim and three of his soldiers at three o'clock in the morning under the light of the stars. It was a six-hour march at a fairly unhurried pace, although Nabih was unable to maintain it and tottered in exhausted some thirty minutes behind me with two of the escort. During the journey I took the first bearings, with an army prismatic compass, for a series of traverses from which I would slowly compile a map of Bayhan.

The purpose of the visit was to discuss the affairs of the Bal Harith, and over the next few days I had long talks with the two principal Bal Harith shaykhs, Ali bin Munassir and Nassir bin Hussain, and several of the minor *aqils*. We talked about their hostage arrangements; their crops and water rights; some lootings they were accused of; their complaints against Sharif Hussain's taxation; the methods of digging and selling salt from their mine at Ayadim; the dissident Ahl Nimran section, who were still outlaws at large in the desert; the discovery of further unexploded bombs; and many other small matters which rankled in their minds. It was their chance to lay down all their grievances and mine to get to know them.

Suspicions of our every act still dominated Bal Harith thinking. Once, as we sat in my room – the two senior shaykhs with Sharif Abdullah, Nabih and myself – I poured out glasses of lime-juice for the two shaykhs, topping them up with water from a Thermos flask. After they had finished drinking, Nabih took one of their glasses and helped himself to the lime-juice, but, noticing a canvas water-bag hanging from a wooden peg on the wall, decided that the water in it would be cooler and topped up his glass from the bag rather than from the Thermos flask. Suddenly Ali bin Munassir leaped up and snatched the glass from Nabih's hand. "Hey! What are you doing, *ya* shaykh?" Nabih exclaimed. The old man said nothing, but sipped from the glass and then passed it to his colleague, who also sipped it. Sharif Abdullah leaned forward and whispered into my ear: "They suspect there is poison in your flask." I poured out water from the flask and drank it to allay their fears. We had to confront deep and primitive instincts when we were dealing with the Bal Harith.

I returned to Bayhan al-Qasab after a week of long, difficult and tiring discussions. The night before our departure it rained again and there was another heavy flood, strong enough to water most of the Bal Harith lands. It made our journey back a difficult one. I was beginning to enjoy a reputation as a rain-bringer, for my movements were frequently coinciding with a downpour. On one occasion some

months later, during a long period of drought, I returned by plane
from Aden and, as we disembarked from the aircraft, a small cloud
above us in an otherwise totally blue sky shed a few drops of rain
over the welcoming party. My stock rose even higher that day, but
the magical powers were unfortunately to desert me during the
severe drought of 1949.

When we got back to the capital a new crisis was awaiting me.
There was trouble in Wadi Markha.

Markha lies south-east of Bayhan and is a wadi of comparable size.
It was never taken under the control of the *hakuma* during my time
in Aden and remained unadministered until the Protectorate was
abandoned. Wyman Bury and Hamilton had travelled through it and
their books mention the Himyarite ruin-sites they saw there,
"where", as Hamilton wrote, "our camels slipped grunting in a rubble of marble and alabaster and where we camped among thin tiles
of blue stone lying on the wadi bed." Only Davey had been there
since.

From Bayhan the journey to the heart of Markha took two days
by camel along a track which left Wadi Bayhan well south of the
capital and climbed over the intervening mountains. A short but
unavoidable section of it passed through the territory of the Bani
Yub (pronounced "Yoob"), a Yemeni tribe. Bayhani merchants
bringing goods up from Aden would use this route in order to avoid
the high duties exacted at the customs posts on the more direct routes
through the Yemen, often plodding huge distances to skirt round the
scenes of local wars on the way. But if Markha were hostile then they
would have to divert very much further to the east through Nisab,
and enter Bayhan from its northern end after a difficult journey
through the Bal Harith sand-dunes. Markha was thus of considerable economic importance to Bayhan, a fact which the rulers of
Yemen, keen to hinder the establishment of a proper administration
in Bayhan, well appreciated.

The main tribe of Markha was the Nisiyin (pronounced Ni-see-
yin). But the wadi also contained a powerful group of armed Sayyids
– or *Sada* to give them the correct Arabic plural – who had a wide
influence as peacemakers and owned the largest village. Like Bayhan,
Markha had been racked with blood feuds, and in 1945 Davey had

begun to work on a plan to bring order to the wadi by using Nassir
bin Muhsin, the leader of the Sayyids, as the head of an administration. But Sayyid Nassir was not another Sharif Hussain. Pride went
to his head, he began to make unreasonable demands and the tribesmen refused to co-operate with him. The plan had to be called off.

The Zaydi leaders of Yemen then grabbed their chance under the
astute direction of ash-Shami, the wily Amil of Bayda. Sayyid Nassir
was bought over with financial and material gifts and placed a hostage
in the Imam's court as a pledge of friendship. Other Markha chiefs
followed him, just as the Musabayn had done in Bayhan. As soon as
the Yemenis felt they had purchased sufficient friendship in Markha
they sent in a military force equipped, quite unusually, with a large
mountain gun. Davey hastily mustered the Government Guards in
Bayhan and marched over the mountains to investigate the reported
invasion. He was encircled and besieged in a small fort, which the
mountain gun started to bombard, and radioed back to Aden for
assistance from the Royal Air Force. The RAF had a very lucky
strike. The barrel of the gun was so heavy that only one camel, a
giant among his race, was able to carry it. This camel was killed by
one of the bombs dropped and, because the Yemeni soldiers were
tribesmen and hence would not consider undertaking the labour of
an animal, the Yemeni artillery was immobilised. At the same time
a force of loyal Nisiyin from the lower reaches of the wadi arrived
to join the battle. The Yemenis and their Sada allies withdrew, leaving their gun behind, and during their retreat the brother of Sayyid
Nassir bin Muhsin was killed.

Had the victory been followed up an administration might yet
have been set up in Wadi Markha, but the opportunity was allowed
to pass and the Nisiyin, interpeting the British government's reluctance to intervene further as a sign of weakness, decided they too
had better make their peace with the Imam, surrendering hostages
in exchange for gifts of money. No British funds were available to
counter this bribery and, in desperation, Seager sought the help of
the Sharif. The Sharif was very willing to help. Encouraged by Davey,
he saw the possibility that he might himself become the ruler of
Markha. With considerable skill he won back the Nisiyin shaykhs in
exchange for a monthly stipend of two hundred Maria Theresa

dollars paid from the coffers of the Bayhan Treasury. But the Colonial Office was unwilling to allow any further consolidation of the Sharif's influence in the wadi and Markha subsided into an uneasy peace, while Sayyid Nassir bin Muhsin brooded on his unquenched ambitions of suzerainty and on revenge for the death of his brother.

My first intimation of further trouble in Markha came with a visit from a wrinkled old Markha *sayyid* named Sayyid Abdullah Dhaifallah, who entered my office with his young son on the morning following my return from Asaylan. He was almost naked and covered with indigo. Crouching down on the floor, with a gnarled walking-stick held between his knees, he pulled a crumpled letter from his belt.

"Mr Davey gave me this. He was my friend."

The letter, in Davey's clear, well-formed Arabic script, expressed Davey's gratitude for assistance the old man had given him during the earlier troubles.

"We need the help of the *hakuma*," the old *sayyid* went on. "Sayyid Nassir bin Muhsin has made new plans with ash-Shami to conquer our wadi and we need arms and ammunition to prevent him. Ash-Shami sent him to see the Upper Awlaqi Sultan in Nisab, where he slaughtered an ox and surrendered two close relatives as hostages. Sultan Awadh has agreed to help him for a reward of money and a share of the loot. Some of Sayyid Nassir's men are already in the Sada village of al-Hajar; they have built fortifications there and are firing on anybody who approaches. Now we have news from Nisab that Sultan Awadh is collecting his tribesmen and preparing to attack Markha in the first week of May. We beg you to help us before it is too late."

The involvement of the Upper Awlaqi Sultan was a new and disturbing development. His domain lay on the far side of Markha and, like Markha, it was still an unadministered area. Awadh, the Sultan, was a strange man who had shut himself up in a fortress near Nisab and refused to have any dealings at all with British officials in Aden. There were ancient traditions behind the origin of his family and that of his cousin, the Lower Awlaqi Sultan, and he was still a ruler of very considerable influence, heading a numerous, vigorous and temperamental horde of tribesmen with a Machiavellian cunning. If the Awlaqis attacked the trouble could be very serious indeed.

On the following day the first of many delegations of Sada and Nisiyin tribesmen arrived to seek government help. They called first on Sharif Hussain, lining up outside his main gate to fire a salute. But Hussain saw this as a matter for the Political Officer to deal with and they were quickly sent over to my *dar* next door. A Government Guard brought them up to my room where, kicking their shoes off at the entrance, they squatted on my striped Bayhan carpet, leaned their indigo–dyed backs against my once white walls and spoke long and passionately about Nassir bin Muhsin's new machinations. They were full of forebodings and exaggerated rumours and it was not easy to piece together quite what was happening, but the problem grew more and more complex as I delved into its intricacies.

There were three groups of Sada, I discovered: a powerful one under Nassir bin Muhsin; a second, called the Ahl Hafeedh, of which old Abdullah Dhaifallah, my first visitor, was the head, and which was loyal; and a third which, while strongly opposed to an Awlaqi invasion, still believed that Sayyid Nassir had a right to seek revenge on the Nisiyin for the death of his brother. If Sayyid Nassir won over the third group then, despite their better feelings, the Ahl Hafeedh would probably change sides in order to save their skins.

The Nisiyin, who lived further down the wadi and would bear the brunt of an Awlaqi attack, had their own divisions. They were part of a loose confederation of tribes known as the Bani Hilal, though none of the other members was likely to assist them. The strength of a tribe in South Arabia was always measured by the number of its fighting men, of which the Nisiyin had six hundred, an average size. They had a high fighting reputation, but unity of plan and purpose was by no means assured. There were three main sections, of which the most powerful, the Ahl Khamis, headed by a young, piratical-looking shaykh with one eye named Ad-Dawshal, was held responsible for the killing of Sayyid Nassir's brother. The Ahl Khamis were at feud with the second section, the Ahl Rajih, while the third section, of less importance, was uncertain which of the first two to support. "They will fight well," Sharif Hussain said when I was discussing the crisis with him, "but each Nisiyin section stands for itself alone. They have strong ideas about rights and *sharaf* and they never act together as a tribe. What they need is a com-mander-in-chief."

If Hussain still saw himself as a potential ruler of Markha he did not reveal it. The crisis was outside his realm and beyond his pow-ers and, in any case, these tribal visitations customarily demanded either a meal or a cash present in lieu and he was content that such an expense should be met from my money-bags rather than from his. "Entertainment of Indigent Tribesmen" was a major item in my monthly cash acount, for every visitor, whatever his information, expected to be rewarded, and I would receive no confidences if I did not uphold the practice. My sack of Maria Theresa dollars dwindled almost to nothing at the time of the Markha crisis, when I made a set speech to each delegation, expressing the hope that the *hakuma* would be able to stop the trouble before anyone had resorted to force, and then presented them with a fistful of the heavy silver coins. But Hussain was not unconcerned and we saw many of the delegations together, when his skill in assuaging their worst fears and sending them away content was of significant help. Together we deliberated over the welter of wild and distorted facts which they fed to us, in order to assess the true position. Afterwards I would return to my room with a much clearer idea of what was happening, open my message pads and the great Bible-like volume of the Government Telegraph Code, and compose lengthy signals to Seager reporting the latest position.

Fortunately the power of the *hakuma* was still held in some awe by the tribes of the North Eastern Area and the Bal Harith bomb-ing was still fresh in their minds. There was no question of taking an expedition into Markha as Davey had done, for we might have fallen into the same trap, but the RAF could reach everywhere and the Awlaqis needed no reminding of this. If we could convince Sultan Awadh that we were determined to prevent his attack and would use force to do so, then there was every chance that he would back down, although much depended on the extent to which he had already committed himself to support the renegade Sayyid, and on the degree of Yemeni involvement.

On this occasion the storm blew over almost as quickly as it had arisen. A signal arrived from Seager with a short, sharp message for the Sayyid which I despatched by runner. A day or two later, on 2 May, an RAF plane flew over Nisab and dropped a longer, more polite letter from Seager for the Sultan. The means of delivery to the Sultan was a strong hint in itself. Four days later, when I flew down to Aden to report, Sultan Awadh had quietly arranged to pull out of the escapade, while a fuming Sayyid Nassir had returned to ash-Shami's court in the Yemen. It was a part of Seager's great skill that he knew exactly in what terms to couch an ultimatum in order to get the desired result while avoiding any subsequent resentment. The Upper Awlaqi Sultan bore Seager no grudge despite the indignity of having to capitulate.

While the immediate danger was averted, the problem of Markha was not resolved and it soon raised its head again. Disappointed with the Upper Awlaqi Sultan, the renegade Sayyid turned to the chief of the other half of Upper Awlaqi, the Upper Awlaqi Shaykh. The Shaykhdom had no contiguous border with Markha, but the aged shaykh, Muhsin bin Farid, received the Sayyid in his capital at Yashbum and was persuaded to lend his support to another plan to occupy the wadi – a revenge, the Sayyid claimed, for the death of his brother, since the killing of a *sayyid*, a descendant of the Prophet, was a heinous crime. Sultan Awadh again agreed to help and reports came in that substantial quantities of arms, ammunition and money had been provided by the Yemenis, including two field guns. Delegations of Nisiyin and loyal Sada poured in once more from Markha with news of the thousands of Awlaqis who were preparing for the attack.

As the new crisis was reaching a head an unexpected visitor arrived from Nisab to see me. He was a lively young man, the nephew of an important "holy man" called the Mansab of Nisab.

"I am here on behalf of the Sultan and the Shaykh and the other leaders of Awlaqi," he said. "We have plans to help the cause of Sayyid Nassir bin Muhsin, but before we take any action we wished to check with you what Sayyid Nassir has been saying to us. His words are that the *hakuma* has agreed that it is right for him to take steps to punish the Nisiyin for the killing of his brother. He tells us he has a promise from Seager that no action will be taken by the *hakuma* if the blood of the Nisiyin is spilled."

"Neither I nor Seager nor anybody else in the *hakuma* has given any such undertaking to Sayyid Nassir," I replied. "If he has been saying that he has been telling you lies. Have no doubt at all that, even though the *hakuma* does not administer Markha, we could never allow it to become a battle-field."

"What would the government do," he asked, "if we entered Markha?"

"I cannot tell you what plans the *hakuma* may be making, but you would risk the worst of consequences if you attempted to create a disturbance for the sake of this foolish *sayyid*."

The young man looked surprised and taken aback. "We thought the *hakuma* was sleeping," he said. "We did not think you would object."

"Please tell your leaders all that I have said," I went on. "They were wise to send you to me. I hope they will now agree to call off their attack."

"Yes," he replied. "I will recommend that they do not listen any more to Sayyid Nassir bin Muhsin."

During our conversation the Mulazim of the Government Guards, who had been listening in as he sometimes did, suddenly got up and left the room. When the young Mansab's nephew departed he passed by a group of Government Guards in the quadrangle of the barracks busily cleaning a Bren gun, as well as another group counting out ammunition, as if preparing for an operation.

"I thought a little display would help to convince him that the *hakuma* has not gone to sleep," the Mulazim said to me later.

Next morning the RAF dropped warning letters on both Nisab and Yashbum. And we were to hear no more of the Awlaqi invasion of Wadi Markha.

Even now the matter had not ended for the Nisiyin, since the Sayyid still had blood to avenge. Any Nisiyin tribesmen could be murdered to obtain that revenge, but it was more likely the Sayyid would restrict his victim to a member of the Ahl Khamis section, which was responsible for the killing. A military attack was still possible, but revenge could also come from the single shot of an assassin. There was one way to avoid a revenge murder and that was to pay *diya*, or blood money. Death had its recognised price and the *diya* for a tribesman was at that time around seven to eight hundred Maria Theresa dollars, an enormous sum to these impoverished people. For a holy *sayyid* the *diya* would probably have to be much more. In the circumstances I would have liked to fund the Nisiyin for this purpose, but government money could not be used in such a way and I could not help.

During my conversations I had established a good "rapport" with ad-Dawshal, the one-eyed shaykh of the Ahl Khamis section, whom I found to be a wise and intelligent as well as a remarkably tough young man. He was one of the few shaykhs prepared to look beyond tribal horizons.

"I want a peaceful settlement for my people," ad-Dawshal said. "But it is very difficult for us. For all the tribes of Bani Hilal the mediators in our disputes are the Sada of Markha. This is our tradition and it would be hard to seek mediation in any other way. But we cannot ask them to mediate in this case, for it is they who seek revenge on us. I think I will wait until Sultan Awadh is no longer angry and then I will seek his help and that of the Mansab."

It was a wise proposal and in due course a settlement was reached, a *diya* paid and a truce arranged, Ad-Dawshal giving the Sultan a hostage as a pledge of his good faith. For the time being Sayyid Nassir bin Muhsin had been muzzled.

The chronicle of this crisis in Wadi Markha typifies the problems which assailed the Political Officers working in the Western Protectorate at that time. While each such major crisis was being resolved, numerous other less important matters would need attention. The Political Officer was *ath-Thabat as-Siassi*, and *siassa* in the Western Aden Protectorate meant politics compounded of intrigue, cunning, duplicity, volatile passion and a frightening readiness to pull a trigger or draw a dagger. Patience and reason were rarely encountered and one was constantly being presented with emergencies calling for rapid decision and speedy action. The Political Officer could not easily postpone his problems and he could certainly not escape them.

Leisure was rare indeed. For days on end I would work from dawn until long after dusk, with periods of travel too rushed to be anything but exhausting. Ahmad produced meals with uncomplaining efficiency at the oddest hours – meals assembled from the tins and dried foodstuffs brought up from Aden, and from the few available local products – chickens so small that a whole bird was a single helping, and eggs of commensurate minuteness. In general he was expected to get on with things without instructions, and I could make no complaint when the Arab cook's favourite recipe, caramel pudding, came up for the fifth day running. The opportunity for culinary variety was very restricted. There were not even any butchers, so that the people of Bayhan could only obtain a joint of meat when they clubbed together to buy a complete animal and then divided the carcass.

At dusk, when Hurricane lanterns pricked the darkness outside, Ahmad would set up my Tilley pressure lamp and I would work, or when occasion permitted, read under its hissing glare. Only in the Sharif's household and the homes of one or two other wealthy personages were there pressure lamps, and at night-time the houses of the more important members of the community could be identified by the occasional bright cracks of light showing through shuttered windows.

When my last tribal visitors had gone and Nabih had finished chatting about some complaint or petition which had just come in; when the Mulazim of the Government Guards had left after discussing a problem about sickness among his soldiers or space on the next plane to Aden; when the Amir or Sharif Awadh or Sharif Hussain had said "good night" after dropping in after their supper to hear my news or warn me of some trouble-maker expected to call next morning; when the evening W/T schedule was over and the wireless operator had called with replies to my signals and I had decoded them and prepared answers to queries in them; when I had filled in my daily office diary of events and put my typewriter back in its case after rapping out a report with four fingers about some new and unexpected information; then at last I could relax with a book or switch on the radio to hear music crackling through the disrupted atmosphere of great distances; or, if I still had the energy, I would write up my own diary or pull out Thatcher's Arabic Grammar, and the notebook in which I jotted down new words and phrases, for a half hour of study. More often than not, however, this was the point of defeat. Carrying the Tilley lamp, I would climb the mud stairs to the tiny room on the roof, grope under the mosquito net, flop down on my "charpoy" and surrender to complete exhaustion.

Sometimes the brightness of the Tilley lamp would attract other visitors. Strange moths flew in and hurled themselves suicidally against its burning glass. Occasionally scorpions worked their way up the surface of the mud walls outside and advanced menacingly towards me with stings poised erect behind them; I would dive for a shoe and execute them swiftly. They usually arrived in pairs, so that after the first had been killed one waited tensely for the mate. More frightening were the huge spiders, some of eight or nine inches' span, their legs covered with reddish-brown hair and as thick as a man's fingers. One variety carried a pair of heavy pole-like antennae before them, giving them three or four inches of extra reach. These spiders moved with alarming speed and were extremely difficult to catch and kill, especially as the high ceiling of my *dar* gave them a large area where they were safely out of reach. There were differing views about whether they were poisonous – possibly one species was and the other was not – but most local Arabs were as frightened of them as I was. When one escaped my wild lashings out and retreated into a safe nook in the crooked *ilb* beams high above my head, the rest of the evening would pass in uneasy apprehension of his return.

At the height of the Markha crisis I received an unexpected visit from the shaykh and elders of the Ahl Nimran (also known as the Ahl Jamiyal), the Bal Harith section which had murdered and fled during the bombing operation. Their action, which I now suspected had been prompted by Shaykh Ali bin Munassir, had made it impossible still for them to return to their lands for fear of reprisal and they had been living in black tents in the sand-dunes near the Yemeni border, too frightened to move any nearer to their fields and homesteads in the wadi.

The Ahl Nimran shaykh was tall and black-bearded, a strikingly vigorous man with a forceful way of speech. "I throw myself on the mercy of the *hakuma*," he said. "My people are exhausted and our food and money are gone. We seek your help in making peace with our tribe."

The other Bal Harith leaders had been firmly assured that the complete submission of the Ahl Nimran would not be accepted until blood money had been paid, with all its related formalities. "I will do my best to help you reach a quick settlement," I said, prevaricating. "I will discuss it with the Sharif and we will approach the Bal Harith *aqils*." I could say no more, but it seemed to be as much as they were expecting. They left at once, without a further word.

I sent a message asking Shaykh Qassim to call. "Before we can go any further towards helping the Ahl Nimran I need to know just what would be entailed in the payment of blood money. Why do we talk of *hasham* with the Ahl Nimran when the Nisiyin of Markha talk of *diya*?" I asked.

"The two are quite different," the old man explained. "*Diya* is paid by the killers to the people of a murdered man. *Hasham* is paid to his protector, or when there is a truce it may be paid to the person who mediated that truce. If a man is murdered while he is living in my house, or while I am escorting him under a safe conduct through my country, then I am responsible to his people and the murderers must pay *hasham* to me. If a truce is broken then they may also have to pay *diya* to his family."

"How much do they pay?"

"With *hasham* it depends how serious the crime was and how well the case is argued. We might get a mediator to decide the amount, or perhaps the protector would decide it. If a woman has been murdered then the sum will be doubled, because that is a very bad crime."

"It seems to be a very complicated system," I said.

"Yes. But it is the custom. We all understand it."

"Let us go to the Sharif to see what we can do for the Ahl Nimran," I said. We called on him that evening, but surprisingly he too prevaricated, as if he were unwilling to discuss the matter.

The Nimrani shaykh had brought news of a threat from a new quarter. "We have heard," he said, "that the Mishqas are preparing to raid towards Bayhan. You should be ready for an attack."

The Mishqas were a confederation, of which the main tribes were the Awamir and the Manahil, who lived in the mountains and desert reaches north of Hadramawt and had a reputation for raiding over

enormous distances. They were a powerful group, far more numerous than the Bal Harith, and their raiding parties, each man on a fast
riding-camel, were sometimes several hundred strong. Wilfred
Thesiger, who moved exensively among these people, has given
details of these raids in his book *Arabian Sands*, having passed through
Awamir territory and that of the Saar tribe (who were, I suspect,
erroneously included in the Nimran definition of Mishqas) only a
few months before at the start of his second crossing of the Empty
Quarter.

Other Bal Harith leaders had already told me of their fear of a
Mishqas raid, because the Abida, a Yemeni desert tribe who lived
immediately to their north on the far side of the Ramlat Sabatayn,
had lost two hundred camels in a recent attack. The most important
of the raiding tribes lived in the Eastern Aden Protectorate, where
the Hadrami Beduin Legion was being expanded to control them
by the simple expedient of placing small garrisons at the desert wells
to deny their use to the warlike. It was desirable and inevitable that
this should be done, but the excitement and danger of the raid was
in the blood of these tough desert warriors and the prospect of
acquiring sudden extra wealth by looting appealed to their cupidi-
nous instincts. If raiding were abolished their desire to go on living
at all in the desert would be diminished unless some alternative could
be found to compensate. "What have we got to offer in exchange,
unless there's an oil strike?" Ernest Kennedy once said to me.
"Nothing but a football! What sort of a substitute is that?"

My visit to Aden early in May enabled me to talk to Seager and
others about the Mishqas threat as well as about the trouble in
Markha, but its main purpose was to be present when the Sharif
made his annual official visit to the Governor of Aden. Such visits
were a convention of the Protectorate system, being the occasion
when, in accordance with the terms of his Protectorate Treaty, the
chief would pay his respects to the Governor, renew his pledge of
friendship, and receive his stipulated annual present of arms, ammunition and cash. Each chief was given a gun salute, varying in number
according to his importance. On this occasion my plane was delayed
and the official visit was over before I arrived, but the Sharif and his
party – the Amir, the Qadhi, a slave and an escort of Tribal Guards

– were to remain in Aden for a few more days to enjoy the flesh-pots. Now it was my turn to be the host. I was sharing the temporary use of a flat with Alistair McIntosh, who was in Dhala, and invited them all to a curry dinner, eaten on the floor with fingers and spoons, after which we moved on to the public cinema in Khormaksar, where the film was a version of Shaw's "Caesar and Cleopatra". It was all a strangely mixed-up compromise between East and West.

Aden in May was always stifling – a heavy, clammy heat in which the smells of drab bazaars, bunkering oil and fishglue, used for careening the dhows on the Maalla foreshore, mingled and lingered inescapably. Surprisingly, the Bayhan party seemed not to mind the heat. Dressed in oddly inappropriate clothes – the young Amir in a blue serge suit – they set out to enjoy themselves with gusto. They required no further attention from me. There was work to do in the WAP Office, stores to obtain, and a fresh supply of Maria Theresa dollars to collect. Soon I was back in an Anson heading northwards once again over the moonscape of the Protectorate mountains.

Three days after my return I set out to visit one of the frontier posts manned by Government Guards.

The "G.G.s", as they were always known, had been formed by Hamilton in 1938 at Seager's instigation. At the start the force was composed of tribesmen from important families who, when faced with trouble, had the influence to deal with it responsibly despite lack of numbers. Sheppard, who became British Agent in Mukalla, was their first Commandant and was succeeded by Dick Tring. In 1948 the British officers under Tring were Jimmy James, Alan Denny and the Quarter Master, Phil Purchase. With a small group of Arab officers of the highest quality, the cream of Hamilton's original recruitments, they had moulded a force which was by then some five hundred strong into a unique blend of soldier-policeman.

The Government Guards were the arm of the Political Officer, providing his bodyguard and promoting stability by their very presence. They were trained, disciplined and administered by their own officers, but their disposition was at the behest of the British Agent and his political staff. They did not interfere in the administration of the Protectorate states, but they helped to preserve them and had their own ways of giving local rulers appropriate *sharaf*.

With trouble occurring almost continuously in one part of the
Protectorate or another, the G.G.s suffered many casualities, but their
morale was always high and their enthusiasm was unbounded. The
good manners and mild and friendly dispositions of these men were
deceptive, because they could be extremely tough. Nor were they
too fussed about drawing-room niceties. On one occasion, sent out
to locate and capture a particularly notorious bandit who had been
terrorising the trade routes north of Aden, they returned in triumph
a few evenings later while Dick and "Bunny" Tring were entertaining the social elite of the Colony to cocktails. The Arab officers of
the expedition walked proudly into the crowded room with a wicker
basket and pulled its lid off with a flourish. Inside was the head of
the brigand.

One of the functions of the Government Guards was to provide
garrisons at important positions on the Yemeni border, either to stress
that it was an international boundary or to deter Yemeni aggression.
Such was Najd al-Mizr, a fort in Wadi Bayhan some seventeen miles
south of Bayhan al-Qasab, which was garrisoned by a G.G. force of
seven men.

The oddity of Najd al-Mizr was that it was not really on the frontier at all but well inside Bayhani territory, in the country of the Arifi
tribe. The Arifi, who had joined the Musabayn confederation only
recently, preserved a very independent tribal attitude. They were tall,
virile, wild-looking men with long hair held back by headbands,
dressed usually in nothing but short *futah*s, with leather ammunition
belts and the inevitable *jambya*s in sheaths at their waists. They
painted themselves from head to foot with indigo and their teeth
showed up in gleaming white against this dark blue whenever they
smiled. Their main village, al-Haraja, was at the south end of the
wide plain of Bayhan, but many of them were mountain beduin and
some of them lived in caves. There were numerous sections of them,
occupying a tribal area of a few hundred square miles of savage
mountains through which the narrow upper gorge of Wadi Bayhan
ran down to the plain.

In 1931, long before the writ of Sharif or *hakuma* had any meaning in Arifi territory, the Imam of Yemen had established a garrison
and customs post in a small village, in the gorge of Wadi Bayhan,

called Nata. This post controlled all movement in the upper wadi, which was an important route for Bayhanis trading with Yemen or Aden. Yemeni forces had occupied Ayn and Manawa at the same time, and also a village called Lakhf in Wadi Khirr. Little was known about these invasions when the Treaty of Sanaa was negotiated three years later and, although the Yemenis eventually withdrew from much of the territory they had taken over in Wadi Harib, their garrisons at Nata and Lakhf remained. The presence of these two forts, exacting customs duties for the Imam from well inside Arifi territory, incensed Sharif Hussain, who never ceased pleading with me to persuade the Government in Aden to take action to help him recover them. But we had had to defer to the likely international repercussions. Instead, it had been decided to put a Government Guard post close to Nata, as a reminder to the Yemenis that this was Bayhan territory and a part of the Protectorate. Accordingly a fort was built at Najd al-Mizr.

I left with two Government Guard officers – the Mulazim and a visiting Rais – and a small escort of G.G. soldiers. The Arifi shaykh accompanied us with several of his tribesmen, to show us his country. There had been rain overnight and a strong *sayl* was still flowing down the wadi bed. At one point, where the gorge narrowed and the flood was deep and difficult to cross, we dismounted and ascended a track with traces of paving which wound round the steep mountain slopes. Part of it had been hacked out of the solid rock. "This road was made by the Himyarites in the Days of Ignorance," the Arifi shaykh informed me.

"Are there writings?" I asked.

"Yes. We will come to them."

On this occasion the writings were no more than a few letters from the ancient alphabet, painted on the rock together with crude pictures of men and ibexes.

The fort of Najd al-Mizr was a tall stone tower, with a few outbuildings, erected on a mound of bare rock which jutted out into the wadi gorge. Less than a quarter of a mile upstream was Nata, a hamlet with another fortified tower.

The hamlet of Nata belonged to a small group of *sayyid*s, the only ones living in Arifi territory, and it was their accession to the Imam which had given him the opportunity to send his troops there. The head of the clan was Sayyid Muhammad Dubbash, who was allowed to collect the Imamic customs duties, retaining a fixed portion of the takings for himself. I met Dubbash many times subsequently and found him an intelligent and sensible man, tall and bustling amidst an ever-present posse of Zaydi soldiers. He was well aware of the anomaly of his situation and strove quite genuinely to maintain good relations with the Sharif while yet continuing to serve the Imam.

We stood on the roof of Najd al-Mizr fort to take stock of our surroundings. An indigo-blue sentry stared at us from the top of the Nata tower. Our buildings and the Yemeni ones opposite were insignificant in the vastness of this landscape, minute specks in the bottom of the chasm, with mountain sides soaring steeply upwards for hundreds of feet on either flank.

The G.G. Nayb (or sergeant) pointed to a tiny cube on one of the peaks high above us. "That is another Yemeni fort," he said. "It is called al-Ghurayba."

"Is it occupied?"

"Oh yes. When we built Najd al-Mizr the Yemenis got into a panic and Kuhlani ordered a *husn* to be built up there so that his troops could fire down on us from it. The Zaydis have about sixty men in Nata and another twelve in al-Ghurayba."

"But surely at that height and distance they would find everything was out of range?"

"That is so. It is no great danger to us. But the Amil has given his orders and they have to be obeyed. When the weather is cloudy they cannot see down into the wadi at all."

"How ever do they get up there?"

"It is a very steep climb. Even a goat would find it hard work. It takes them about an hour-and-a-half."

"They must find it difficult to keep in contact!"

"They send runners," the Nayb said, "and they also sound bugles." The Yemeni army always made much use of bugles.

"Some time ago," the Nayb went on, with an impish grin beginning to spread over his face, "we discovered that one of their bugle calls was an order for the commander of the post in al-Ghurayba to come down immediately to Nata. So we watched the relief garrison climbing up the hill and just as it reached the top we blew that call on our own bugle." He added mischievously: "It is a very long way down when you are already tired out."

"Do you still do that?" I asked, rather hoping for a demonstration.

"No. We did it several times, but then Sayyid Muhammad Dubbash sent a letter asking us not to. We respect him, so we have not blown our bugle since."

We spent only a short while in Najd al-Mizr on that occasion, having already been pressed, as a matter of *sharaf*, into accepting a luncheon appointment with the Arifi shaykh in the village of al-Kurra, some three miles down the wadi. There was *masub* and boiled sheep, the first meat that many of the banqueters would have tasted for weeks, and afterwards we drank coffee in an upstairs room while long-stemmed, gurgling water-pipes were passed from mouth to mouth in a thickening cloud of sweet tobacco-smoke. When we left in the evening the whole village turned out to stare at the Political Officer. Our horses were fretting for their stables as we slithered over patches of slippery rock and splashed through the flood-stream on our way home; once we reached the sand plain they seized their bits in their teeth and covered the remaining six miles at a hair-raising and uncontrollable gallop.

On my next visit to Najd al-Mizr I spent the night in the fort, dossing down on the floor with a blanket, for I had found that on the odd night away the elaborate business of arranging a baggage caravan to bring Ahmad, his cooking pots and my camp kit was not worth the trouble. But night stops at Najd al-Mizr involved some hazard, for the building was overrun with savage and apparently starving mice. Throughout the night I was repeatedly awoken by mice burrowing inside my blanket to get at my feet, while Nabih was bitten quite severely. The *askaris* – the soldiers – seemed to have resigned themselves to getting no sleep at all during the night, though none of them complained, accepting the discomfort as an integral part of the misfortune of being posted to Najd al-Mizr at all. When I was next in Aden I bought spring traps, which I presented to the garrison, but the mice soon learned how to remove the bait without getting caught. Finally, having failed to find any suitable poisons, I arrived at the post with a small kitten purchased in Suq Abdullah and tied up in a bag. "That is a wonderful gift," said the Nayb. "Now at last we can get some sleep."

The cats of South Arabia are a wild breed, with unusually square dog-like faces and a tendency to mew persistently in a whining and very irritating manner, and the Bayhan kind seemed to be especially noisy. On my next visit I saw no sign of my gift.

"What has happened to the cat?" I asked.

"He talked too much," the *askari* replied sheepishly. "Especially at night-time he just went on talking. We could not make him stop. He kept us all awake. He was worse than the mice."

"What have you done with him, then?" I enquired.

The Nayb came forward and pointed to one of the out-houses. "We have banished him," he said. "He lives over there on his own. He is quite wild now, but there are plenty of mice for him and he has become very, very fat."

"He must be very unhappy on his own!" I observed.

"No! Not at all!" the Nayb replied with feeling. "He is very lucky compared with us. After all, he eats meat every day, and he can go over to Nata whenever he wants to visit his wife."

6

"Bread and Salt"

Away from the coastal plain, the heat of May and June in the
Protectorate was not normally very uncomfortable. In Bayhan the
nights were cool and the daytime heat, rarely much above one hundred degrees fahrenheit in the shade, was dry, so that one did not
suffer from the enervating listlessness induced by the high humidity
at sea level. It was hot enough, though, and the short trips I was
making for mapping purposes at that time required some effort and
evoked little enthusiasm from the unfortunate Government Guard
askaris detailed as my escort. Mapping meant steep climbs up burning rocks and avoidance of the larger inhabited places, for I soon
found that if I came too close to a village the local *aqil* would come
bustling out to put all his complaints and aspirations to me and,
inevitably, to trap me into staying for a meal.

To help the map along it seemed a good idea to climb Jabal Raydan
and take an overall view from the top. The mountain towered over
Bayhan al-Qasab and dominated the whole wadi plain, the last and
highest of a chain of peaks dividing Wadi Bayhan from its tributary
Wadi Khirr. It was capped by a massive cone of rock which had the
appearance of a huge fortress and there were remains there, so everybody said, of the Himyarites. When Alan Denny, a Government
Guard officer, flew up to Bayhan to inspect his posts, I took the
opportunity to abandon my other duties for an afternoon, and
together we climbed Jabal Raydan.

The remains of a carefully engineered zig-zag footpath helped the
approach up the steep lower slopes. Clustered in a saddle below the
huge peak we found the ruins of ancient houses, possibly Islamic

rather than Himyarite. Around the peak was an elaborately constructed system of rainwater run-offs leading to two cisterns, almost
certainly made by the people of Qataban. One of these still retained
water. A constructed pathway led round to the far side, but part of
it had disappeared, leaving a terrifying stretch of smooth, steeply-
sloping rock-face dropping down to a precipice, with a rock
overhang at one point which could only be negotiated by crawling
along beneath it on one's stomach. There was no time to overcome
that final obstacle with Alan Denny, but on a later visit with Charles
Inge we got over the awesome slope using the long, red *mushadda*,
or turban cloth, of a Tribal Guard as a rope. From there the pathway led round the peak to a wide natural platform near the top. On
the edge of the platform, where the mountainside dropped sheer for
several hundred feet into Wadi Khirr, was a huge, smooth-faced, egg-
shaped boulder, like a gigantic beach pebble some twenty feet high;
it was balanced so precariously that it looked possible to push it over
the side without effort, but it was in fact too vast to be moved by
wind or man. The Himyarites too had evidently marvelled at this
phenomenon and given it divine associations, for strange symbols
and animal heads were painted on its face in the red pigment of
Qatabanian graffiti.

Raydan may have been a religious shrine of some importance in
the days of Qataban. Its striking shape, its significant position and
this spectacular boulder near its peak would certainly have favoured
such a development. In the later centuries of the Himyarite era the
kings began to use the title "King of Sheba and Dhu Raydan". By
that time Raydan was also the name of the royal fortress of the
Himyars at Zafar, in the Yemen near present-day Yarim, but that
nomenclature may have derived from the sanctuary at Jabal Raydan
after Qataban had been conquered. Some traditions of this sanctuary seemed to have lingered through the centuries. There was the
legendary treasure concealed in a cave halfway down the precipice
on the northern face, to which Qassim had once been lowered on
the end of well-ropes. And there was also the custom still surviving
among the more pious Bayhanis that they would spend the first night
of the Ramadhan fast high up among the ancient remains on this
mountain fastness.

I could not remain in Bayhan al-Qasab for long. The Bal Harith were again claiming attention. When they abandoned their rebellion Seager had promised that I would give their problems special study, and the time had come to spend some while with them, commencing with a tour of their black-tented villages. Shaykh Qassim and Sharif Awadh were enthusiastic about this, for it would bring *sharaf* to the tribe to be singled out for such attention, but Hussain, when Seager put the idea to him in Aden, agreed only reluctantly; he did not want the *hakuma* to take all the prestige.

Early in June we rode to Asaylan and I took up residence once again in the little room beside the central tower. In a wise redistribution of his Naybs, Hussain had moved Abdullah to Ayn and brought Salih bin Nassir to Asaylan in his place. The Bal Harith would now get a more understanding and sympathetic hearing from their local governor. Salih greeted me with his individual form of salute, firing his rifle when I was only three feet away from him, and with Nabih and his second son, Haydar, who was standing in as a scribe in his elder brother's absence, we sat down to discuss our plans.

"It will be very hard work for you," Salih said. "Each of the eleven sections will have to be treated equally, for only old Ali bin Munassir believes there should be a *shaykh min shiyukh*. They will all insist on slaughtering sheep and goats in your honour and you will have to feast with each section in turn."

The greatest problem was to limit the zeal of the Bal Harith, for these impoverished tribesmen, who lived almost permanently on the borders of hunger, would kill their last goat, empty their last grain bag and pour out their last cruse of *simsim* oil in order to provide the traditional hospitality of the desert. I wanted to restrict them to reasonable limits. "It will not be easy," Salih said, "but when I write to tell them of your coming I will say that it is your desire that they should slaughter no more than one or two animals. We will impress on them that you have come to eat 'bread and salt' – *aysh wa milh* – for that is the custom of the desert. Once you have eaten 'bread and salt' you are their honoured guest, and all the time you are with them they will protect you, even with their lives."

So the days of feasting began. We would leave Asaylan at about seven o'clock in the morning, while the sun was low. Sharif Salih,

Shaykh Qassim, the Mulazim, Nabih and I, and one or two others, rode horses, while the retinue of Government Guards and Tribal Guards and miscellaneous followers, of whom there always seemed to be far too many, jogged along with us on foot, happily dreaming of the orgy to come. We headed into the cultivated area, where the seed corn, planted only a few weeks earlier, had grown at astonishing speed in the rich silt; there were now acres of high green crops ready for harvesting, with millet stalks eight to ten feet tall and thick enough to be used as walking-sticks.

As we moved through the fields, the Bal Harith ryot, sometimes women as well as men, would rush up to greet Sharif Salih, and we would halt, our horses stamping impatiently in the dusty ground and tossing their manes to shake off the flies, while he heard some tale of broken irrigation rights or field encroachment and gave judgement on the spot. After a while we would emerge out of the greenery into scrub-topped sand-dunes, until we reached the tribesmen we were visiting that day, drawn up in a long line in front of their tents. There would be desultory rifle shots as we approached and a crescendo of firing as we dismounted about fifty yards in front of them. This was always a moment of tension, because a tribesman still feeling disgruntled could so easily have fired at us instead of over our heads.

We walked towards the tribesmen, Salih keeping a pace or two behind me, and as the firing died down I called out the usual greeting, "Salaam alaykum!" and the tribesmen muttered the reply "Wa'alaykum assalaam!" in a low-voiced unison. From the middle of the line the aqil advanced, followed by all his men, down to the smallest boy, to shake and sometimes to kiss our hands, at the same time making a soft kissing noise with the lips as is customary in this part of the desert. The aqil then led us towards a large, open-sided black tent, floored with all the strips of carpeting he could muster. At the entrance way two men held a goat tightly, with its neck pulled taut, and as I reached it one of them slit its throat with his jambya, so that I stepped over the spurting blood. We kicked off our sandals and squatted down in the shade while the still shuddering corpse was dragged away to be skinned and boiled for lunch. The Bal Harith goats, born and bred on soft sand, had hooves which curled out in front of their feet for several inches, like ornate Turkish slippers. I even saw horses with this strange defect, for there was nothing to wear their hooves down, no thought of cutting them back, and no blacksmith; none of the Bayhan horses was shod.

We sat cross-legged in the tent, leaning against camel saddles arranged around the sides, whilst coffee was poured from slender copper pots into small, handleless cups. Tribesmen and peasantry crowded round the edges of the tent to watch and listen. Small children scampered round excitedly, and sometimes the women, veiled but less bashful than their sisters higher up the wadi, peered round the tent walling to stare at the strangers.

Among the desert tribes the greeting ceremony continues long after the guest has sat down, with a series of formal enquiries about health and well-being, exchanged in a monotonous undertone. The Bal Harith questionnaire went as follows:

"*Kayf haalak?*" − "*Sallam haalak.*"

"*Guweet?*" − "*Ingeet.*"

"*Allamoona?*" − "*Wa allamuzeen.*"

"*Anta bil khayr?*" − "*Gaalik bil khayr.*"

These phrases, sometimes with additional ones, would be put by the host to his guest and then by the guest to his host, and then each would exchange them with others in the tent. While going the round both host and guest would have an ear cocked for any interesting news coming up in the conversation elsewhere. The tent became filled with the sound of low mumbling.

The guest who has travelled is also honoured by the Bal Harith with a foot massage while he drinks his coffee and exchanges his greetings. This is the ancient ritual of anointing the feet with oil. Taking the right leg first, one of the younger men of the tribe cleans off the sand by a brisk rubbing and then applies *gilgil* (the oil of *simsim* or sesame) with his hand and works it into the skin with a vigorous massage, starting at the sole of the foot and extending up to the knee; finally he returns to the foot and stretches each toe in turn with a sharp tug. After the left leg has been similarly treated, a small amount of *gilgil* is sometimes poured on to the top of the guest's head and rubbed into his hair − one of the few occasions when a man will remove his headdress.

So we sat and exchanged our greetings and talked and held out our feet for massage, while the sea of faces on the sand outside stared at us and the empty cups were swilled out with a splash of coffee and a brisk wipe of the thumb and then refilled for another guest. Crockery and cooking utensils were in short supply. Nabih, who found the bitter taste of beduin coffee disagreeable, announced his preference for tea, and thereafter a blackened tin kettle followed us around from camp to camp, its load of tea-leaves added to but never emptied out; when the thick sediment blocked the spout someone would clear it with a lusty blow, like a trumpeter, before pouring Nabih another cup.

For two hours or more we talked and waited, until the *masub* arrived, steaming hot, and we tunnelled into the thick pudding domes with our bare fingers, conversation suddenly ended. Then the meat was carried in on flat basket trays and the shaykh, dispensing hospitality with beaming pleasure, divided the pieces among the diners, carefully placing a mound of extra delicacies – heart, liver, kidneys – on top of my substantial allocation of ordinary flesh. Eating required dedication.

In ten days we feasted with ten sections of Bal Harith, the eleventh, the Ahl Nimran, still being in hiding. The sections varied greatly in size and some mustered only a few dozen men. For the first nine days our reception was uniformly warm and friendly. Despite their deeply felt suspicions, our hosts clearly wanted to show that they wished no ill of the *hakuma* and were relying on it to resolve their differences with the Sharif. My object was to win Bal Harith confidence and I was anxious to avoid any political wrangling. Sharif Salih and Shaykh Qassim did their best to steer the conversation on to innocuous subjects, and Nabih, setting himself up as a clown, provided a diverting sideshow. There was other entertainment too: a mad Harithi poet who followed us round reciting an endless stream of completely nonsensical rhyming verse; and a deaf-mute, a highly intelligent young Awlaqi, who mimed the actions and characteristics of Bayhan notables with a devastating accuracy. The heavy dialect of the Bal Harith was difficult to understand, but for once the limitation of my Arabic was useful, for it discouraged the more politically motivated from trying to get me to one side for a whispered intrigue.

On the last day we were to pay a visit to the Ahl Ali bin Ahmad, the section of Shaykh Ali bin Munassir. This was the most powerful group among the Bal Harith and included the young instigators of the rebellion. Ali had been away in the sands when I reached Asaylan and was cross because his rival, Nassir bin Hussain, had been allowed the honour of entertaining me first. To overcome that loss of face and to press his claim to be *shaykh min shiyukh* he arranged for a reception superior to any we had had from the other sections. He invited all the other *aqils*, although several of them refused to come, and besides slaughtering seven goats, far more than anyone else, he also sacrificed an ox. Gastronomically the ox had no significance, for the flesh was considered inferior and distributed among the poor, but its slaughter represented an underlining of the importance of the occasion.

Nassir bin Hussain, who had refused to attend Ali's feast, took grave offence and came storming over to Asaylan next morning to see me. "Is it true that Ali bin Munassir slaughtered an ox for you? What right had he to do so when no one else among us was allowed to? Why was I not given permission when he was? *Ya* Groom, I swear on my face that I, Nassir bin Hussain, would have slaughtered *four* oxen had you only allowed me to!"

Qassim and Salih calmed him down with smooth words. Fortunately he had other business to take his mind off the slight. He had brought with him his tribesman Awadh bin Aiyadh, the brother of the man who had been murdered by the Ahl Nimran. Awadh said: "There are Nimrani camels near at hand. I seek the agreement of the *hakuma* to capture them. We can do so with little trouble."

"Neither I nor Sharif Hussain could agree to that," I replied. "We want to settle your case against the Nimran. What you propose would only make a settlement more difficult."

Awadh seemed to be a more philosophical man than his shaykh and shrugged his shoulders. "A pity," he said. "It would have been so easy. But we are the children of the government. We shall do as you say."

The Ahl Ali bin Ahmad were by far the wealthiest of the Bal Harith sections, owning most of the area of land first reached by the flood water when it entered the wadi delta. Shaykh Ali himself lived in a small hamlet south of Asaylan, which had in consequence escaped the bombing altogether, but he received us on this occasion in a marquee made out of several black tents pitched together. His son Abdullah al-Bahri, who had covered me with his rifle during our peace conference, sat close by with a dour and hostile expression and we were aware of black looks from several of the younger tribesmen. Qassim seemed to be unusually tense and I was reminded of Seager's warnings about Bal Harith treachery.

Among our hosts was a man of wide renown – Shaykh Ali bin Ghurayba, the head of a sub-section of the Ahl Ali bin Ahmad. Ali bin Ghurayba had been one of the Bal Harith party which helped Hamilton to eject the Imam's forces from Shabwa and Hamilton described him as "a doughty warrior ... who had once, single-handed, out-manoeuvred a raiding party of the Simian-like Sei'ar of the outer sands and brought back with him more than twenty of their rifles." His reputation had grown with many other deeds since that exploit and he was now recognised as a desert knight, a revered figure to whom all the desert tribes gave honour. "That man is a lion among lions," Qassim said to me, pointing out a large, well-built, barrel-chested man, grey-haired but still immensely strong. "Last year he went off in pursuit of a raiding party from the Mishqas. He took on three men who had become separated from the rest. He was alone with them in the dunes, but when they saw who their adversary was they threw down their rifles and *jambya*s and surrendered without shame. It is an honour to be taken prisoner by such a warrior and it would be a disgrace to kill him. *Wallah*! There is no greater warrior than Ali bin Ghurayba."

Ali bin Ghurayba looked relaxed enough, but I noticed that there was no sign of his son Alawi, who had been one of the principal instigators of the rebellion.

My feeling of unease increased and I began to watch the glowering figure of Abdullah al-Bahri carefully out of the corner of my eye, noticing incongruously that he had six toes on each foot. Presently a Tribal Guard entered the tent and whispered to Sharif Salih, who stood up and left a few minutes later. When he returned he said nothing to me and we resumed our feasting. It was difficult not to feel apprehensive, but nothing could be said in front of our hosts.

We did not get back to Asaylan until the evening. As we dismounted outside the gate, Salih said: "I will come with you so that we can talk in private."

"I was called out by Alawi bin Ali Ghurayba," Salih said as soon as we reached my room. "He wanted to talk to me where no one could overhear us. He has spoken his heart to me."

"I thought he might be plotting something against us," I said.

"No. There are still black hearts among his section, and I too was frightened at first when I saw their faces. But they would not do anything against the *hakuma* – even Abdullah al-Bahri appreciates the dangers of that."

"What happened, then?" I asked.

"Alawi realises that he has been mistaken. He told me he now sees that the Bal Harith will gain nothing from resisting the Sharif further and it is best to accept him and co-operate with him. But he is frightened of the punishment he may yet have to face for his misdeeds. He has some secret knowledge of the Nimran killing, but he would not tell me more about that. He has asked for a *wajh*, a written pledge, from the Sharif and Seager saying that his past is forgiven and he can now travel safely in Bayhan. In exchange he will do all he can to ensure that the Bal Harith remain peaceful and loyal."

"Do you believe him?" I asked.

"Yes," Salih said. "I think he is sincere. I think his father has been talking to him. Ali bin Ghurayba is a very loyal man."

Quite what had brought about Alawi's change of heart we never discovered, but it was a significant and encouraging development. On my next return from Aden I brought Seager's signed *wajh* and some weeks later Alawi bin Ali Ghurayba rode into Bayhan al-Qasab on a camel alongside Sharif Salih to offer his loyalty to Sharif Hussain.

Before we could return to Bayhan al-Qasab a radio message arrived from Aden saying that the Sharif, still on holiday there, had purchased a Jeep which the RAF proposed to bring to the Jaw al-Milah landing ground in a Dakota. Would I arrange to receive it?

Hamilton had come over in a lorry to Asaylan from Shabwa on a one-day visit, but no other vehicle had ever been seen anywhere in the North Eastern Area except for Philby's car when he drove from Shabwa to Marib in 1936. The arrival of the Jeep was therefore a sensation. Sharif Awadh, acting as Regent, came up to witness the event and direct the labour force. With a great deal of shouting and disorganised heaving the vehicle was lifted out of the Dakota's wide doorway by a forest of brown arms and lowered gently to the ground. The Government Guard Mulazim took the wheel, with a beaming Awadh at his side and the RAF crew and a number of retainers in the back. Following behind in procession on horses and camels, like a sovereign's escort, we crossed the sand dunes and Bal Harith fields towards Asaylan. A new stage had been reached in Bayhan's history. The machine had caught us up. Soon the horses would go and eventually even the camels would lose their role and a whole way of life would be changed. "From now on," Brian Hartley, the Director of Agriculture, said to the Sharif jokingly a few weeks later, "you will know your subjects less and less. On horseback anyone can come up and say "*salaam alaykum*" to you and you will stop and talk to them. But now you will not even hear them. Instead you will throw up dust in their faces and drive on without stopping." It was an earnest warning.

But Bayhan did not yield to the motor car without a struggle. Sharif Awadh had decided it was a matter of *sharaf* that he should be driven right into Asaylan, despite the presence across the gateway of a barrier of heavy stones designed to prevent hobbled camels from wandering outside. Yielding to his petulance the Mulazim charged the boulders, the front wheels of the Jeep reared up and the body came down on them so heavily that part of the gearbox casing cracked and broke off. That evening Awadh insisted on being driven back to the capital. The gears soon choked with sand and for some weeks, until a mechanic had been recruited, the Ashraf motored everywhere in bottom gear.

Tunis, the Sharif's powerful grey stallion, seemed to sense what was in the offing. He was the strongest and fastest horse in the Protectorate but wild and highly temperamental. "He is a *shaytan* today – a devil," the groom would say as I moved up to mount him, and Tunis would respond by threshing wildly, with gleaming eyes, and jerking his head round to bite. On the day after Awadh's departure Tunis was saddled ready for my own return. "Today he is *shaytan ibn shaytan* – the very son of a devil," the groom said. Three men were holding him with the utmost difficulty and all my attempts to get a foot in the stirrup were successfully resisted. "We'll get him over to that wall," one of the men said breathlessly, "and you can climb up from the other side." I had dropped on to the saddle before Tunis saw me and in a moment we were away. Only one other person was already mounted – young Haydar, Salih's son, riding his father's chestnut stallion.

Tunis usually became responsive after a wild start, but this time the devil was truly in him and he galloped headlong towards a clump of *ilb* trees, hoping that the low branches would sweep me off. I ducked the first and managed to pull him round the second. Then he set off on a straight course for Bayhan al-Qasab. I gave him five minutes flat out and then tried to curb him by drawing harder and harder on the reins, but he would have none of it. "I can't slow him down," I shouted out to Haydar, who had stayed close behind me, suddenly aware of his responsibility as my only escort. "I'll let him run until he gets tired." "You won't tire him," Haydar called back. "He never tires. He's a *shaytan*."

We thudded on, veering round the patches of *rak* bush, kicking up the dust in two swirling clouds. A party of *sayyid*s pulled their donkeys anxiously to one side as they heard us coming and Haydar yelled out an apologetic explanation.

We passed the Ashraf and Sada villages and the mound of Hajar bin Humayd, hurtling over fields and banks, and, while I strained with legs and arms to steer my devil-horse round the more dangerous obstacles, Haydar dropped further and further behind. As the peak of Jabal Raydan grew larger, I managed to reach a patch of flat and firmer soil, not seeing the great irrigation dyke which straddled across it further on, a dam of earth scraped up by oxen, a quarter of a mile long and some ten feet high. I remembered that on the far side the sloping banks had been eaten away by the recent floods into vertical cliffs. Tunis would not deviate from his course and I could do nothing but hold my breath as he scrambled madly up the slope. But his instinct was uncanny. Along the whole length of the dam there were only three points where the flood-side had not been eroded. He had gone straight to one of them. We soared over the top triumphantly and scampered down. Within ten minutes we were back in Bayhan al-Qasab and Tunis had stopped, all at once quiet and obedient, near his stable door. We had covered some sixteen miles at lightning speed and my hands were raw and bleeding from the effort of steering him round obstacles in our way. "That," Tunis seemed to say, "is what I think of your Jeep!"

Sharif Hussain returned with the rest of his party a few days later, coming as far as the foot of the great *kawr* precipice by lorry and then travelling on horseback through the Yemen and down the Bayhan gorge. We went out in the Jeep to al-Haraja to meet them, with a crowd of soldiers and elders, and escorted them back through the growing shadows of the evening sun. People ran out from distant villages along the way to watch their royal family pass by in the new machine, which was grinding along noisily and slowly in bottom gear. Some of the more timid, alarmed at what was approaching, fled for their lives.

Hussain was in an indignant mood. His party had been stopped at the Awdhali customs post on the Yemeni border. "They would not let us go through until morning," he expostulated. "We had to spend the night sleeping as best we could in the cold on the open ground. We did not even have a blanket. It was an intentional affront to my *sharaf* and it can only have happened on the personal instructions of the Awdhali Sultan. He is an insolent young man and needs to be taught a lesson. I am writing a strong letter of complaint to Seager and I hope, *ya* Groom, that you will send one too. It is a very serious matter." We never did establish the Awdhali Sultan's motive and the insult rankled with the Sharif for many years to come.

I had a meeting with Hussain and Awadh the following morning, when we went over a number of matters which had arisen since Hussain's departure. In the course of it I mentioned casually that we might think of organising a simple postal service between Bayhan and Aden. No such service existed anywhere in the Western Protectorate at that time, and the only way a Bayhani could send a letter to Aden was by persuading a friend to carry it for him. I had already sounded out Awadh, who strongly supported the idea. To my surprise Hussain greeted the suggestion with an angry torrent of abuse, almost as if I had insulted him. That evening Awadh came over to my room. "You must forgive my brother," he said, "and you must try to understand him. He is still very angry because of the treatment he received from the Awdhali Sultan. But you made a mistake when you put this to him as a suggestion. I should have warned you. My brother will never accept a suggestion. You have to explain the problem to him and lead him to propose the solution. Then you must flatter him a little for thinking of it. That way you will get him to do anything you wish." The question of a postal service was not mentioned again.

At least Hussain had agreed that we should lose no more time in trying to settle the Ahl Nimran feud. My feasting in the Bal Harith encampments had persuaded the *aqils* of our good intentions and even Abdullah al-Bahri had thawed before we left his father's marquee after the last of our meals. The Bal Harith were now in a more helpful mood and we were hopeful that they would co-operate in an attempt to restore tribal unity. But Ramadhan, the month of fasting, was close upon us and if we did not act soon we would have to delay until after the feast of the Id four weeks later. Messages were sent out summoning all the Bal Harith leaders to attend the court of the Sharif. They arrived a day late, a matter of no concern in the slow life of south Arabia, and it was decided after a long discussion that nothing could be achieved until the offenders were present. The next meeting was then deferred for two days while runners were despatched into the desert sands to locate the Ahl Nimran leaders and bring them in under a *wajh*, a pledge of safe conduct, from the Sharif and the Political Officer.

I knew already about *hasham* and *diya*, the forms of blood money payable for murder, but the Bal Harith were now talking about something I had not heard of before – *ya ayba*. "It is a public admission of shame," Qassim explained. "If the aggrieved party demands it, then the guilty one must say a *ya ayba* – that is the start of the form of words used for it. Once it has been said the aggrieved party will accept an arbitrator proposed by the guilty one and a truce is declared until the time of arbitration."

"Will there then be a *hasham*?" I asked.

"Yes. The arbitrator works out the *hasham* in accordance with certain rules, but he will be allowed to help the murderers by declaring that the *hasham* can be paid in kind, in camels and cattle and rifles perhaps, and giving each item a value far greater than its real worth. He may allow the *hasham* to be paid over a period of several months, which will help them even more."

"And what about the truce?"

"Once the *hasham* is agreed then the arbitrator declares the truce as binding for a fixed period. After that the two parties have to renew it. But unless there is a *diya* payment as well, the blood that has been spilled is not forgotten. If they do not renew the truce then the feud continues and somebody else will be murdered. That is the way of the tribesmen, *ya* Groom. Revenge is a matter of honour."

Sometime later I learned of another Bal Harith custom for dealing with murder. The young man arraigned before us denied most vigorously that he was responsible for the killing. The Sharif had brought several of the Bal Harith shaykhs over to assist him with the case and they were unanimous on what to do next. "The *bishar*," they all said. "He must be given the *bishar*." This was a trial by ordeal. His tongue would be touched with a piece of red-hot iron. If it showed no more than redness, he was innocent. If it burned or blistered, then he was guilty. "Certainly I will have the *bishar*," the young man said. "I have sworn to you that I am innocent. The *bishar* will be my proof. Come! Lead me to the fire and let me show you!" His absence of fear was evidence in itself and after further deliberations his protests were accepted without the ordeal being imposed on him.

The Ahl Nimran deputation, led by their tall, black-bearded shaykh, duly arrived and we settled down to long and intricate discussions. Sharif Hussain took the lead and there was little for me to do but lend him my support and try, through the whispered translations of Nabih, to understand what the venerable old Bal Harith elders were saying. We had promised them that no settlement would be agreed without a *ya ayba* and a *hasham* payment. This seemed to be very much in the better interests of the Ahl Nimran as well, but for some reason they appeared to be protesting against such an arrangement.

For some time I had suspected that old Ali bin Munassir had instigated the Ahl Nimran, because the murdered man came from the section of his arch rival, the phlegmatic Shaykh Nassir bin Hussain. Alawi bin Ghurayba's apparent admission of implication seemed to strengthen my suspicion. I had hoped that Ali, using the influence and wealth of his section, would secretly persuade the Ahl Nimran to accept the settlement proposed by promising to help them pay for the *hasham*. But it did not happen that way. Everybody was talking round the subject. There were long, impassioned speeches. But the Sharif seemed to be prevaricating, as he had done when I saw him with Qassim earlier, and no one would get down to the bones of the problem. The Ahl Nimran stubbornly refused to make the opprobrious admission of *ya ayba* and resisted the payment of *hasham* with equal obstinacy. We were getting nowhere, and I decided the time had come to intervene and ask some pointed questions.

As soon as he saw what I was about, Hussain said suddenly: "*Ya* Groom! I would like to speak to you." Giving me no time to reply, he turned to the assembled shaykhs and adjourned the meeting.

"Come with me," Hussain said, and led me to a small, empty room nearby. Nabih, who tried to follow, was politely deterred.

"There are things you should know which I have not said before," Hussain whispered, his dark eyes glancing at the doorway to make sure nobody was near. He spoke slowly and deliberately, mouthing his words with care to make sure I understood.

"It was I," Hussain went on, "who arranged this killing."

"*Ya* Sharif Hussain! What are you saying?" I exclaimed, not sure that I had understood him correctly.

"I persuaded the Ahl Nimran to undertake this murder," he said. "While you were in Asaylan for the bombing, Awadh wrote to me saying that you thought to split the unity of the Bal Harith as a way of bringing them to submission. I too was thinking of that. I sent messengers secretly to the Ahl Nimran shaykh. I told him that, if he wished to avenge the blood he had against Nassir bin Hussain, now was a good time. I said I would make sure he need never pay a *hasham*."

"But what of Nassir bin Hussain?" I said. "Was he not at truce?"

The Sharif replied: "He was my enemy then, for he was one of those leading the Bal Harith in rebellion against me."

Now I began to understand the attitude of the Ahl Nimran and the extraordinary reluctance of Sharif Hussain to allow the discussion to take a practical turn. No word of his intrigue had passed to Abdullah Hassan or myself while we were in Asaylan. He was faced with settling a feud which he had secretly reopened himself and in which his secret promise to the Ahl Nimran that there would be no *hasham* conflicted with our publicised undertaking to the Bal Harith that a *hasham* would be enforced. He dared not allow the true facts to emerge, but he could not rely on the Ahl Nimran to keep the secret unless he kept his pledge to them about the *hasham*. I wondered how much further it all went. Was it knowledge of this matter which Alawi bin Ghurayba was using to secure the Sharif's forgiveness for his past misdeeds? I was caught up in another devious Western Protectorate intrigue, a *siassa*, and I could think of nothing to suggest which might help to solve it.

"Let us go back and continue the hearing," I said. "I will simply sit quietly by your side. You understand the mind of the beduin and no doubt you will be able to find a way out of the problem. But I do not think I can help."

"Yes. You can help," he replied. "There is no need for you to say anything, but if the Bal Harith see that you support me, that will be all the help I need. Trust me! I will find a way. But show them that the *hakuma* is with me!"

A lesser man would not have been able to extricate himself from the predicament Hussain was in, and it was a measure of his political skill that he was equal to the task. There were long discussions with all the Bal Harith shaykhs together and private sessions with each of them in turn, which I did not attend. There were long waits while groups of them whispered to each other in far corners. Men moved secretively from one group to another and sometimes there were angry words. But at last, somehow, all were agreed. The settlement included a *ya ayba* and a *hasham*. The Ahl Nimran were released from their outlawry.

We moved out of the courtroom that evening with a feeling of relief after a day of tension. Hussain looked triumphant. "You see, *ya* Groom," he said. "With the beduin you need patience. They are difficult, like children. But Allah will find a way." I wondered how much it had cost him in secret bribes to bring the matter to a successful conclusion.

In an inner room another banquet had been set out for all the Bal Harith shaykhs.

"What happened when you went out with Hussain?" Nabih asked me while we ate.

"He had some ideas for different ways of getting a settlement," I replied. "He just wanted to know what the Government's reaction would be to them."

"Were they good ideas?" Nabih asked.

"I'm not too sure," I said. "Without you to interpret I can't be certain I really understood them."

Then I realised that I too was undulging in a *siassa*. South-west Arabia now had me firmly hooked.

7

Fasting, Feasting, Plotting

Unlike their Islamic successors, the Himyarites and their forebears observed a calendar year in which the months corresponded with the seasons.* Such a year was also observed elsewhere in pre-Islamic Arabia. The Muslim month of Shaaban, the month of separation, is thought to have derived its name from an ancient Arabian month which fell in the heat of June, when the people were often obliged to disperse in search of water. Its successor, Ramadhan, the month of burning, may also have originated as a calendar month which fell during the searing days of high summer. With the adoption by Muhammad of a lunar year, the twelve months shifted round the natural calendar by eleven days every year, so that Shaaban and Ramadhan fall at the same point in mid–summer only once in about every thirty years. 1948 was a year when Shaaban started during June.

In South Arabia the lunar months were still held to commence with the actual sighting of the new moon. Although nobody worried about lunar observation at other times of the year, this was the signal which commenced Ramadhan, the month of fasting. Radio was already creating confusion about this custom – should one start to fast as soon as Cairo Radio reported that the new moon had been seen in Egypt? – but in Bayhan the old arrangement still prevailed and the ordeal did not officially begin until the Imams in the local mosques gave the word. In 1948 Ramadhan began on 8 July.

* The Himyaritic year is in fact thought to have been a 360-day one, divided into twelve months each of thirty days, with a periodic addition of extra days to keep the calendar in line with the natural year. The details of the calendar, which varied in the different kingdoms, have been worked out in a fascinating study by Professor A.F.L. Beeston in his *Epigraphic South Arabian Calendars and Dating*, (London, Luzac, 1956).

I had been expecting a total observance of the religious obligation to fast, but had not anticipated the effect it would have on our
way of life. Between dawn and dusk not a drop of water, a morsel
of food or a whiff of tobacco smoke may pass the lips of a devout
Muslim. In westernised communities like Aden the response varied
from the strict to the frankly lax, but in these remote tracts it bordered on the fanatic. Religion was a very real part of life in these
areas and the Bayhani held God in great awe. He felt no bashfulness
in suddenly breaking off a discussion at midday in order to go outside, face Makkah and, kneeling until his head touched the ground,
start to say his prayers. During Ramadhan a man in Bayhan seen to
break his fast would receive a warning shot from a fellow tribesman
to make him appreciate the enormity of his crime. Over the twenty-
eight days of Ramadhan the entire population practised an asceticism
which would have taxed the willpower of the most zealous Trappist.
But they did so in this fiery midsummer heat by altering their entire
mode of life.

During Ramadhan the population of Bayhan spent the day in the
shade as motionless as possible, if not actually sleeping. Even travel
came more or less to a halt, despite the dispensation allowed by
Muhammad to those genuinely on the road. When I looked out of
my windows, the sandy spaces between the groups of houses were
almost empty. An occasional figure loped slowly along, head stooped
and muffled up in a cloth as if suffering from toothache. One or two
small groups sat disconsolately in shady corners waiting for something to happen. Even the animals sensed the atmosphere and lay
down patiently to await the end of the day. In the evening, as the
sun began to reach behind the western hills, an air of expectancy
animated the scene as everyone awaited the call of the muezzin from
the mosque announcing that the sun was properly set. In many places
this signal was given by a gun. When it came, life suddenly erupted.
I would hear the *askaris* of the Government Guards below cheer as
they scrambled to drink and prepare their evening meal. Out of all
the doors of the *suq* people appeared, laughing and chattering, to
visit their friends, to shop and to carry on with the deferred business of the day. Until the small hours of the morning the noise and
bustle continued and sleep was difficult. When at last I dropped off

exhausted it was to be awoken only a few hours later by the glare of the rising sun and the buzzing of flies, to find that everybody else in Bayhan had once again disappeared.

In such circumstances my own activities were inhibited. I could take a few short walks out into the empty fields on my own to gather further bearings for my map, but no lengthy journey was possible, for my *askaris* were in no condition to provide an escort and I would not have been welcomed at the other end. In the evenings, as the time of breaking the fast approached, Sharif Awadh and Sharif Hussain would sometimes call on me, looking pale and haggard after the day's ordeal, for a chat or some matter of business. Once or twice I joined Hussain for an evening stroll in the little garden he was developing behind high mud-brick walls at the back of his *husn*. Here a boy led a camel up and down a ramp all day to draw water from the well in a goatskin bucket and empty it into irrigation runnels. The main crop was tomatoes, which Ahmad was allowed to use for my meals, and Hussain was endeavouring to cultivate papaya and other fruit-bearing trees. But most of my time had to be spent indoors, catching up on reports and filing, and studying Arabic grammar. There was also one job to be done which I had delayed for some time and which the circumstances now suited. This was the inspection of the Bayhan state treasury, known as the Bayt al-Mal or "house of money".

In March 1944 Sharif Hussain had been the first Protectorate chief to sign an Advisory Treaty with the British Government. These treaties marked a dramatic change in our policy towards the Protectorate. No longer were we content with the friendship of its chiefs. In addition it was now accepted that we had reponsibilities for the welfare of their people and must exercise some measure of control over the chiefs to secure it.

The Sharif's new treaty contained two main articles. Under the first, he agreed that he would "at all times co-operate fully with and accept the advice of the Governor of Aden in all matters connected with the welfare and development of the territory of Bayhan". Under the second, he pledged that "being desirous of participating in the cost of agricultural, social and security services in the territory of Bayhan" he would "accept as a proper charge upon his revenue such allocation therefrom for these purposes as shall be determined annually by the Governor of Aden in consultation with him." In effect he was obliged by his treaty to do what the Political Officer, as the Governor's representative, formally suggested, in particular over the working out of his budget – not an unreasonable requirement in view of the growing subsidies he was being given. This was not a control which could be exercised without tactful diplomacy, but there was a strong move in Aden and Whitehall to ensure that the system of Advisory Treaty relationship set up in Bayhan should be seen to be a success, for it was hoped that all the other rulers would eventually come under the same form of control. Success had to be measured in two ways. The Sharif must be satisfied with the arrangement. But so, too, must the population.

In the four years since the Advisory Treaty with the Sharif had been signed, progress had not been all that was intended. The very close relationship which Davey had established with Hussain, especially after Davey became a Muslim and married a Bayhani girl, meant that he could not take a very detached view of Hussain's administration. At the same time he had encouraged Hussain to believe in a personal destiny which went far beyond the ruling of Bayhan. When Davey left Bayhan to stem the troubles in Dhala, where he met his death, he was not replaced and Hussain was left to his own devices. Despite the terms of the Advisory Treaty Hussain had never yet submitted his annual budget for consideration.

At the end of 1947 Alistair McIntosh was sent to Bayhan on a brief visit to make a critical inspection of how things were going. He found signs that much of the state revenue, beyond that allocated for the civil list, was being retained by Hussain as a personal income. Hussain, he reported, was getting too big for his boots. When I arrived in Bayhan a few weeks later my directive was to find out more exactly what was going on, to keep Hussain under a tighter control, to prepare for further constitutional changes designed to give the tribes more say in the administration, and to see that the affairs of the Bayt al-Mal were being properly conducted. The Bal Harith rebellions, symptomatic of the need for changes, had distracted us and I had needed time to find my feet, but now I was ordered to subject the accounts to a detailed scrutiny.

In my five months in Bayhan it had not been easy to establish a close relationship with Hussain. He was always friendly, cordial and courteous, but he was forthcoming only when it suited his purpose. I felt that he resented my presence, regarding it as an indignity to have a young, newly arrived Political Officer thrust upon him after he had been so long without one. He knew very well that I was reporting to Aden about his own attitudes and activities and was frightened that I might listen to the complaints of his enemies. A lot was being kept hidden from me and Bayhanis were discouraged from seeing me. He undoubtedly feared that his position was being undermined. Old Shaykh Qassim had no illusions. "The Sharif," he said, "does not want me to come to see you. He knows I may tell you things he does not wish you to hear and it makes him angry." But Qassim continued to call.

After Seager's telegram arrived asking me to start the inspection, I went to see Hussain. "The British Agent, the *Matamad*, has asked me to send him details of the taxation schedule," I said, for this was the way we had decided to broach the matter with him. "Could you", I continued, "ask Sayyid Abdullah to provide me with a list?" Sayyid Abdullah was Hussain's private secretary and privy to almost all his confidences.

"Of course," Hussain replied disarmingly. "You must come over and talk to Sayyid Abdullah. He will tell you everything. Better still, why not examine all the accounts? Makintoosh has already seen some of them and everything is in order. It would be good for you to study this information and learn how we manage things. I will ask Sayyid Abdullah to get the papers ready for you."

This was not the reaction we had expected, but I thought he had probably got wind of what was afoot while he was in Aden and hoped to get the matter over and done with as quickly as possible. We arranged that I would present myself to Sayyid Abdullah in two days' time.

Late next evening Nabih came up to see me in a highly excited state.

"The Sharif sent his slave round for me," he said. "I went over and the Sharif took me to one side where we were alone and started to use honeyed words. He promised he would be my greatest friend and look after me. He asked me if I would like to earn a lot of money – I think he meant several hundred dollars. I said: 'What for?' and he replied: 'It will be very simple for you. All you have to do is keep Groom's eyes blind tomorrow'."

"What did you tell him?" I asked.

"I just said that I wouldn't be able to do that, because if you wanted to see something I could not prevent you, and I could never stop you asking questions."

"So what have you arranged?"

"Nothing. When I said that, he changed the subject. It was not mentioned again."

Over ten successive mornings we tackled the books of the Bayt al-Mal for an hour or two before the rigours of fasting took too tight a hold on Nabih and the Sharif's clerks. The books were produced by the Clerk of the Bayt al-Mal, but all my questions were answered by Sayyid Abdullah. He was vague and elusive, and it was soon apparent that we were dealing with an accountant's nightmare. The accounts were cooked as a matter of routine, but so incompetently were they being kept that it hardly noticed. There were numerous entries under the wrong head, others rubbed out and reinserted with quite different figures, and there were whole pages tightly glued together so that they could no longer be read. Quite clearly much of the revenue was not appearing in the books at all, while much of the recorded expenditure was an improper charge on the state. There was no doubt that the state revenue was being treated, as it always had been in the hereditary chiefdoms of the Protectorate, as a private income of the ruler. Very little of the taxation we had enabled the Sharif to collect when we put him in power was getting back to the people in public services. In fact, the whole purpose of the Advisory Treaty was being circumvented.

I wrote out my report to Seager. I was not an accountant and, in the hope that the position might not be as black as it seemed, I suggested he send up the accountant who ran the financial affairs of the WAP Office to confirm my findings. Somehow we had to get the Bayhan Treasury running on sound lines, but it had to be done in a way which would not seriously weaken Hussain's standing, or the country would slide back into tribal anarchy. There could be no open showdown. Nothing could be done too abruptly. But we could not afford to leave things as they were.

Hussain kept very much to himself after my audit of his Bayt al-Mal and it was hard to tell his reaction. But a few nights later Qassim called on me very late one night.

"I have come now," he said, "because it is best if my visit is not noticed by anybody in the Sharif's buildings next door. I have come to tell you that Sharif Hussain is engaging in some secret correspondence with ash-Shami. There is a messenger who has had to travel several times between here and Bayda carrying letters. I do not know what they are about, but I have learned that Hussain has insisted that great care should be taken to avoid you or the *Matamad* finding out about it." I thanked the old man warmly, though I did not tell him that the Rais of the Government Guards had already reported the same information.

While Ramadhan lasted I could do no more than take note of what I was told. The conduct of political business after nightfall gave it an unreal, conspiratorial air and matters of minor significance began to loom grotesquely large. The Ramadhan way of life was a strain on everybody and people were becoming irritable and impassioned. I reported Qassim's news to Aden, but it was impossible in these conditions to say whether it was significant. I was beginning to feel a prisoner in my *dar* and my judgement was becoming cloudy. For once it came as a considerable relief when I was suddenly summoned back to Aden. Kenneth Bell, just back from leave, had been co-opted into the Secretariat and I was needed to fill the seat which had been awaiting him in the WAP Office. For three weeks I became a headquarters man.

The office in Captain Haines' old residence was as bewildering when I worked in it as it had seemed when I was first taken round it. Seager still kept well away, and vehicles shuttled constantly from the office to his house in Khormaksar with despatch boxes full of files and papers. The over-crowded and dusty untidiness was made worse by the effect of the fast on the Arab clerks and by the gusting winds of the summer monsoon. Ahmad Hassan Mudhaffar was in charge of the noisy scene and in the side office a new Confidential Secretary was installed – this was Kitty Maclean, the wife of Aden's

Commissioner of Police. To the Political Officers of the time "Mrs WAP", as we called her, fulfilled with unfailing cheerfulness the additional, voluntary role of buying and forwarding agent, for she was our vital link in Aden for all our petty requirements from grocers, stationers, chemists and other shopkeepers. No request to her ever went by default.

My stay in Aden ended as abruptly as it had commenced. Two weeks after the Id festival had celebrated the end of Ramadhan an Immediate signal reached the WAP Office from Sharif Hussain. "I have discovered a plot by Musabayn leaders to assassinate me. There may be a Musabayn uprising." I returned to Bayhan at once.

The assassination of the Sharif was planned by the Salihi Shaykh, Salih bin Ahmad, the head of that section of Musabayn which had been most loyal to him. The plan was a cowardly one. On Friday, the holy day, Hussain always attended midday prayers in the main mosque. He was to be shot during the service. Fortunately a member of the section who was loyal to the Sharif heard about it and warned him. Hussain sent out his Tribal Guards immediately to round up the assassins, but they were seen approaching and the conspirators fled to the Yemen. Their flight confirmed their guilt. There were four ring-leaders, one of whom was an Arifi. From details Hussain passed on to me and information from others it looked as if the Zaydis in Yemen, in particular ash-Shami, with whom Hussain had so recently been exchanging letters clandestinely, had some knowledge of the plot, while the Rassassi Sultan, a Yemeni vassal, appeared to have played a part in it too. Intricacy was an intrinsic feature of all South-west Arabian intrigues.

It so happened that we had been planning to hold talks with the Rassassi Sultan over a number of small disputes between his subjects and those of Bayhan. Hussain, with my full assent, had already made some arrangements for these discussions through Sayyid Muhammad Dubbash in Nata. Despite our suspicions about the Sultan we decided to carry on, and towards the end of August the Sharif and I set out with a large escort which included a bodyguard of three mounted slaves who, from now on, were never far from the Sharif's side, as he felt he could no longer trust his Tribal Guards.

Moving at a slow walking pace, we travelled to Rafaa, at the entrance to the Bayhan gorge, where the shaykh would give us lunch. Sharif Hussain had a new Mauser rifle. After we had eaten our *masub* and boiled goat and were idling the time away, he started to fire through one of the small loophole-windows at a white stone on the mountainside some three hundred yards away. He fired several shots, but was unable to hit it. Then he passed the gun over to me. By good fortune rather than special ability at marksmanship I shattered the target with my first bullet. My Government Guard *askari* acclaimed the success with a roar of delighted approval. The *hakuma* had shown its superiority over the *dawla*, the state. Hussain's face clouded. He could not hide his annoyance. Unwittingly I had diminished his reputation as a marksman and lowered his *sharaf*. He took the rifle back and wasted another half dozen bullets before he hit the next target.

Hussain spent the night at al-Kurra and I went on with my G.G. escort for another sleepless night with the mice in Najd al-Mizr, which we reached at dusk. We were not expecting the Rassassi Sultan until noon the next day and were late in rising. While I was still shaving, Sayyid Muhammad Dubbash put his cheerful face round the corner unannounced, calling out: "We are expecting the Sultan to be here in an hour-and-a-half." Then, as abruptly, he withdrew. We settled down to breakfast. Twenty minutes had passed and I was still eating when we heard voices faintly chanting a marching song in the distance. Presently the Sultan, a wild-looking indigo-blue figure on a spirited pony, rounded the bend of the wadi with his son, also mounted, surrounded by a jogging escort of thirty blue tribesmen armed with ancient rifles. I had intended to conduct him to al-Kurra, but we were caught unprepared. We kept still and hidden away, hoping he would not call, and watched with relief as his cavalcade swept past us, their high-pitched voices echoing in the gorge, and disappeared down the wadi among the *rak* bushes. My party followed thirty minutes later. It was not yet nine o'clock.

Custom ordained that there could be no business with the Sultan until he had eaten with us. Accordingly we sat all morning on cushions on the floor of an upper room in al-Kurra drinking gingered coffee and engaging in small talk with him. The room was crowded almost to suffocation and the Sultan sucked nervously at a large "hubble-bubble" with a long, coiling pipe, dutifully kept stoked up with tobacco and charcoal by an old henchman named Sayyid Munassir bin Ali. I had seen Munassir bin Ali before, when he came to Bayhan with the Sultan's son at the time of Seager's visit to seek support for a rebellion. The Sultan was not an old man, but his face was aged, perhaps by the debauched life he was reputed to lead, and his eyes were red and full of guile.

I sat next to Dubbash, who was in an agreeable mood and repeatedly asked me to visit him in Nata. He had brought with him a small, hawk-nosed man who stayed to one side and kept glancing anxiously at Nabih and myself. After about an hour this man rose to leave the room, for there was much coming and going, and as he passed Nabih I noticed him wink in the manner which signifies to the Arab of South-west Arabia a desire for a secret conversation. Nabih got up and went out a few minutes later and was away for over half-an-hour. When he returned, deciding he could not converse in English with me without arousing the suspicions of Dubbash, he asked me in Arabic for a piece of paper so that he could write a letter. The "letter" recorded his discussion with the hawk-nosed man, a Zaydi clerk. "He says he has just arrived in Nata to take charge of the customs post," Nabih wrote. "He hates the new Imam and Dubbash. He is getting married and needs money. He says he has valuable information for us and will supply it regularly. He's already given me some quite useful scraps. More promised soon. Wants a monthly salary, first instalment immediately. Worth trying I think." I laughed as if what I was reading was a joke and surreptitiously told Nabih to give the man thirty rupees *ex gratia* when a suitable opportunity arose to do so covertly. Later in the day the man signified with a nod of the head that he was well satisfied. I felt I had done a mean trick to Dubbash. Without stirring from the cushion alongside him I had, I hoped without his noticing it, recruited his chief clerk as a spy. But, like many others who offered such services, my new intelligence agent never fulfilled his promises. One or two reports of minor interest arrived from him, but his enthusiasm then flagged with a growing realisation that payment was by results and that espionage was unlikely to prove very lucrative for those who were not able to produce the goods.

We finished our meal and drank tea. Dubbash then excused himself to say his noonday prayers and, after the nonentities had been hustled out, we began serious discussion. The Rassassi Sultan had never been on the best of terms with the Imam's government. His grandfather had abandoned the ranks of the Protectorate chiefs because he thought he saw advantages in becoming a Yemeni vassal, but soon regretted his action and the Rassassis had been on the verge of rebellion on many occasions since. They still had much to be discontented about. But the present Sultan had a reputation for untrustworthiness and treachery, which included murdering a guest in his house, and for all his outward, roguish charm, we knew we must tread warily in our dealings with him.

We were not discussing anything very significant – the Amil of Bayda would never have allowed that – but it was all of consequence to the security of Bayhan: a feud between a Musabayn section, the Ahl Jaradan, and the Bani Yub, who were nominally subjects of the Sultan; several outstanding cases of looted camel caravans; and a claim by the Sultan that Bayhanis had taken over land on his side of the ill-defined frontier. We talked at length about the situation in Markha, which bordered Rassassi country, but could get no new information. When I mentioned the Salihi's plot to assassinate Hussain, the Sultan said: "I have heard of that, but I know nothing about it. On my face, I have had nothing to do with these people. It was a terrible thing they planned." We left it at that. Leaning forwards conspiratorially, he went on: "You must know that I am your friend against Dubbash and your friend against ash-Shami. They wish evil of me and they oppress me. By Allah, how they oppress me! Soon there will be blood between us and the Zaydis." We kept our silence and he said no more. It was difficult to tell where his real feelings belonged. There were many times when he had not been truthful. I wondered also how much Sharif Hussain was withholding from me of what was said in the whispered asides which the two exchanged and especially during their evening in al-Kurra together after my departure. In this land of the *siassa* nothing was straightforward and little could be taken at its face value. Next morning it was no real surprise when the Sultan and his cortège passed our fort at Najd al-Mizr and, instead of proceeding up the side wadi on the road homewards, called on Sayyid Muhammad Dubbash. Later I learned that Dubbash had paid him the signal honour of slaughtering an ox and that the two had been closeted together in secret conversation until late that evening. Hussain said: "He cannot be trusted. His face is a mask. His thoughts are quite different." But on one thing the Sultan had not deceived us. Within a few weeks the Rassassis were at open war with their Yemeni overlords.

We had further negotiations to conduct with the Yemenis, this time with the Amil of Harib, Sayyid Ahmad Kuhlani. The date for these was drawing near and I was keen to make my approach to Harib by the northern, desert route, which I had not yet travelled. Apart from adding to my map I hoped thereby to smooth some of the Sharif's ruffled feathers, for such a journey by the Political Officer would reinforce Hussain's claim to border areas which the Yemenis had seized from Bayhan.

On 2 September I rode up to Asaylan on Tunis with a Tribal Guard escort to prepare for this journey, leaving Nabih to accompany the Sharif later on the more direct route through Mablaqa. On these short journeys I had by now found that it was easier to travel without any kit at all, sleeping on the floor with a borrowed blanket and accepting the hospitality which everyone making a journey in these parts expected as of right. Nabih could not tolerate such a mode of travel, for the Arab townsman enjoys his comforts and dislikes going without them. On the way I visited the ruins of Hayd Kuhlan (ancient Tumna) once again and was able to collect a few fragments of inscribed alabaster lying in the ground and to take photographs. For once the Tribal Guard Nayb accompanying me, a Sayyid from Awlaqi country, was interested in the ancient ruins and helped me to acquire two alabaster carvings from an Ashrafi tomb robber we encountered – one was a crude crouching figure, the other a beautiful relief carving of a girl's head. I hoped that a price of three dollars against the thirty he sought would diminish his enthusiasm for digging among the Qatabanian graves. The carvings went to the Aden Museum.

Even when I fled alone to places like Asaylan there were visitors who followed me. A young Sayyid from Markha arrived, seeking an introductory letter to Seager to discuss the affairs of his wadi. Shortly afterwards Sharif Salih brought in a man who was recognisable at once from his appearance and the dignity of his bearing as a desert tribesman of some eminence. "This is Shaykh Abdullah bin Ali al-Hammami," Salih said. "He was a great friend of Colonel Hamilton. There are some affairs of his tribe which he wishes to discuss with you." We exchanged greetings and spoke of ordinary things, but his beduin dialect was not easy to grasp and I suggested we wait until I had an interpreter before we talked of serious matters. He agreed to accompany me to Ayn.

The Hammamis live some two days' journey east of Bayhan in an area of sand, wadi and gravel plain at the mouths of Wadi Markha and Wadi Hammam, which flows past Nisab. They were a desert tribe, well known as the providers of camels for trading caravans, and they had an extraordinary reputation for honest dealing. For a long time they had been friendly towards the Aden Government and in earlier years they had been of much assistance to us. Wyman Bury spoke highly of them; Philby had stopped among them; to Hamilton they were a tribe *par excellence*; Colonel van der Meulen, on Hamilton's advice, used their camels for part of his journey of exploration in 1939;* Davey had maintained the friendship, but had not been able to visit them. Although acknowledging a measure of fealty to the Awlaqi Sultan, they were not Awlaqis and were jealous of their tribal independence. In recent years we had had to ignore them and I hoped that something of the earlier relationship might be restored through my meeting with this important shaykh.

Shaykh Abdullah bin Ali was an impressive man – intelligent, friendly and able to see far beyond the politics of his tribe. Over the months which followed I was able to get most valuable advice from him, but the opportunity never presented itself for us to use the Hammamis in the way he offered, as a base from which to take over control of his region of the Protectorate.

Early the following morning, while dawn was still picking out the tops of the great sand-dunes of the Ramlat Sabatayn, I left Asaylan on horseback with Sharif Salih, my Tribal Guard companion and Abdullah al-Bahri, the Harithi who had once singled me out with

---

* See *Aden to the Hadramaut* by D. van der Meulen (London, Murray, 1947)

his gun. Abdullah was now our *rafiq* over this desert route, pledged to escort us safely through his tribal teritory. For so short a journey this was little more than a formality, but it was part of the customary law, like the eating of "bread and salt", which regulated desert life. Under the care of a *rafiq* of influence a desert traveller could move through areas to which he might otherwise be denied access on pain of death. The Arabs have a saying, "*rafiq qabl tariq*", "companion before road"; in the context of the desert beduin this means that the selection of a good *rafiq* is more important than one's choice of route.

Cantering a winding course through *rak*-covered dunes, we soon caught up with Abdullah's father, old Ali bin Munassir, and the redoubtable Shaykh Ali bin Ghurayba, who had gone ahead on camels. There were Bal Harith affairs to discuss with Kuhlani and we needed their presence. The Hammami shaykh had taken a more northerly route in company with Shaykh Nassir bin Hussain, for Ali and his rival did not care to travel together. I had powerful escorts.

We reached the edge of the mountains on our left, which threw long spurs northwards into the sand-dunes. Between each spur a small wadi led out into the desert, with stones and thorn-bushes along the stream-bed. Near one of these were the remains of a small building, recognisable at a glance from the quality of its stonework as Himyarite; part of it had sunk into the soft bed of sand, so that the remaining masonry courses curved downwards into the ground. It seemed likely to have been a fortified post guarding the entrance to Bayhan.

We crossed over a flat gravel plain and headed north into lofty dunes, following the tracks of camels to a small encampment of the Bani Sayf bin Murad, a Yemeni tribe who were friends of the Bal Harith. Abdullah clearly had his eye on a good lunch. As soon as they spotted us the Muradi shaykh and the few tribesmen with him advanced towards us, cupped their hands to their mouths and started to shout a long welcome at the top of their voices, a custom I had not witnessed before. The water supply for this encampment came in goatskin bags carried by camel and donkey from a well some miles away in Wadi Harib and a youth was immediately despatched on a camel to supplement it. As we walked towards the black tents there was much gesticulation and pointing towards our horses and I was surprised to see another Muradi tribesman mount one of them and gallop off on it. "Where's he going?" I asked. Salih said: "Their flocks are pasturing some miles away. He has gone off to fetch sheep for our lunch."

We sat in the shade of a tent, leaning against camel saddles and drinking camel's milk, while more and more of the Bani Sayf bin Murad arrived, from hidden tents scattered among the great hills of sand, to greet us. I was stared at as an object of enormous curiosity, the first European most of them had seen. Presently the equestrian tribeman returned with two sheep stretched across his saddle, which were summarily slaughtered in front of us and dragged off to the cooking pots.

It was some hours before our meal was completed and, as there was not enough water for our horses, we left as soon as we could in order to reach the well before they began to weaken. We moved back on our tracks and then turned up the rocky course of Wadi Najd Marqad for about two miles towards a low pass in the hills. As we reached the pass I realised that it was a significant Himyarite site.

Some five hundred yards before the head of the pass a wide road-way had been levelled and paved, with walls on either side forty or fifty feet apart at the start but drawing closer together as one climbed upwards. This continued over the pass and down the other side for about three hundred yards into Wadi Harib. A little beyond the end of the walled roadway was another short stretch of walling with a paved platform in front. On a hill to one side were the remnants of what appeared to have been a small fort. There was no time to examine these broken ruins in any detail on this occasion, but there seemed little doubt that they must have been constructed to control camel caravans, the walls probably designed to force the animals into single file so that customs duty could more easily be assessed. It looked altogether older than the pass at Mablaqa and I have since suggested that the Mablaqa pass was constructed to replace it.* But what was the trade which merited such significant public works? It could hardly be other than the trade in frankincense and myrrh. Najd

---

* In "The Northern Passes of Qataban", *Proceedings of the 9th Seminar for Arabian Studies*, Vol. 6, London 1976.

Marqad must have been the first control point on the incense road after the caravans left Tumna on their long journey to Gaza.

I was probably not the first European to pass through Najd Marqad. In 1935, a year ahead of Philby, a young German traveller, Hans Helfritz, had become the first explorer to see Shabwa, moving on through the north of Bayhan to Wadi Harib, where he was taken prisoner. In his book he described the pass which led into Wadi Harib:* "We arrived at a pass which is formed by the junction of two ranges of hills. On the summit are two parallel walls formed of huge stones, many of which are covered with ancient inscriptions, and both walls rise to a height of nearly one thousand feet." There were no inscriptions, the pass was a low one, and the height of the walls was less than ten feet, but Helfritz must have been describing Najd Marqad. He was writing from recollections, much affected by heat and exhaustion at that stage of his journey.

On the far side of the pass we debouched into a rapidly widening gravel plain and cantered along a track edging the mountains on our left. We passed several low mounds, the ruin-sites of small buildings, but there was no time to examine them, as we still had far to go. The gravel plain led to the sand and silt plain of Wadi Harib proper. Though similar in many respects to Bayhan, Harib narrows considerably at its mouth, where the flanking mountains are only about two miles apart, and the great sand-dunes of the desert beyond, menacingly higher and closer than those around the Bal Harith fields, cover much of the wadi delta. But the wide plain within is fertile, with *ilb* trees, patches of bright green crops irrigated from wells, stretches of field watered by the floods, areas of *rak*-covered sand-dunes, and villages of square mud-brick houses dominated by central stone forts. Most of the villages we could see belonged to the Ahl Abu Tuhayf, who occupied the northern end of the wadi, a tribe similar to the Bal Harith, though more settled. They had a bitter feud with the Bal Harith and Abdullah al-Bahri was anxious to move away quickly out of their reach. To the south-west we could see the distant towers of Darb al-Ali, usually known as Harib, and, a few miles closer, the Tuhayfi stronghold called Darb Ahl Abu Tuhayf, a

---

* Hans Helfritz, *Land Without Shade* tr. Kenneth Kirtness, London, Hurst & Blackett, 1935.

village about the same size as Asaylan. We headed towards a well some two miles distant known as Bir Ahl Aqil (Aqeel), round which from afar we could see huge herds of camels.

The Ahl Aqil had come in from the desert to water their camels and were encamped around their well; their black tents dotted the plain, interspersed with huts made of branches thatched with thorn foliage. The arrival of four strangers on horseback was something of an event and we were quickly surrounded by an inquisitive crowd of men and boys who stared at me remorselessly. We sucked water greedily from goatskins while the work at the wellhead went on. It was a large well, with four skin buckets on separate wooden pulleys; the men heaved at the ropes with a rhythmic chanting and their women deftly flicked the heavy skins over to pour the water into troughs for the waiting herds. We were taken to the shade of a mud building, the only one there, where I was kept busy handing my watch round to incredulous old men and young boys who wanted to hear it tick. Soon the shaykh arrived, tall and authoritative, and led us into his thorn-walled hut, where we sat down on carpets, with camel saddles to lean against, and drank coffee. The Harithis and the Hammami shaykh joined us there an hour later.

For the first time since I had arrived in Arabia our coffee was carried in by a woman – the shaykh's wife. She was veiled up to her eyes and wore an indigo-blue dress and headcloth, with a thick belt, decorated with cowrie shells and bright red cornelian stones, round her waist. From her forehead, projecting from under the headcloth, was a stiff rope ornamented with more cowrie shells, which hung down in front of her face like an elephant's trunk. I was stared at disconcertingly by bright kohl-rimmed eyes determined to miss nothing.

The shaykh of the Ahl Aqil tried hard to persuade us to spend the night in his camp, but this would have been unwise and, as he did not force our hand by slaughtering a goat, he was probably hoping we would refuse. Although we were in an area the Sharif claimed as his own, the Ahl Aqil paid their taxes to the Imam and, until some settlement determined otherwise, we had to accept that they were Yemeni subjects. To have spent the night there without the Amil's permission would have pressed the Sharif's claim too strongly and the Ahl Aqil would have suffered. We moved on while the sun began to set.

The Bal Harith, always happier in the tents of fellow beduin, were leading us towards the camp of a small section of Ahl Shurayf hidden among distant *ilb* trees when we ran into a large party of Manawa *ryot* on their way back to their homes. Manawa was a mile-wide valley extending for some six miles into the hills to the east. The Yemenis had occupied it in 1931, but it was now Bayhani territory again. It was not a wadi but a *shaab*, which in this sense meant that it had no main watercourse and such flood irrigation as was possible was undertaken by tapping the water-flow directly off the mountainsides. The surrounding hills were steep and, although there was a difficult track through them to Mablaqa and another even more perilous one to Wadi Bayhan, the only practicable route in and out lay through Wadi Harib. While the Yemenis dominated that wadi they exercised a stranglehold over Manawa and could imperil the Sharif's control of it. Hussain's desire to recover the rest of his lost territory in Harib was understandable. "Everything on this side of the *sayl* bed is Musabayn country and should belong to Bayhan," Salih explained to me, adding: "One of these days, *ya* Groom, you must get it back for us."

Our Manawa acquaintances were insistent that we should spend the night at Shahza, the main village of Manawa, and we conceded. It would, after all, help to emphasise that Manawa belonged to Bayhan, while there were rain clouds gathering, which made the mud walls and roofs of the village a more attractive proposition than a wet night in a tent. We pushed on up the *shaab* and reached Shahza just as it was getting dark. Tea was brought in, followed after a long wait by *masub* and mutton, which we ate by the light of a Hurricane lamp; for two hours afterwards we listened to an impromptu song-ster with a repertoire of ribald lays, who accompanied himself on a small drum. The rain kept off and we chose the roof-top rather than the stuffiness of the dining-room for what was left of the night, lying down on the bare mud surface, without blankets, and pillowing our heads on our arms. I was far too exhausted to feel any physical dis-comfort. We arose before dawn and left with the first light, our party swollen by numerous tribesmen of Manawa.

The last part of the journey occasioned some risk. From Najd Marqad to Manawa we had moved over wide, open, uncultivated country. Now we had to pass through the heart of Wadi Harib and within a mile of Darb al-Ali itself. The track clung tightly to the mountainside, the fields pressing close up on our right, and there were several Yemeni habitations to pass by. Immediately opposite Darb al-Ali our path went within a few yards of a small hamlet called Shaqir. "The *aqil* of Shaqir is a Musabayn," Sharif Salih said, "but the Zaydis have a garrison there. Sometimes they stop anybody from Manawa who passes by and make them pay customs duty there. If Kuhlani wants to turn us back that is where he will stop us."

One of the Bal Harith killed a snake which he swore would cause a man to die within twelve hours of biting him. Further along, as we were getting close to the danger point, a fox suddenly ran across our path. Salih hastily aimed his rifle and fired a fusillade at it as it dashed away up the mountainside. The shots echoed from hill to hill and the peace of the morning was shattered.

I called out: "*Ya* Salih! The Zaydis will think we have come to attack them!"

"It is good that they should hear it," he replied. "I want to make sure they are awake. It would be a pity if they do not see us when we pass them by."

We approached Shaqir with some apprehension, quite expecting the soldiers in it to open fire. Fortunately, despite Salih's aggressive noises, all was well. A blue-skirted Zaydi sentry was standing on the roof of the square stone fort. As we drew level with him he came to attention and acknowledged our greetings with a sleepy wave of his arm. For the time being an international crisis was avoided.

On a later visit to Ayn I probed into the hills behind Shaqir and found the necropolis of the Himyarites of Harib. The slopes of the mountain, known as Jabal Dhahat Shaqir, were covered with the eroded remains of square mausoleums, usually divided into narrow chambers on either side of a central passage. In one valley, called Akimat adh-Dhakhr, a well-constructed paved pathway led upwards to a bowl in the mountainside, in the centre of which was a large rock with an inscription of several lines (RES 4328). My guide on that occasion told me: "There is a great treasure buried here beneath this rock. Many years ago a man called Mansur bin Rugayyi of the Beni Abd tribe was digging here to find it when a terrible jinn suddenly sprang out and chased him away. Nobody has ever dared to dig here since." The word *dhakhr* means "treasure". I copied the inscription, which was translated by Professor Beeston. It records the construction of a pass road which had been commanded by the god "Amm of Shaqir". Once again the ancient name has survived into modern times.

We moved with lighter hearts after we had passed Shaqir and our horses, sensing the end of their journey, began to frisk impatiently, but the camels of the Bal Harith grunted complainingly now that the sandy tracks had given way to rough-edged stones. Wadi Ayn was visible, with the huge dome of Jabal Qarn Ubayd guarding its approaches. The mound of Hajar Hinnu az-Zurir looked bigger and more impressive from this angle and I was surprised to see another mound not far to the north of it, which I visited later and found to be larger in area and covered with the tumbled remains of more humble buildings. Had this perhaps been the abode of the townsfolk, while the king, with his priests and nobles, lived in a temple and palace in Hajar Hinnu az-Zurir? The question has still to be decided.

We rounded Qarn Ubayd and headed for the distant towers of al-Hajb. A large party headed by Sharif Abdullah had formed up outside the village to greet us and there was much firing of rifles as we approached them. Sharif Hussain and the young Amir were nowhere to be seen. After a while Nabih detached himself from the crowd to join me.

"What has happened to the Sharif?" I asked him.

"He got married last night."

"What, here in al-Hajb?"

"Yes. He decided to avail himself of the right of a traveller to make a marriage while he is on a journey. Last night there was a wedding and the festivities went on until a late hour. His bride is from a local tribe and her kinsfolk will be very honoured by it."

"Will he take her back to Bayhan?"

"No. I don't think so. The marriage is just for the time he stays here. I expect he will divorce her this morning. But at the moment he is still asleep."

It was nine o'clock, when all the world was normally afoot, and there seemed to be no excuse for the Amir to be sleeping too, but I said no more. Nabih was clearly envious of the Sharif's privileged good fortune.

Hussain joined us an hour later, while we were drinking coffee, and was courteous and agreeable despite the tension now developing between us. We lunched, and after the last clean-picked bones had been thrown over our shoulders to the waiting flies, after we had washed greasy hands in a proffered bowl of warm water, regurgitated loudly and muttered our *al-hamd l'Illah*s, and after the last guests had been tactfully persuaded to leave, we got down to some business. Then Hussain's mien suddenly changed, and with a challenging glare he flung down a letter in front of me.

"Look at that, *ya* Groom!"

I picked it up and asked Nabih to summarise it to me. "It is addressed to ash–Shami," he said after a quick perusal. "It is from the shaykh of the Ahl Fujara. It is about some goats looted by the Bani Wahb." The Fujara were a Bayhani tribe and the Bani Wahb a Yemeni one. "The shaykh is asking for ash–Shami's help in getting the animals returned."

"Read out the last sentence," Hussain demanded.

The last sentence of a local letter was always written in flowery phrases, but this one went rather further, suggesting fealty to the Imam.

"Do you know in whose handwriting that letter is written?" Hussain asked. I had recognised it all too easily, but said nothing. "It was written by the Qadhi of Marib," Hussain continued. "It is a gross interference in the affairs of Bayhan."

Letters blazoned with crosses were continuing to reach me for Seager from our arch-spy and the Sharif, knowing this, looked as if he would happily have had him murdered. I counselled restraint in any action he might contemplate and said I would suggest that Seager raised the complaint with ash–Shami. I could understand Hussain's feelings.

The anger fading from his face, Hussain turned to a more serious issue. I had agreed with Seager to let the Sharif go into Harib on his own for the discussions with Kuhlani, while I hung on in al-Hajb to be available only if required. This would greatly boost his *sharaf* as a Treaty Chief and should have pleased him immensely. But there was a new complication. Picking at the few grey hairs in his otherwise black beard, a habit of his when he was nervous, he leaned forward and said in a low voice: "I have some information of great importance about our visit to Harib. There is an old shaykh in Ayn whom I trust implicitly and he has just come back from a visit to Bayda. He was told there by one of ash-Shami's officers that the new Imam believes I took part in the plot to assassinate Imam Yahya. Perhaps that is why the Salihi shaykh was being paid to kill me. Now Imam Ahmad has sent twenty men from a special military unit in Ta'izz up to Harib for my visit. I am very suspicious that the Zaydis are plotting against me."

"Do we know that the Imam's soldiers have reached Harib?" I asked.

"Yes. There is no doubt about it. They have arrived. The Ashraf in Harib have confirmed it."

"And what about Kuhlani? Do you think he would allow them to do you any harm? After all, he was your guest."

"He is a treacherous man. Besides, he might not be told."

"What do you think we ought to do?"

"They would not dare to harm me if the Political Officer and his Government Guards were with me. I would like you to accompany me to Harib."

On 7 September we left in the cool hours of early morning for the Yemeni border.

We were a sizeable party. The Sharif had brought the Amir and the Qadhi of Bayhan, together with his bodyguard-slaves and household servants; with us were the Bal Harith and the Hammami on their camels, and several dignitaries of Ayn and Manawa; and we were escorted by twelve Government Guards and twenty Tribal Guards – in all some sixty-five persons. We moved slowly to the marching songs of our military, the horses frisking with excitement and breaking into short bursts of agitated trotting. Kuhlani, making his own gesture about the location of the frontier, was waiting for us on the ruin mound to the north of Hajar Hinnu az-Zurir and advanced to meet us with a large entourage as we drew close. We met in a small clearing and, as we dismounted, there were sharp bursts of rifle fire in greeting, while Kuhlani heaved his fat little body off a mule and ran forwards to shake our hands. Behind him were a hundred unkempt, indigo-covered, light-blue-skirted soldiers, together with some four hundred tribesmen and townsmen.

There was a wild melée of hand-shaking and then we began to move towards the town. The Zaydi troops had brought a bugle with them, which they started to blow tunelessly. The young boys of Harib school had turned out with a song of welcome which they sang without cease. A group of *shahadh* cavorted in circles in front of us with drums and pipes. Loose rifle shots from late-comers barked and echoed. Our own soldiers renewed their songs. The Yemeni cohorts, disregarding their bugler and marching ten abreast, burst into shrill songs, peculiar to the Zaydis, which rise higher and higher in pitch until they end with a scream. Our horses whinnied and shied, and camels and donkeys added their protests. Yemeni flags, red with white stars and the sword of Islam, waved from sticks and rifle barrels. Our progress, made difficult enough by the thorn thickets in our path, was further confused by the *nidham*, the Zaydi troops, who would stop suddenly, without warning and regardless of who was behind, and gather into small groups, like rugger scrums, to debate the words for the next verse of their chorus. It took us an hour of deafening bedlam to reach the town.

Darb al-Ali, or Harib town, was built in the centre of the wadi, and *sayl* beds carried the flood-waters past it on either side. In appearance it was very similar to Bayhan al-Qasab. Its stone and mud houses had the same square towers, pinnacles, flat roofs and loophole windows; it possessed the same unhygienic sewage system and the same indigo-stained mounds crested by earthenware pots where cloth was dyed; it had just as many flies. But a closer acquaintance showed up differences. There were larger, better-built houses than in Bayhan, some of them with walled courtyards. The streets were wider. There were even walled gardens irrigated, like the Sharif's garden, with water drawn by camels – but here the main crop was *qat*.

We regarded *qat* as the scourge of South-west Arabia and had persuaded Hussain to ban it in Bayhan. It is a small bush, and sprigs of it are stuffed into the mouth and munched. "It makes you feel good. You forget all your worries. You can do anything." So the *qat* chewers would claim. But under its influence they became garrulous, aggressively quarrelsome and so constipated that they felt no need for food. Addicts were recognisable by their wan complexions and lean appearance, and their families were often left totally impoverished, because, like all drugs, it was a costly habit. *Qat* was widely consumed in Aden and the Aden Protectorate, as well as in the Yemen, and was the cause of much trouble. Davey had been murdered in Dhala by a man under its influence. I had not known before now that it was cultivated on this substantial scale in Harib for local consumption.

The best house in the town had been emptied and placed at our disposal and we lodged in it for a week. I was given a tiny, newly white-washed room at the top, and Sharif Hussain, the Amir and the Qadhi of Bayhan shared a large room below where we ate communally. Our meals were of a luxury unknown in the Protectorate, for we were guests of the Imam and the Yemenis had higher feeding standards. We breakfasted on a flaky chapatti soaked in honey, and a large omelette, which we attacked with our fingers. At lunchtime and in the evening the same dishes would be served with the addition of bowls of boiled chicken, round, flat loaves of heavy bread, and baskets laden with segments of boiled mutton.

"They must be slaughtering a lot of sheep to feed all sixty-five of us like this every day," I said to Hussain at one evening meal.

"We are eating ten sheep a day," he replied with relish.

"So we are putting the Imam to great expense," I continued.

"*Aiwa*. That is indeed so," Hussain said. "But the Imam is wealthy. Besides, some of it is paid for by customs duties which I should be receiving and not him. What's more, Kuhlani owes me a great debt, for I fed him and his whole party in Bayhan for three months when he took refuge with us and altogether he consumed three thousand dollars from the Bayt al-Mal. So do not worry about the cost, *ya* Groom! Eat! Enjoy youself! There is no need to praise the Imam for his bounty."

We received a continuous stream of visitors wishing to pay their respects – officials, down to the most menial clerks, and many citizens and merchants of the town. Prominent among them and a frequent visitor was Sharif Sayf bin Abud (Abood), a tall, imposing man with a grey beard and a complete set of gold teeth. Sayf was the eldest of a family of twelve brothers and the leader of the Ashraf of Harib, kinsmen of the Habilis, Sharif Hussain's family. He had written many letters to Hussain in the period of confusion which followed the Imam's assassination, suggesting that the time was opportune for his clan to capture the town, break away from the Zaydis and join up with Bayhan. Hussain had wisely cautioned restraint, knowing that if Imam Ahmad won the day his reaction against those who had rebelled would be merciless. Now Sharif Sayf was as loyal a Yemeni citizen as any, which at least meant that he rendered to his Caesar the things which were Caesar's.

Another of our visitors was the Keeper of Kuhlani's Treasury, and therefore a person of considerable importance in the Harib set-up. He came up to my room with Nabih to introduce himself and, after we had exchanged the normal courtesies, said: "You know my brother. He is the customs clerk in Nata and you met him with Sayyid Muhammad Dubbash." No more was said during the course of that meeting about my would-be spy, but the brothers had evidently exchanged confidences. Within twenty-four hours he had sidled up secretly to Nabih and been corrupted himself for the sum of fourteen Maria Theresa dollars. For that amount I was given, in addition to some general and useful items of news about the political situation in the Yemen, details of the special measures taken to watch my movements. It was not the Sharif but the Political Officer who was now under greatest suspicion. An evil-looking youth who had already presented himself as my personal servant was under instructions to sleep outside my door in order to report on any midnight visitors. Another, older man, who served the food, was there to assist him. Ten of the soldiers sent up by ash-Shami from Bayda had been ordered to escort me everywhere I went outside the house and ensure they overhead every conversation I might engage in with any member of the local populace. It was all very symptomatic of Yemeni fears and mistrust.

The most important matter for discussion with Kuhlani was the Bal Harith feud with the Ahl Abu Tuhayf. The truce between them had been broken by a Tuhayfi who had wounded a Harithi with his *jambya*. The crime was particularly heinous because the Harithi had already given the Tuhayfi *aysh wa milh* and was acting as his *sayyar*, or guide through Harithi territory, when the murder attempt occurred. Under an agreement Davey had worked out with Kuhlani, the offending tribe was obliged in such case to pay the assessed value of the injury as compensation, together with a similar amount as punishment. But the injury was not severe and the compensation assessable under Sharia law would have been no more than eighty-five Maria Theresa dollars, whereas under tribal custom the Bal Harith would have expected at least one thousand dollars because of the special circumstances. The Tuhayfis had insisted on settlement under the agreement, while the Harithis demanded an award based on tribal custom. It was for this reason that we had brought the four most powerful Bal Harith leaders to Harib. Discussion went on for hours and there were moments of high passion when the Harithis and then the Tuhayfis vehemently affirmed their rights. To break the deadlock we finally persuaded Kuhlani to order the Tuhayfis to pay a total fine of five hundred dollars, a sum which the avaricious Bal Harith could be induced to accept only with the greatest difficulty. They left next day, looking extremely disgruntled, and I feared we might yet see revenge taken against the Ahl Abu Tuhayf.

I had hoped to leave Harib as soon as the Bal Harith dispute was settled, for Hussain's worst fears of a plot against him now seemed to be dispelled, but he was insistent that Kuhlani expected us to stay longer and would be insulted if we left too soon. He was probably determined that the cost of entertaining us should have time to exceed the huge sums he had spent on Kuhlani. There was not much more for me to do and my escort of Yemeni troops, together with the surging crowds which thronged around me every time I stepped out of the front door, made it difficult to explore the surroundings. To avoid giving offence I had to leave my camera behind me when I went out: not only was photography regarded as tantamount to spying, but it was still widely held here, as in many parts of the Protectorate, that photography of a person breached the Islamic ban on the pictorial representation of a human being, while to allow one-self to be photographed by a *nasrani* – non-believer – was sinful. In Harib there were even deeper superstitions. Above the door of Sharif

Sayf bin Abud's house was an alabaster stone inscribed with five lines of beautifully carved Himyarite letters, probably stripped from the temple ruins at Hajar Hinnu az-Zurir. I was politely refused permission to photograph it and with equal courtesy was denied leave to copy it down with pencil and paper – to do so would spoil the good luck which this stone brought to the establishment. Before we left, Nabih slipped out in the early morning hours to copy it secretly for me by moonlight, but it was high above his head, the light was inadequate, and he did not know the Himyaritic letters, so that his copy was too inaccurate to be decipherable.

On two occasions Hussain and I managed to get out for short rides on horseback, but our escort made sure we did not go far. On one of these journeys we rode to the far side of Jabal Hashfah, an isolated hill north-west of Darb al-Ali. Here Wadi Ablah, after flowing through a wide, open plain, passed through a narrow gap in the mountains flanking Harib to join the main wadi as a tributary. Crossing the valley between one hillside and the other over a distance of about half-a-mile was a line of enormous boulders. "The remains of a fortress of the Himyarites," one of Kuhlani's men said, but to my eye this looked very much like the remains of an ancient dam. I was politely restrained from going on to look at the site of a Himyarite town said to lie about a mile away in the Ablah plain, but at least I had the discovery of this relic of a major irrigation scheme of Himyarite times to report to Inge on my return.

I had resisted the worst attentions of the flies in Harib, but there were other germs around and by the time we returned to Bayhan I had a cold and a cough. An Agricultural Officer, Jimmy Congdon, came up on his first visit to Bayhan and I spent five days with him talking about agricultural matters to farmers and merchants while my ailment got worse. After he was gone I was gripped by an overwhelming lassitude and signalled for a plane so that I could see a doctor in Aden. Almost immediately Bayhan was blanketed by low clouds, wrapping the whole land in a cold fog which no aeroplane could penetrate. The white-out persisted for over a week. I was short of stores and rations, but no longer had much inclination to eat. News arrived that the Rassassis had gone to war with the Imam, but I no longer cared.

I reached Aden on 5 October. "You are just getting over a bad attack of jaundice," the doctor said, pulling back my eyelids to reveal blood-shot saffron eyeballs. "What have you been eating?"

"For the last week," I replied truthfully, "I had nothing left in my store cupboard except tins of sardines."

"In that case you ought to be dead," he said, and sentenced me to remain four days in hospital and not to leave Aden for another three weeks. It was disconcerting. I had planned to return to Bayhan in two or three days with fresh stores and a bottle of pills. Yet for once I was glad of the comforts Aden had to offer and even more grateful for the opportunity to be on my own. In the Protectorate a Political Officer could not expect privacy.

8

A Variety of Troubles

In the last week of my convalescence Basil Seager called me over to discuss a new plan for the administration of Bayhan. It was a simple enough scheme. In line with arrangements already carried out in other states, he proposed to ask the Sharif to promulgate a formal state constitution. We knew that this would be a bitter pill for Hussain to swallow, but something more had to be done to curb his increasing "hauteur", while the Colonial Office was demanding constitutional advances and better financial controls as a pre-requisite for more money for development in the Protectorate.

The British Government, a Labour one at that time, did not take very happily to Arab despots, who could sometimes be utterly corrupted by power. In Dhala, Peter Davey had been involved in the ejection of a tyrant Amir in 1947 and since then Alistair McIntosh had been obliged to undertake a full-scale military operation with RAF support to oust another petty dictator from the neighbouring state of Shaib. An RAF plane had been lost in that operation and the pilot killed. In both these cases arrogant rulers had turned efficiency into a grinding tyranny when, because of the shortage of Political Officers, they were left to their own devices. The Shaibi Shaykh had made his subjects crawl backwards on their hands and knees whenever they left his presence, while the catalogue of Amir Haydara's cruelties and injustices would fill a book. Once they were ousted, constitutions of a sort were introduced into their states. In Dathina a constitution had already been promulgated with the full co-operation of the local tribes and was working well. A fourth constitution existed in Fadhli. Thus a pattern for the Protectorate was being established, acceptable to post-war notions of colonial rule. If it was to have meaning and validity then the Sharif of Bayhan, who was not a ruler at all until we made him one, had to be the next to succumb. He was not expected to like it.

By the time I was ready to return to Bayhan the first draft of a constitution was ready for discussion with the Sharif. It was a compromise and by no means as tight as we would have preferred. It aimed to set up a small Executive Council and a large Advisory Council, both voting by secret ballot, for no one would have dared to vote against the Sharif publicly. We decided to leave the question of control of the Bayt al-Mal for a later stage, for the constitution alone was probably as much as the Sharif could take at once and would be difficult enough in itself to put over. I had Arabic and English versions of the draft with me when I returned, and had been instructed by Seager to bide my time for a favourable moment before planting this bombshell in front of him.

In the month since my departure, Bayhan had become surprisingly cold and I had to don extra clothes to keep warm. Amir Salih met me at the landing ground and told me that his father was ill. We lunched in the white tower and Sharif Hussain joined us afterwards, looking pale, exhausted and feverish. I signalled for medicines without delay, and they came up on a Government Guard relief plane the next morning.

After my long absence there was much to do and a lot to catch up with. One big event was being discussed everywhere. Shaykh Salih Ahmad Sayf, who had plotted Hussain's murder, had returned to Bayhan, under a *wajh* from the Sharif, following the representations we had made to Kuhlani and ash-Shami for his extradition. Pending a decision on how to punish him, he was living at home, quite freely, having surrendered hostages who now repined in manacles on his behalf in the Sharif's airless prison. Such manacles, hammered on round the ankles by a blacksmith and held up off the ground by a leather thong, so that the prisoner could just shuffle along in them, were a normal feature of Protectorate prisons. The mud brick and mud-mortared stones of local buildings made it all too easy for anyone to dig a way out of his cell and escape without this extra restraint. But it was not normal for manacles to be used on hostages and Seager had already asked me to try to get them removed from these luckless Salihis.

Imprisonment in the Protectorate had another unusual feature. The prisoner's food and other wants had to be supplied by his friends or relatives. The state locked him up but felt no obligation to feed him. When Shaykh Salih Ahmad Sayf came to see me next day, he asked me to intercede with the Sharif in order to secure the release of his three existing hostages in exchange for one much more important one, his brother. "It is not just that I must pay for the food of all three hostages," he said, "but also I have to pay for the maintenance of their families. With hostages that is the custom. But it is expensive and I do not have much money." The shaykh could not talk to Hussain direct and I was his intermediary. I passed his request on that evening and Hussain's expression clouded. "I will have the hostages unchained," he replied, "because that is what Seager wishes. But I cannot agree to their release. No. Not even in exchange for the shaykh's own brother. The shaykh has agreed to give me these hostages and it is too late for him to change his mind." Two days afterwards the Salihi shaykh called on me again. "If the Sharif refuses to let me exchange my hostages, it cannot be helped," he said. "But they are still in manacles. That is a great *ayb* – a stigma. They are hostages, not prisoners. I beg you to ask the Sharif to have their manacles removed." Amir Salih called on me a little later and I told him what the Salihi shaykh had said. "I will go to my father's sickbed at once and ask him about it," he said. "He must have forgotten to give the order." But he returned in a few minutes looking very sheepish. "I am sorry," he said "but my father is in a difficult mood. He will not allow the manacles to be removed. He says that all three hostages have defaulted on their agricultural loans and they must remain manacled until the loans are repaid." I forbore to protest that these were loans from the *hakuma*. "Why is the Sharif being so difficult about these hostages?" I asked Amir Salih later. Salih replied: "He is disgruntled over everything to do with hostages. While you were in Aden, Sharif Awadh and I sought his agreement for the Bal Harith hostages to be allowed a few days with their families during the Id celebrations. He would not permit it and there were angry words."

That evening I made a mistake which worsened my relations with the Sharif even more. A young soldier of my Government Guard garrison was, unusually, a Bayhani. For some time he had been trying hard to persuade me to give him *sharaf* by having supper at his house. I finally consented, for the morale of my Government Guards was most important. But I had not appreciated, and had carefully not been told, that my young host was a relative of the Salihi shaykh. To all appearances, when the Political Officer went over to ar-Rawna for supper that evening he was consorting with the enemies of the Sharif. The life of a Political Officer abounded with such pitfalls.

Obviously this was not an appropriate time to present the new constitutional proposals to Sharif Hussain and the drafts remained in my keeping. But there were plenty of other matters requiring my attention. One in particular was close to my heart because it concerned the correction of an enormous injustice. This was the problem of mortgaged lands.

More than a quarter of all the agricultural land in Bayhan was, I had discovered with profound concern, mortgaged to the small and thoroughly unscrupulous group of merchants who controlled the country's trade. A peasant farmer would get into debt and approach a merchant for help. A deal would be arranged at great speed, often with no documents at all to record it, whereby a sum of money, or perhaps a quantity of grain, was advanced to the peasant in exchange for complete control over his land, including all its produce. The peasant then became an employee of the merchant, tilling what had been his own land for wages consisting of a small fraction of the produce. One good harvest might well be enough for the merchant to recoup all of his outlay, and thereafter everything he received was profit. Qassim had explained the iniquities of this system to me and subsequently I found that the Qadhi, too, was passionately concerned about it. "It is a great evil in this country," the Qadhi said to me. "The injustice is even worse than you think. Most of these peasants who have lost their land in this way no longer have any money at all, so they can only repay their loans in kind, from their wages or by handing over some of their livestock. Then the merchant says: 'These goats are not worth forty dollars, on my oath. I can give you no more than ten dollars for them.' So ten dollars is all that will be deducted from the loan. It is wrong, *ya* Groom. It is against the Sharia law. But these merchants are wily and have many clever tricks with which they can get round the Sharia."

It was not a matter which could be quickly solved. We decided that before any new measures could be imposed we would need to compile a register of all existing cases, a substantial enough task in itself. As Hussain was still ill, we went to see the young Amir, feeling that it was a good opportunity to give him some practice in ruling. Salih was flattered. "This is a bad thing you tell me of," he said. "I will write to the Wakils and ask them to start making their lists." The Sharif, who must have known about the system for a long time without concern, did not overrule him and so the long process of reforming the mortgage system was commenced. For some months, while various schemes were considered and discarded, there seemed to be no viable solution to the problem. Then the wisdom of learned men in Lahej was invoked and a dictum of the great Islamic jurist Ibn Hajjar was brought to light. "Ibn Hajjar is acceptable to us in Bayhan," the Qadhi said. "What he decrees shall be and no one can find fault with it." The so-called *uhda* sales, which formed a large portion of the contracts concerned, could now be settled. The landowners would have the right to work as *batul* on their land, receiving half the crops as their wages, while the merchants took the other half, accounting fifty per cent as profit and the other fifty per cent as a refundment of their debts. It was a simple solution on traditional lines, satisfactory to both merchants and their victims, although there were to be many minor difficulties in applying it. "Why did no one ever think to deal with this grievance before?" I asked the Amir. "We are all bedu," he said. "We do not have the wisdom for such things." It seemed a very lame excuse.

One of my most frequent visitors from Markha was Sayyid Nassir bin Ahmad, a likeable young man who kept me well-informed about the affairs of his troubled wadi. His face badly marked by small-pox, he had small, intense eyes which stared at me earnestly and, as far as I could see, honestly. He was always bare to the waist and dark blue with indigo. One day he came to me with a companion. His first news concerned a Nisiyin deserter from the Aden Protectorate Levies who had absconded with his army rifle and ammunition.

The Levies, usually known by their initials as the "APL", were the military force used in the Western Protectorate when disorder got beyond the control of the local state forces and the Government Guards. They had never been needed in Bayhan and I had little to do with them at that time, but their officers, men of the RAF Regiment on secondment for a few years, were a friendly bunch and their mess in Shaykh Uthman was always hospitable to Political Officers visiting Aden.

We were prepared to close our eyes to this desertion from the APL, but the theft of the rifle and ammunition could not be tolerated: these items were of enormous value at local rates and if one Levy got away with such theft then others would be encouraged to make a quick and handsome profit in the same way. I had entrusted to Sayyid Nassir bin Ahmad the job of personally handing over to the deserter a letter from me demanding the return of the stolen arms, and I had also asked him to advise the man that my threats should be heeded. In addition I had written to the Nisiyin shaykhs asking them to help. When Sayyid Nassir read out my letter, the deserter at first declared that he had already sold the rifle and spent the money he had received for it. After much deliberation he had changed his attitude and undertaken to return it to me personally provided I would guarantee his readmission into the APL without punishment. This was of course quite impossible, but I asked the Sayyid to tell him that if he handed over the rifle I would not attempt to apprehend him while he remained in the Protectorate. These negotiations had been going backwards and forwards for some time.

On this occasion the young Sayyid had a broad grin on his face as we shook hands. After we had exchanged greetings, he said: "I have brought something which will please you – a present for the *hakuma*," and, returning to the entrance way, retrieved a Lee-Enfield rifle, which he held aloft in triumph. It was a small success, but a significant one, for it showed that even in uncontrolled areas like Wadi Markha the *hakuma* could extend the long arm of its influence. The word would soon get around.

But the matter of importance that day lay with the visitor who had accompanied Sayyid Nassir. He was a frightened-looking shrivelled-up little man of middle age. Sayyid Nassir said: "*Ya* Mister

Groom, this is Sayyid Abdullah bin Muhsin." Then I knew that my confidence in Sayyid Nassir had been justified. He had brought in the brother of the notorious trouble-maker Sayyid Nassir bin Muhsin. As this unexpected visitor sat on the mud floor beside me, his spindly toes pointing inwards to those of the other foot and his mouth barely able to open or shut for fear I would imprison him, it was difficult to appreciate that his presence represented a significant political event. One of the most important of the rebel Sayyids of Markha had defected from Sayyid Nassir bin Muhsin and submitted to the *hakuma*, quite possibly bringing Sayyid Nassir bin Muhsin's influence in the wadi to an end and leading to a reversal of the Yemeni policy of support for him. To visit me was an act of notable courage, because his brother would very probably try to kill him for it. He was not in a communicative mood, but there was little that needed to be said, as the very fact of his visit said everything.

For some time there had been signs of a grain shortage in my area and the failure of the autumn rains was disturbing. Early in November I was visited by an old man from Manawa called Hishla, whose lively personality made him a natural spokesmen for his people. He came with a complaint from the people of Manawa against a heavy new customs duty which the Yemenis had suddenly imposed on grain exports, probably to conserve their own supplies. Quite properly, he had gone to the Sharif first of all, but Hussain had sent him on to me. "This tax is very harsh on us in Manawa," he complained. "The mountains cut us off from Bayhan, as you have seen for yourself, and the only way we can get into Wadi Ayn is through the customs post at Shaqir. We have no irrigation wells in Manawa, because the water is so salty, so when the rains fail we have to buy all our grain. We usually get grain from Darb al-Ali. But now we can only do that if we pay an export tax, and the tax is so high that we cannot afford it. If we buy grain in Ayn the Yemenis will make us pay the same tax on our way back when we pass their customs post at Shaqir."

"Could you not buy grain in Bayhan and bring it through Najd Marqad?" I suggested.

"No. The journey is too far. We have no camels in Manawa and it would cost too much to hire them."

I suspected the Sharif had sent Hishla on to me because his complaint fortified the Sharif's own case against the Yemeni occupation of Shaqir, but these were people living almost from hand to mouth and one felt sympathy for their predicament. I told Hishla I would try to help, but there did not seem to be much any of us could do. The public funds, whether from government or state, were quite inadequate in those days to permit subsidies for such cases, while protests to the Yemen would probably fall on deaf ears.

Hardly had Hishla left my room, when a Bal Harith shaykh, Nassir Fahdan of the Ahl Said section, called. His section was a small one, but I had found him the most friendly and far-seeing of the Bal Harith leaders and was beginning to win his confidence. "I have come to talk to you about the shortage of grain," he said. "It is becoming a very serious matter for us. Our people are beginning to suffer hunger."

"Yes," I said. "We are all worried about the grain situation."

"I want you to help us."

"In what way?"

"By asking the Sharif to let us take our salt direct to Darb al-Ali."

The rock salt which the Bal Harith dug out of their mine at Ayadim was their main source of wealth – if wealth is a suitable term in regard to such an impoverished people. Most of it was purchased by the Yemeni merchants in Harib, but in order to appease the powerful merchant community of Bayhan al-Qasab and at the same time to facilitate the collection of his customs duties, Sharif Hussain had insisted that the Bal Harith must bring their salt to Suq Abdullah rather than take it direct to Harib.

"Why will it help you to take your salt to Darb al-Ali?" I asked.

"Because the Yemenis need a lot of salt at present and with the money we can buy grain to bring back."

"But you will have to pay a very heavy export tax on the grain," I said. "Someone has just protested to me about that."

"No," Shaykh Nassir replied. "Kuhlani has let it be known that we can buy wheat to the value of the salt we sell without having to pay the new tax on it."

I remembered Kuhlani's fulsome expressions of friendship and cooperation during our talks in Harib only a few weeks earlier. Now, without any consultation, he was trying to bottle up Manawa and tempt the Bal Harith to smuggle their salt directly into Harib against Hussain's orders. It was a mischievous action, calculated to embarrass Hussain in his difficult relationship with the Bal Harith. The Bal Harith would have benefited, of course, and their shaykhs, as I discovered later, had selected Nassir Fahdan as their emissary to me because of my friendship with him. But he had to be sent away empty-handed. "I am sorry," I said, "but the regulations must be obeyed. I could not support any arrangement for you to avoid the duties in Suq Abdullah." He shrugged his shoulders, showing no resentment, and repeated the phrase I had heard so often from the Bal Harith before: "We are the children of the *hakuma*." With that he departed.

That evening, while I was still feeling indignant about Kuhlani, a Yemeni youth arrived who worked as a messenger for Kuhlani and who had on several previous occasions called on Nabih under the cloak of darkness to sell information about the activities of his master. He brought some trivial news about comings and goings in Harib and then added the pointed advice that I should avoid eating any foodstuffs which Kuhlani or ash-Shami might send me as gifts. I told Nabih to give him three Maria Theresa dollars, as a sum commensurate with the value of his information. Nabih returned to my room a little later and said: "He is very angry, Sahib. He says he has saved your life and it is an insult that he should be paid such a paltry amount. He has gone off in a huff and I do not think he will return." We did not see him again and the poisoned comestibles proved to be a figment of his imagination.

The Bal Harith did not fall to Kuhlani's lure and continued to bring their salt into Bayhan al-Qasab. I had been visited some days before by Alawi bin Ghurayba, who told me that they had news of a large raiding party from Hadramawt which had been preparing to set out from the watering point at al-Abr with the intention of attacking the Bal Harith. The main purpose of his visit was to seek permission to launch a counter-raid against the Ahl Kurab. The attack from al-Abr had not materialised and I had, rather to Alawi's surprise, forbidden their counter-attack, but raiding parties were out and about and the Bal Harith were frightened of being caught unawares. Usually the salt camels arrived in Suq Abdullah in small caravans of about a dozen animals. Now, for security, they were being kept together. On 8 November a convoy of a hundred salt camels reached the Suq under a strong escort, and the next day the largest caravan ever seen in Bayhan entered the town – more than six hundred camels guarded by over a hundred armed tribesmen. The sight was impressive: long files of camels, tied nose to tail, winding slowly through the dusty fields and the plain beyond out of the distant heat haze. Soon the area around the small, open-sided customs house in front of the Sharif's court was a forest of long, brown camels' legs, with a throng of customs clerks and white-skirted tribesmen bustling among them – counting, weighing, sorting and shouting at each other above the snorts and grunts of the animals. If one disregarded the long, old-fashioned rifles, which the Bal Harith carried horizontally on their shoulders, muzzle forward, then the scene went back some two thousand years, when the commodity being carried was not salt, but incense.

While I was watching this animated picture from my window, a Government Guard *askari* came up to my room with a curious item in his hand – a small, square plate of heavy red metal with a straight line crossing it on one side and a Himyarite letter "K" on the other. It had been found in the graveyard outside Hayd Kuhlan and I suspected he had acquired it as a speculation. "Is it gold?" he asked me. I was not too sure, but could not in any case suggest it might be, for that would have started another rush to rob the tombs. It looked to me rather like a merchant's weight. Could it, I wondered, have been used to measure out incense?

The threat of a raid from the east induced the Bal Harith not only to travel in convoy but also, once I had rejected their proposed counter-attack, to ask me to arrange a truce with their eastern neighbours. It was not a request which could be easily met. The history of feuding and raiding between the Bal Harith and these Mishqas tribes went back into distant generations, but within remembered times there existed a stain on the Bal Harith honour which it would be most difficult to eradicate. Many years back the Nahd, one of the Mishqas tribes, had killed a Harithi *sayyar* in Hadramawt. Despite arrangements taken to restore the truce, the Bal Harith had never

forgotten that murder and had not given up the idea of revenge.
About ten years ago some Bal Harith had been acting as *sayyars* to a
Nahd caravan in the desert north of Harib. On a pre-arranged signal the *sayyars* deserted the caravan, the safety of which they were
pledged to guarantee, and a mob of Harithi tribesmen charged in
with a burst of rifle fire. There was a brief orgy of murder and looting and eight of the Nahd were killed. The Nahd had still to avenge
this treacherous slaughter. In 1943 Davey had made great efforts to
negotiate a new truce, but the stubbornness of the Bal Harith, who
had entrenched ideas about the terms, defeated him. In five years
nothing had changed. While there was still no settlement with the
Nahd there was little chance of the other Mishqas tribes mainly
concerned, the Saar and the Kurab, agreeing either. I spent a lot of
time during the next few weeks sounding out the situation, but the
Bal Harith, despite their request for a truce, remained as stubborn as
ever about its terms and I could get nowhere. Until we were able to
use military forces to compel the observance of peace terms there
was nothing we could do in the face of such intransigence.

During the same period a domestic feud also engaged a great deal
of time. It centred on a new schoolmaster. During his long stay in
Aden after his "official visit", Sharif Hussain had recruited one
Abdullah Muhammad Jalal to take over the school in Bayhan al-
Qasab. When he first arrived I suspected that one purpose the Sharif
might have in mind was to secure translations of such of my papers
written in English as fell into his hands, but this soon proved to be
a calumny when Abdullah's knowledge of the language was found
to be no better than that of the Second School Reader seen lying in
his house. Instead he turned out to be a competent and most dedi-
cated teacher and a veritable ball of fire.

The school in Bayhan al-Qasab was the only one in the whole of
Bayhan. It had been run by untrained local men under a Quranic
teacher named al-Alimi – "the learned one". The boys sat in small,
dark rooms and were taught the Quran, through which they learned
to read and write, together with a little elementary mathematics.
Abdullah Jalal had more progressive ideas, and in a very little time
he had arranged a proper timetable, launched classes in unheard-of
subjects like history, geography and art, organised Swedish drill,

started the boys on play-acting and even produced a competent school band. His pupils revered him. It was all too much for al-Alimi and for the forces of conservatism and reaction. Al-Alimi was fat and slow-witted, jealous of Jalal's success, and angry because he had been earning a small private income in the classroom during school hours, settling minor disputes between the townspeople, and this was no longer tolerated. After a few weeks al-Alimi barely attended the school, even to teach religion, and was gathering support for a protest movement. The *casus belli* was a quarrel over carpets. Before Jalal's arrival al-Alimi had used the best classroom in the school and had had it furnished with locally-made carpets. In the abnormally cold weather the mud floors became chilly to sit on and Jalal distributed these carpets round the classrooms so that all the boys could benefit from them. Al-Alimi returned to the school, grabbed all the carpets, announced that the new school timetable was contrary to the teachings of the Quran, and stumped off to complain to the Amir.

All might have been well if Hussain had not been ill. Amir Salih, lacking the wisdom of years, jumped to the conclusion that Jalal had stolen the carpets and reacted by sending al-Alimi back to the school with a posse of Tribal Guards to eject the new headmaster by force. This was an exciting event for the students, whose support for Jalal was total, and they set out *en masse* to the Political Officer's *dar* to seek my assistance. Jalal ran out to intercept them and persuaded them to return, but they would do so only after passing a resolution that if he were not reinstated within a few days they would boycott the school. It was the sign of a new age dawning, an indication that the idea of demonstration and strike was taking root even in these remote Arabian districts.

Next morning Jalal called to tell me his story. "I beg you most earnestly to intercede on my behalf with Amir Salih," he said. "He will not listen to me, but I am sure he will pay attention to you."

"I will do what I can," I said, "but it is really a matter for the Amir and the Sharif to decide."

"There is another problem I have," Jalal went on. "I have not complained about it before, but now things have got so bad that I am in very desperate circumstances."

"What is the trouble?"

"When the Sharif appointed me as headmaster, while he was in Aden, he told me he would not pay me until I had proved myself. I agreed to that. I thought I would have to wait only two or three weeks for my wages. But I have now been here for two-and-a-half months and the Sharif has refused to pay me anything. Whenever I go to the Bayt al-Mal they say '*Bukra* – tomorrow'. It is always '*bukra*'. I have run up debts with the merchants and now al-Alimi is making trouble for me with them and they are refusing to let me have anything else until I have paid them what I owe. My family is going hungry, because we have very little food left and I have no money to buy more. I beg you to ask Amir Salih to tell his clerks to start paying me what I am owed."

I agreed to lend him ten dollars privately so that he could meet his most urgent commitments at once and he left as happy as if all his problems had been resolved. A few days later, after I had made some tactful remonstrations with Amir Salih, the whole affair was debated in a *majlis* – a gathering of people for discussion – in the Sharif's court. The Qadhi and a few of the elders of Bayhan were invited to see fair play. Hussain was by this time sufficiently recovered to deal with the case and once again his brilliance at settling a dispute was demonstrated. A clear-cut victory for Jalal and the side of progress, which Hussain favoured, was made to look like a delicately balanced compromise, and both parties left contented and convinced that the moral victory was theirs. Next day Jalal returned my ten dollars.

Ever since Ramadhan I had been without the help of Shaykh Qassim, who had fasted with puritanical zeal and after the Id festival had gone off on the *hajj*, the pilgrimage to Makkah. Following the old pilgrim trail, which itself followed much of the more ancient incense route, he had set off with a party of about sixty Bayhanis on camels and donkeys on the road to Marib and Jawf. Joining with many hundreds of others from the Protectorate, the Yemen and the Hadramawt, he would eventually change to motor transport on the long final stretch through Saudi Arabia, but at their start, which I missed that year but saw the following year, the obvious pictorial analogy was with the pilgrims of Chaucer. Now old Qassim was back, his hair and beard dyed henna-red in the traditional style of one who has made the pilgrimage, and he would henceforth be known as Hajji, or al-Haj, Shaykh Qassim.

Long before Qassim left, Seager had discussed the proposals for a constitution with him, so he knew exactly what was entailed. His advice now was very definite. "You must put this proposal to Sharif Hussain without any more delay," he said earnestly. "Otherwise he will believe it is I rather than Seager and the *hakuma* who has conceived the idea." On 9 November I sent a note to Hussain stating that I would like to talk to him about a matter of some importance, provided he was well enough to see me. A Tribal Guard came round next morning to say that he was ready.

Seager and I had planned how to broach the topic and I went through my rehearsed speech with as much conviction as I could muster. Everything had to be laid on Seager's head, though whether Hussain would believe that Seager alone was responsible seemed rather doubtful.

"The British Agent was seriously alarmed by the plot of the Ahl Salih to assassinate you," I began. "He is particularly concerned because the Ahl Salih have always been the most loyal of the Musabayn tribes. If they were prepared to do that, then what might the feelings be among some of the others of your former enemies? You and the British Agent between you will increasingly have to make decisions which are in the best interests of your people but which may not be popular among them. But we cannot allow misguided opponents in Bayhan to threaten your position; you are a valuable influence in the whole North Eastern Area and we must protect you. Major Seager has asked me to tell you that he wants other men of importance in Bayhan to share some of your responsibilities, because in that way they will also attract some of the inevitable criticism of unpopular decisions, criticism which would otherwise all be directed at you personally. He wants a *majlis*, a Council, to be set up which will assist you in making some of the decisions."

This, in brief, was the line which I had to take in my stumbling Arabic, for on a matter so personal and delicate I could not allow Nabih to be present. The Amir gaped open-mouthed as I spoke, while Sharif Hussain listened intently, narrowing his eyes into slits and tugging nervously at the end of his beard. He was crouched up against the doorway in a white suit, with a handkerchief tied round his head in place of his turban to show that he was still a sick man.

"The British Agent suggests two ways by which a constitution, a *dustur* (pronounced "dustoor"), setting up the *majlis* can be introduced," I went on, still speaking to my brief. "Either we can keep the whole matter secret until he himself comes up to Bayhan in about three weeks' time, when an announcement can be made by proclamation about it. Or else you, *ya* Sharif Hussain, can make a request for such a *dustur*, which he will then have published widely in the newspapers and on the radio as an example of your concern for the progress and advancement of your people. He hopes that you will choose the latter course." I handed him the Arabic copy of the draft I had been given. "This is the constitution which Seager would like you to have. Please think about it very carefully. When you are ready we can discuss the detail and see if any changes are necessary."

While I was speaking Hussain had sent for Awadh, who sat by his side with an expression of growing horror and disbelief. It took some while for either of them to collect their thoughts. Then Hussain said: "It won't work. I could not possibly govern Bayhan in the way you propose. Nobody would understand it. As for the idea that I should be seen to ask for such a thing – I could never do that; if I did and then things went wrong you would turn round and declare it was all my fault."

Very soon they had turned to the subject of finance and begun to realise from rapid questioning that the proposed Executive Council, the *Majlis al-Tanfidhi*, would have considerable control over the public purse. Awadh began to get vehemently emotional. "If you force an arrangement like this on us," he said, "by Allah, it will be better for Bayhan that we the Habilis should hand over the administration to you and leave the country." Hussain reserved his deepest thoughts for himself, but it was quite clear that he saw the proposal as a major *kassar sharaf*, an ignominy which he would do his utmost to avoid. I left two hours after we had begun, having failed to persuade them that there was any merit in our proposals at all, and went back to my room to prepare a signal for Seager reporting that we had another crisis on our hands.

That night there were signs of a fearful agitation in the Sharif's court. "I don't know what you have told the Sharif," Nabih said next morning, "but extraordinary things are happening there. The main group of pilgrims arrived back from Makkah yesterday evening and called on the Sharif to give him their respects, as is customary, and he refused to see them. Sharif Awadh was there all night. Now Sayyid Abdullah has just told me that he was summoned by the Sharif long after midnight to write down a letter to the Governor of Aden, but then he was sent away before the letter was composed. In the Suq they are saying that something terrible has happened to the Ashraf. What is it all about?" I refused to tell him, but asked him to keep his ears open. All day there were comings and goings of Hussain's closest henchmen. "The four *wakils* have been sent for," Nabih reported. Later he came to tell me: "The Sharif called for the copies of all his Government treaties, and Sayyid Abdullah says there was a frightful scene when one of them couldn't be found," while the Rais of the Government Guards told me: "Some of the Tribal Guards have been detailed to carry heavy boxes from the Bayt al-Mal into the Sharif's private quarters. They must be full of dollars."

In the afternoon Sharif Awadh appeared in my room unannounced. "No," he said with a disarming smile, the anger and anxiety of the previous day no longer apparent, "I don't want to talk about the *dustur*, not yet. My brother is still thinking about that. I want to talk about the Bal Harith." He too had been approached by Bal Harith *aqils* eager to take advantage of the grain tax concession which Kuhlani was offering them. Awadh always had a better understanding of the beduin point of view than his brother and showed some sympathy to the Bal Harith case. "But I can do nothing," he said, shrugging his shoulders. "It is for my brother to decide."

Hussain came round to see me a little later, looking much calmer and more relaxed. "I believe my brother has spoken to you about the Bal Harith," he said. "We cannot allow them to take their salt directly to Harib. They are greedy for profit, *ya* Groom. They are not really short of grain. In the last harvest they had a very good crop – at least forty thousand *mads*." (The *mad* was a grain measure peculiar to Bayhan). "There is no reason why they should not continue to bring their salt to Suq Abdullah. Besides, I have just had another report from Sharif Abdullah about Kuhlani's misdeeds. He has put military patrols on the track between Manawa and Najd Marqad and they are taxing every trading caravan they meet. It is a blatant violation of the frontier."

"Why do you think he has done that?" I asked.

"It is a retaliation for your march along that track with Sharif Salih. I am writing to Kuhlani to protest in the strongest terms."

"I too will write to Kuhlani," I said. "And I will ask Seager to complain to ash-Shami."

He seemed pleased at that. But he did not mention the constitution and I refrained from raising the subject. Instead, in an obvious move to maintain an outward semblance of camaraderie with which I was happy to co-operate, he suggested that we went off for a ride in the Jeep. Awadh joined us and we set off, armed but without an escort.

The landing ground at ar-Rawna, on the far side of the *sayl* bed, was maintained with great difficulty by an elderly labourer provided with a wheeled water-sprinkler and a camel to pull it. The surface was a crust of mud on a silt foundation, and when the planes turned round at the end of the runway their wheels sometimes broke through the surface and sank so deeply into the silt that armies of men had to be brought in to pull them on to firm ground. South of the town, on the line of the track to al-Haraja, was a long stretch of firm, open plain which the Sharif hoped might take a Dakota once the tufted sand-dunes along it had been smoothed out. Hussain had it in mind that if a Dakota could land there then the new airline, Aden Airways, might bring Bayhan into their schedule. We drove round the area and, with a range-finder I had borrowed from the RAF for my mapping, I measured the most suitable stretch at about 1700 yards – more than adequate for the purpose. A few years later this became the airfield for Bayhan and Aden Airways were indeed landing there.

While Sharif Hussain continued to ponder over the constitutional proposals, unwilling to commit himself, there were other distractions; increasing numbers of people were coming to call on me with their complaints, petitions, and grumbles. One day I was visited by a pathetic, shrivelled-up little man who announced vehemently that he had been unjustly treated by the Qadhi in a Sharia law suit. I had considerable respect for Sayyid Muhammad Aatiq al-Bakri, the Qadhi of Bayhan, but every Protectorate subject had a right to appeal to the Sharia court in Aden against the decision of his local Qadhi, and Seager was most emphatic that this right should be maintained as a protection against the graft and corruption found in so many of these courts.

"What is your case?" I asked my visitor, whose name was Suwayra.

"My father and mother died about three months ago," he said, "and the Qadhi has distributed the property they left quite unfairly, so that I and my four sisters only get one-third of the estate, while my brother, who is a deceiver, has obtained two-thirds. My brother owed money to the merchant, Nassir Awadh, and together they have bribed the Qadhi. I have complained to the Qadhi and to the Sharif, but they will not allow me to appeal to Aden, so I have come to you. By Allah, everything I say is true." It certainly all sounded very plausible.

I called on the Qadhi next day to hear his side of the story. Sayyid Muhammad Aatiq greeted me with a wry smile. "I was expecting you to ask me about that case," he said. "It is a very difficult one, because Suwayra is a very troublesome fellow. First let me tell you that the matter came to me three years ago, not three months, and it is not really a Sharia case at all. These people are always coming to me with disputes which need to be dealt with by tribal custom and are nothing to do with the Sharia, but they do not understand if I refuse to accept them. I have agreed with Sharif Hussain that I will deal with them, but if they are not really Sharia cases then they cannot be allowed to go to Aden on appeal, because they will simply be thrown out. So if the *hakuma* insists that there is a right of appeal to Aden against all my judgements, then I would have to refuse to accept any case that is not properly one for the Sharia court. If I did that a lot of people would never get their cases settled at all. Suwayra's case is a good example. He had already taken over most of his father's goats before the case came to me and then claimed that they were his – and his father had debts which his brother paid for. It was all very complicated, but I did my best."

On the Qadhi's invitation I went to watch him dispensing justice.

His courtroom was a small, high-ceilinged room in the Sharif's main building, where he sat on a carpet behind a box-wood chest covered with case-books and scribbled petitions. A throng of would-be litigants squatted impatiently around him awaiting their turn after the case in hand. The exchanges were often heated, and the presence of armed Tribal Guards in the background was a reminder of how quickly and easily, among these volatile people, argument and anger could lead to the drawing of a dagger, even in the religious court. I felt sympathy for the Qadhi over his working conditions, but he had a good sense of humour and seemed unruffled by the continuous shouting. At least justice was being dispensed under a public scrutiny so close that corruption would not have been easy. Thankfully, too, justice in the Sharia courts of the Aden Protectorate was mellowed by our western influence and the punishments were not brutal, although in the Yemen and Saudi Arabia the Quranic precepts still meant that a thief could have his hand severed by an axe – the stump then being cauterised in boiling oil – and an adulterous couple could be stoned to death, the Qadhi and the witnesses to the crime flinging the first stones, for such was ordained by the law of the Prophet.

By mid-November the affairs of the Bal Harith were again becoming pressing and another visit to Asaylan was necessary. We loaded our baggage onto camels at six o'clock in the morning; it was extremely cold and the teeth of our cameleers chattered while they struggled with the saddles and ropes of their grunting, wheezing and throughly bad-tempered animals. I now had an addition to my staff, a small boy in tattered rags called Khamis bin Ali (Khamis – pronounced "Khamees" – denoting that he was Ali's fifth son). He was an orphan who had attached himself to Ahmad and my kitchen and by degrees had become a salaried employee. He was about eight years old and I never discovered the circumstances of his past, but he was a useful retainer with a remarkably lusty voice which he used to maximum effect. Khamis was a tribesman by birth, with all the tribesman's self-assurance, and able to talk to Bayhanis on their own terms. For the rest of my time in Bayhan he gave me his total devotion and would argue for my interests against anyone. When the first baggage camel lurched complainingly to its feet, Khamis was astride its neck in a moment, his thin, bare, leathery legs flailing away to urge it forwards faster than it had ever marched before.

On this occasion I was to travel in the Jeep, leaving much later. Nabih sat in the back with the Sharif's driver, one of the Sharif's cousins, a slave and two Tribal Guards. Hussain insisted on driving, his first venture on the open highway after a few short lessons on the ar-Rawna landing strip. He had not yet learned to change gear, and tended to go as fast and straight as he could in low gear, disregarding the sand-dunes and pot-holes on the way.

When we reached Asaylan we found the Wakil and his officials, together with the villagers and a considerable number of Bal Harith, assembled outside the village to greet us and fire their salutes. Unfortunately the Sharif had forgotten how to stop, and we hurtled past them and out of their sight at speed. With a sudden twist of the wheel he managed to fling the vehicle through the narrow portals of the main gateway, catching one side a heavy blow on the mud-brick wall, and we came to rest within inches of demolishing one of the houses of his subjects.

"There, *ya* Mister Groom," the Sharif said proudly, "You couldn't beat *that* on a horse, could you?"

I wondered what Tunis, now neglected in his stable, and the proud and powerful black stallion Nijm, Hussain's own mount, would have thought if they had heard him.

We ate our *masub* and mutton in Sharif Salih's dining-room, and while we were regurgitating and patting our bulging stomachs in appreciation, the Bal Harith leaders were called for and began to arrive in twos and threes until the room was crowded. Coffee was served, the heavy tube of a water-pipe was passed round, I lit my own pipe and Sharif Hussain offered cigarettes. His tin was soon empty. The Bal Harith were conscientious about the Islamic ruling that tobacco must never touch the lips. A tube was formed out of the clenched fist, the cigarette held in place at one end with the little finger and the smoke drawn through it from the other between thumb and forefinger. Like the "hubble-bubble" pipe, cigarettes were passed from one person to the other to be savoured in this way. Soon the room was cloudy with tobacco smoke.

Shaykh Fuhayd bin Hussain, white-bearded and voluble, had

interrupted the murmured exchanges of the long greetings formula
with a passionate tirade about a debt which his fellow shaykh, Nassir
bin Hussain, was claiming following the settlement of a looting case.
Nassir wanted his money, but Fuhayd and his ally, Ali bin Munassir,
thought the matter should be forgotten without payment. Even
Sharif Hussain was defeated by Bal Harith intransigence in this case
and finally brought the dispute to an abrupt halt by declaring that
the shaykhs would have to settle the matter among themselves. It was
the first time I had ever seen him completely floored. But the debate
had served as a pot-boiler for the greater argument to come, the
problem of the Bal Harith salt trade.

Hussain was still reluctant to talk about the new constitution, but
before we left for Asaylan we had agreed on a plan for dealing with
the Bal Harith over the issue of their salt caravans. The Yemeni
Treasury official in Harib who was working as my spy had reported
that two Bal Harith salt caravans had arrived in Harib despite the
Sharif's orders that they must all go to Bayhan al-Qasab. I could not
tell the Sharif this without revealing my source to him, but I had no
doubt that he would already be aware of it, quite probably from the
same person. Instead I said: "*Ya* Hussain, I suspect that the Bal Harith
are smuggling salt into Harib. We could bluff them by telling them
we know they are doing this, and we should be able to tell from their
reaction whether it is indeed true."

"You speak well," Husain said. "I too suspect that there is much
smuggling. They are going to Harib because Kuhlani is letting them
buy grain there so cheaply, but I still believe they have good supplies
left. It is greed, not hunger, which makes them go there. They will
sell it all for a great profit. If they really need grain to eat rather than
to sell, I will sell it to them at the ordinary price. I will offer them
grain from the Bayt al-Mal. *Wallah*! Then you will see if they really
need it."

The *ushur*, or crop tax, usually assessed at one tenth of the total
crop, was stored in the state granaries inside Hussain's administrative
buildings in Bayhan al-Qasab. Presumably Hussain was calculating
that his proposal to the Bal Harith would find no takers. I already
had my doubts. The Tribal Guard officer, Ruwayshan, had told me
some days before that grain was getting short not only among the

Bal Harith but also in Awlaqi and elsewhere in the North Eastern Area. But Hussain seemed very confident of his position.

When we started to put our plan into effect by accusing the Bal Harith of smuggling, their consternation was such that their guilt became quite apparent. But when Hussain went on to tell them that he would not countenance this, but was willing to sell them a certain amount of grain from the Bayt al-Mal, they did not react at all in the way he had predicted. Far from ignoring the offer, or accepting it grudgingly, they started to protest vigorously that the quantity he was offering would not be sufficient. Suddenly it became apparent that their shortage was a real one. The Sharif was non-plussed. There was not enough grain in the Bayt al-Mal to meet their demand. He would have to think of another solution.

I played for time by questioning the Bal Harith about their plight while I waited for Hussain to come up with a new proposal. He was sitting on the far side of the room and I could not go over to whisper in his ear without the resultant offer looking like something I had forced on him. Our relationship was too delicately balanced to risk what he might regard as a further *kassar sharaf*. The next move had to come from him. After nearly an hour in which the Bal Harith grew more and more angry, he tossed over a note to me, carefully folded into a spill in the local manner, suggesting that we revert to a solution I had already proposed at Awadh's instigation before we left Bayhan al-Qasab. I nodded agreement. "Very well," he called out above the hubbub. "Listen! I will offer you a concession. Once a month you can take a caravan to Harib to sell your salt and buy your grain without paying customs duty to me." The Bal Harith were silent for a moment and then, always avaricious, some of them started to bicker further. But they knew they had won a victory and they were not long in accepting.

We had been talking for three hours. Immediately agreement was reached Sharif Hussain, looking cross with the outcome, rose to return to Bayhan al-Qasab. I let Nabih go with him, for I knew that what I planned next would not be to his liking. Presently I heard the roaring of the engine as Hussain's jeep disappeared over the dusty fields. For the first time ever a journey to Asaylan had become an afternoon's outing.

It was my intention to visit the Ayadim salt mines. The Bal Harith would now see this as an honour, and it would at the same time help to deter the tribes in the East from any lingering thoughts about raiding us. The same calculations as before had to be made about the size of my escort and the number of camels we would require. I proposed to take as many Government Guards as possible, so that the Mishqas tribes would hear rumours of a great army, while I knew that the Bal Harith would insist on accompanying me with a large party for the sake of their own prestige. There would be a lot of camels to pay for, but as my supply of dollars was limited, we could not afford to be too lavish and careful preparation was necessary.

The Ayadim mines lay in Bal Harith tribal territory but had been discovered within the remembered past, possibly after a sandstorm had removed the dunes which concealed the salt dome, by members of the Ahl Aqil, the tribe at whose well in Wadi Harib we had watered on the way to meet Kuhlani. The Ahl Aqil still had an agreement with the Bal Harith, consequent on this discovery, that they could help hemselves to any salt they needed for their own persons and herds. In his little yellow notebook, Peter Davey had recorded:

> The Bal Harith tribe claim the Aiyadim salt mines to be their sole property and indeed they have the sole right to mine the salt. Any other tribe, either from Beihan, other parts of the neighbouring Protectorate or the adjoining Yemen, can only take salt from Aiyadim by obtaining permission to do so from the Bal Harith; this permission is obtained by firing off a salute before one of the Harithi headmen and placing an *aqira* of a few dollars before him. Rarely is this request refused. As regards the Beihan tribes, it is expedient for the Harithis not to refuse them free access to the mines, as the latter own the most succulent *rak* pasturage, without which the Bal Harith camels would probably die. If the Bal Harith refuse Beihanis access to the salt, the latter will refuse the Harithis permission to graze their camels in their *diras*. Those Beihanis who are accustomed to digging and selling salt include the Ashraf, the Sada, Ahl Hudeyb and Ahl Luqait.

In fact, by my time, only a few years later, salt was rarely dug from Ayadim by anybody but the Bal Harith.

I worked on preparations for the visit with Sharif Salih and Shaykh

Ali bin Munassir until dusk sent them scurrying off to say their evening prayers. "You will put in a good word for me with Seager about my right to be *Shaykh min shiyukh?*" Ali kept saying, as if the repetition of it was bound to ensure my doing so. Shortly after their departure a messenger arrived from Bayhan al-Qasab carrying an official envelope for me. It contained a radio message from the WAP Office: "The Protectorate Medical Officer, Dr Walker, will arrive at ar-Rawna tomorrow for a ten-day tour. Please accommodate him and make arrangements for his travels." I debated with myself whether to pretend that I had not received the signal, but decided reluctantly that Bayhan's interests would be best served by advancing the cause of medicine. Sadly, I called Salih back and cancelled all our elaborate arrangements. There was never another opportunity to visit Ayadim.

Walker, whom I had first met on the troopship which brought me to Aden, was a member of the Keith Falconer Mission run by the Church of Scotland in Shaykh Uthman, a town within the Colony of Aden. At that time the Mission provided the only medical services available in the Protectorate – a few dispensers and a touring doctor – while the worst of the curable cases were found beds in its small Shaykh Uthman hospital. Walker had a Danish wife and several children. He had spent two years as a doctor in Sanaa before being appointed Protectorate Medical Officer and this was one of his first visits into the Protectorate.

There was an air of patient optimism about these kindly medical missionaries, who had tackled their huge task with little direct help. They were barred from proselytising in the Protectorate, although there were sometimes protests that Arabic translations of the Bible had been left behind on their journeys, and it was said that in all the years since the Mission was founded, in 1885, they had converted only one Arab to Christianity.

Once the word got round, Dr Walker was almost overwhelmed by patients both male and female. Normally I saw little of these people, for the Arab likes to hide away when he is ill, but suddenly the Political Officer's *dar* became a centre for some most distressing cases – ulcers and septic wounds, gynaecological deformities, yaws – known also as desert syphilis – and, in vast numbers, trachoma and

other eye diseases, the scourge of all Arabia. For the majority there
was little that could be done without a consistency of treatment
which was impossible, but some of the patients benefited quickly
from a skilled application of proper dressings, a few were noted down
for hospital treatment in Aden, and many went home clutching pills
and powders with a faith which it was hoped might in itself provide
the cure. Another sudden crisis compelled me to send the doctor off
on his tour alone, but reports told of growing armies of sick persons
converging upon him wherever he went. There had never been a
doctor in Bayhan before.

The new emergency was on the frontier. The long murmurs of
discontent in Rassassi country had erupted into rebellion, and now
ash-Shami, with Zaydi troops and field guns brought down from
Sanaa, launched an attack on the Rassassi Sultan's stronghold in
Miswara. In the still of the morning we were just able to hear the
distant thunder of gunfire echoing in the far hills.

I discussed the position with Sharif Hussain. We both discerned a
danger to Bayhan from the possibility that the Sultan, if compelled
to retreat from Miswara, might bring his wild tribal army down the
gorge of Wadi Dhuba into the Bayhan plain. Hussain had no sympathy for the Sultan; politically it was expedient for him to back the
Zaydis, who were bound to win, while he was still convinced that
the Sultan had been implicated in the Salihi plot and had not forgiven him for it. "We had better go and talk to Sayyid Muhammad
Dubbash," I suggested and Hussain agreed, but said he would like
his son to represent him. I rode off to Nata with Amir Salih and Rais
Hussain Mansur, who had just arrived to take charge of the
Government Guards in Bayhan. A large contingent of Zaydi soldiers
was drawn up in line just beyond Najd al-Mizr and greeted us by
firing one after the other at a rock on the mountainside. We were
then led to Nata for lunch, for Dubbash would not talk business,
however urgent, until the courtesies had been observed.

"I don't think it is very likely that the Rassassis will come down
Wadi Dhuba," Dubbash said once the room had been cleared, "but
it is possible and I would like to be able to prevent it." In the Sharif's
estimation Wadi Dhuba was Bayhan territory, but we were not sure
whether Dubbash agreed.

"Presumably you would know in advance if they started to head in this direction?" I queried.

"Yes. Of course. We would hear the shooting getting nearer."

After some discussion we agreed that once he knew the Rassassis were on the way he could send his troops past Najd al-Mizr and up the side wadi to intercept them before they could debouch into the plain. With that we returned home. The distant guns could be heard booming as we left.

Next day the news arrived that Yemeni forces had moved up Wadi Dhuba in strength. Hussain said: "I do not trust them. It may be just an excuse to occupy more of my territory." But shortly afterwards a letter arrived from Dubbash: "Thank you for what we agreed yesterday. I have now sent my forces into Wadi Dhuba to intercept the Rassassis. Do not worry. I will pull them back immediately the danger is over. Indeed, they will withdraw at any time if you wish." In due course, when Miswara fell and the Sultan drew back to the remote fortress of Am Quwa instead of down Wadi Dhuba, Dubbash was as good as his word and all his troops returned to Nata. Sharif Hussain was delighted. "That means," he said, "that the Zaydis have now admitted that Wadi Dhuba is part of Bayhan."

The Rassassi defeat at Miswara was not the end of the Rassassi rebellion and, with some ingenuity, the Sultan managed to embroil a number of Protectorate tribes in his dispute, mostly on the basis of old fears and ancient alliances. Several Arifis went off to fight for him, frightened that the Zaydi troops might turn next to Arifi territory and that they might not be paid wages due to them from Rassassi farmers. Hussain had a simple remedy for this. He immediately sent Tribal Guards to occupy their houses, eating out of their larders and threatening their wives, until they returned. They were quickly back. But other tribes outside our control were joining the Rassassis: the Ahl Khamis and the Ahl Jaradan from Markha and the Dayyanis, Fathanis, Illayihinis and Maraziqis from the eastern parts of Upper Awlaqi. Suddenly there was a distinct danger that all Awlaqi would be waging war with the forces of the Imam, a situation which the Imam would attribute to our own intrigues.

I wrote many letters to Sayyid Muhammad Dubbash, expecting him to pass them on to ash-Shami, which explained how we were trying to prevent this assistance going to the Sultan, while relays of messengers moved backwards and forwards as we sought to convince the leaders of the Awlaqi tribes that it would be suicidal to let the militants in their flocks have their way. In the event the Sultan was driven out of Am Quwa in mid-January and forced to retreat to Nuquq, almost on the Protectorate border. At this stage most of his Protectorate allies began to desert him, but a group of Dayyanis in Wadi Khawra, who already had his family, his possessions and his supplies of grain and cash in their safe custody, remained loyal to him. I sent them a letter of warning which they passed on to the Sultan, and the Sultan sent it back to me with a defiant protest, underlining his anger in the local manner by burning a hole in it with a cigarette.

Wadi Khawra was by then seething with trouble as the bully-boys of the area took the opportunity to settle old scores. One day an elderly shaykh, Nassir bin Muhammad Lajrab, arrived with his family to plead for government help in restoring law and order. Rais Hussain Mansur came up to my room to tell me he was outside. "He is very distressed," the Rais said. "It was his intention to sacrifice a camel in front of your *dar* as a gesture of his earnestness."

"I am glad you dissuaded him," I said.

"No. I did not dissuade him. But while he was on the way his camel was killed and eaten by a leopard. Now all he has to sacrifice is a goat. He fears it is not enough."

When the shaykh came in I assured him that his plea would receive no less attention because of the substitution, but I do not think he was convinced.

The shortage of grain was beginning to make itself felt, and the situation took a sudden alarming turn for the worse when the Yemenis decreed a complete ban on the export of all grain and other foodstuffs. A few days later Hussain called on me waving a report from the Wakil in Wadi Ayn. "The Zaydis have constructed new customs posts in Wadi Harib. There is one at Najd Marqad, another at Jabal Bulayq and a third in Wadi Maqbal, all manned by soldiers. These places are all in Bayhan, *ya* Groom. This is Kuhlani's doing. He is going out of his way to insult me. Please tell Seager as soon as possible that I cannot hold myself responsible for what my tribesmen may do if these posts are not removed quickly."

I signalled to Aden and both Hussain and I sent vigorously worded letters to Kuhlani, but he did not reply. As the days went by we were faced with a growing list of angry complaints about extortion and improper tax collecting by the new garrisons, mainly from tribesmen of the Ahl Abu Shurayf, who were worst affected. When a Shurayfi, returning to Manawa with a gazelle he had shot in the Ramlat Sabatayn, had half the carcass confiscated at Najd Marqad, a group of their headmen stormed into Bayhan al-Qasab seeking permission to attack the posts, and we dissuaded them only after long and passionate argument.

It was irksome to have to persuade the Sharif that we must remain passive in the face of such blatant provocation, but the politics of the day demanded it. Only a short while before, the Governor of Aden, Sir Reginald Champion, had visited the Imam in Ta'izz for discussions, and the official bulletins spoke of the "spirit of mutual accord" which had been reached. To Political Officers this phrase had a very hollow ring, but this time there had been agreement on holding further detailed talks about Protectorate/Yemeni disputes and Seager was now negotiating with ash-Shami to commence these as soon as possible.

In mid-November an Immediate signal reached me on the early morning wireless schedule. Suddenly the talks had been arranged and Seager was flying to Bayda that morning to start them. Briefs on everything we might wish him to raise must be sent directly to Bayda for him at once. I gulped down a hasty breakfast, ordered the Government Guard sentries to allow no one in except the Sharif himself, and sat down to work with my typewriter. The briefs, a thick wad of them, were finally ready and sealed by eight o'clock that evening, when I handed them to a young Arifi tribesman, who had been squatting outside my door for the previous hour, and he scampered off into the darkness. The precious package, which contained significant secrets, was wrapped in an old cloth tied round his waist. When he reached Bayda, after a long journey through "enemy" territory, he would receive only a few *riyals* and a meal. Yet there was not the slightest cause to fear he might breach his trust and I knew without any doubt that the package would be delivered safely into Seager's hands next day, for it was a matter of honour that this should be so.

I had assured Hussain that all would be well once Seager got down to details with ash-Shami. He was wise enough not to comment. The days passed while we waited for results, but, apart from a few minor queries, nothing happened. Finally a terse message reached me. The affairs of other areas had taken up so much time that the problems of the North Eastern Area had not been reached and would have to await another meeting still to be arranged. There would probably be several weeks' delay. It was bitterly disappointing and Hussain showed his feelings about it in his face. We were neither solving his problems nor letting him solve them himself. All his rancour and resentment over the constitutional proposals now came flooding back and he became sullen, uncommunicative and bitter. Seager had spoken some time before of a visit to Bayhan in December to inaugurate the new councils. I sent a signal to say that his presence before then was becoming very necessary.

9

Intrigue and Death

One evening during the days of waiting for Seager to arrive, Rais Hussain Mansur came up to my room, saluted smartly and said: "I want to discuss a small difficulty I am having with the *askari*s. It is about attendance at the mosque."

"What is the trouble?" I asked.

"As you know, we parade for the Friday midday prayers when Sharif Hussain is attending them. He and his party go with his slaves and the Tribal Guards as an escort and we accompany them."

"Yes. I had noticed that."

"We have been doing it thus since Davey's time. When Davey, may the Prophet bless him, became a Muslim it was arranged that on Fridays we would go with him to the mosque, while the Tribal Guards accompanied the Sharif. We were two separate parties, but we always went together. When Davey left Bayhan, Sharif Hussain insisted that we should continue to turn out for Friday prayers. Now I am faced with a problem. My men are saying they do not see why they should parade for Sharif Hussain. They are soldiers of the *hakuma*, not the *dawla*, and Hussain does not command them. They do not parade like this for any other ruler in the Protectorate. They want the mosque parade abolished, and unless it is I fear there may be trouble."

"Are they refusing to attend the mosque?"

"Oh no! It is not that. *Wallah!* Are we not Muslimin? But it is a *kassar sharaf* for the Government Guards to be made to march to the mosque as if they are the slaves of the Sharif."

As an ex-soldier I could understand the feelings in the ranks against compulsory church parades. I knew that if I referred the matter to Dick Tring, the G. G. Commandant, he would insist that the practice cease at once. Perhaps it was a sign of the times that there now appeared to be a barrack-room lawyer stirring things up, and that the Rais sympathised with him.

"Very well," I said, after we had gone over the situation carefully and I had been assured that the garrison was full of pious men who would not dream of missing the Friday prayers, "if we stop making the parade a compulsory one and leave it to those men wishing to attend the service to go in a separate party, would that satisfy them?"

"Yes, indeed. That would be quite acceptable."

He saluted again and left looking very pleased.

I should have known my soldiers better. I should have had the tact to phase the system out over a period. Next Friday there were no Government Guards at all at the mosque service and Hussain, ever watchful of his *sharaf*, took their absence as a personal affront ordered by the Political Officer.

When I went to see Hussain a few days later his pent-up feelings suddenly exploded in a wild outburst of recriminations. "*Ya* Groom, you seem to be doing everything you can to harm me. You and Shaykh Qassim, you are working together to humiliate me. I had thought the constitution came from the *hakuma*, but now I see that it is you and Shaykh Qassim who have arranged it. You have sided with the Bal Harith against me. You have supported the Salihi shaykh, who tried to murder me. You have conspired in secret with other Bayhanis against me. You have interfered in the Bayt al-Mal. You have even ordered the Government Guards not to go to the mosque when I am there. You are trying to destroy my *sharaf* and bring the power of the Habilis to an end. It is shameful that I should be treated like this." In his anger he spoke fast, in a high-pitched voice, the accusations tumbling out in staccato sentences, his eyes on fire with rage. Overwhelmed by passion, he would not listen to my reassurances and there was nothing I could do to placate him.

As soon as I got back from this stormy meeting I sent a message to Sharif Awadh, who was in his house in al-Wusta, and he came over at once. I told him what had happened and his eyes widened in astonishment. "My young brother becomes angry so easily," he said, "and he has been worrying about some of these things for a long time. Sometimes he sees matters differently to others and sometimes he gets things wrong."

"You will have to mediate between us," I told him. "Nobody else can do that. It is very bad for Bayhan if the people see me quarrelling with the Sharif. I do not want that to happen."

"My brother is a very clever person," Awadh went on. "He is very shrewd, but at times he is too petulant. I'm just an old beduin, and I look at things in a simple way, but sometimes I can see his mistakes when he can't see them himself. But you must give him *sharaf*; it is important."

"You must try to settle things between us before the British Agent gets here. We must remove our misunderstandings before then. I do not think your brother has appreciated that the *dustur*, the consitution, is of Seager's making, Seager's and the government's, and that what I have said about it was what I was asked to say on their behalf. We must make him realise that the *dustur* will be good for him, and good for Bayhan – not bad. And it is very important for him to understand that Shaykh Qassim had no part in it."

Over the next two days the three of us, Hussain, Awadh and myself, met privately to thrash out Hussain's accusations. Nabih was excluded, for he could not be privy to discussion of such a personal nature. Nor could I bring in Shaykh Qassim, much though I would have valued the old man's help, for that would have strengthened some of Hussain's worst suspicions. Slowly, over hours of tense and sometimes bitter dialogue, Awadh placated his brother. Finally we shook hands and called the matter closed. Awadh had done his best, but Hussain was still reserved and sullen, unconvinced that we really had his interests at heart. Seager's visit was more than ever necessary.

Still the British Agent was held back by other commitments. Instead I was visited by a series of officials who came and went in rapid succession. The Director of Agriculture, Brian Hartley, was the first, and his arrival was opportune, for no one other than Davey knew Bayhan or the Sharif better, and I hoped he would help to regain the Sharif's confidence.

Hartley's main concern was the business of the thriving Bayhan Farmers' Association, set up by his department, through which loans

of government money were advanced to the farmers and some
co-operative marketing was organised. On this occasion he came to
arrange a large loan for the development of the communally managed irrigation canals on which Bayhan's main grain production
depended. We went out for a ride through the fields, and were discussing the arrangements for the loan as we passed an aged Bayhani
who was placing heavy round boulders from the *sayl* bed on to the
sloping side of a dyke. These boulders would take the main force of
the water when a flood roared down the wadi, and the technique of
laying them had come down from the days of the Himyarites, the
ruins of whose ancient canals and sluices littered the plain further to
the north. "The greatest difficulty with these loans," Hartley was
saying, "is in ensuring that the money is properly spent." He pointed
to the old Bayhani. "That man there is working hard at the moment
to put his section of the revetment into good repair, but give him
half a chance and he will take a loan, even at a high rate of interest,
in order to pay somebody else to do the work while he sits back and
watches." As Hartley spoke I saw the man turn and suddenly recognise us. I spurred my horse and called out to Hartley: "Quick! You'd
better get away as fast as you can. He can read your thoughts!" We
cantered off, and a booming voice followed us: "*Ya* Hartley! *Ahlan
wa sahlan*! May it please you! Can you lend me some money to help
me build this dam?"

On one subject Hartley, the recognised expert on equine matters,
could criticise Sharif Hussain with impunity, and that was the state
of the Sharif's twelve horses. "They are in a disgraceful condition,"
Hartley opined quite bluntly, after we had been shown round the
stables, and added: "They have been given too little food and not
enough exercise." Hussain mumbled: "It's the shortage of barley,"
but we knew quite well that, like Mr Toad, he had lost all interest
in them since the arrival of his Jeep. "Not one of these horses is fit
to be ridden again on a long journey until they have regained
strength, " Hartley went on. "It is a shame on you that you should
let them fall into this state." The Sharif nodded meekly. Only Hartley
and Seager, who had both known him before he became an effective ruler, could speak to him like this without causing offence.

Seager had promised to come up to Bayhan in the Anson which

was to take Hartley back, but the day before a signal arrived stating that Halali, the Yemeni Prime Minister, had turned up quite unexpectedly in Aden for urgent talks. I broke the news to Sharif Hussain with trepidation. He nodded and said nothing. Perhaps it was what he had expected. Instead, a flurry of signals told us to expect a short visit from the newly arrived Chief Secretary in Aden and then, in another plane, the commander of the RAF at Khormaksar, Group Captain Keenes. As the guard of honour was being drawn up on the landing ground, a G.G. *askari* came running over with a message from Aden stating that one of the planes had broken down, but it did not say which. We waited expectantly to see which of the VIPs would arrive, and it proved to be Keenes, accompanied by the commander of No. 8 Fighter Squadron, Squadron-Leader Jenson.

I had special cause to be grateful to Jenson, because during the bitterly cold weather a few weeks before he had brought his entire squadron on a training flight over Bayhan with the object of dropping a pullover for me, but now he was here at the Sharif's request to receive a presentation *jambya* in recognition of No. 8 Squadron's part in the Bal Harith operations. There were short speeches and Jenson pleased the Sharif immensely by announcing that he had been made an honorary member of the Squadron and pinning a squadron badge on to his shirt front. We lunched in the Sharif's *diwan* and were relaxing pleasantly when sharp ears caught the distant drone of an aeroplane engine – the Chief Secretary's plane had been repaired. There was a wild scramble back to the landing ground and the guard of honour reformed breathlessly, just in time to twitch to attention as the second Anson landed.

In the British colonial empire, the Chief Secretary, second only to the Governor in status, was a very senior official indeed. I had been dreading the visit of Ambrose Thomas in consequence, but it proved to be a relaxed four days. He was a Colonial Office man who had not served in a Colony, so his long discussions with the Sharif and his *wakils* were a gentle fact-finding exercise and my role became that of interpreter. Our difficulties with the Sharif were not mentioned and he knew nothing about them. The boys of the school gave a theatrical performance and a P.T. display, and, to celebrate the visit, nine small Harithi boys still held as hostages were allowed to

return to their tents and bounded away like escaping gazelles. Finally
we took Thomas to see the ruins of Tumna; it was the last and
supreme effort of the Jeep, which broke down on the return journey, and for the rest of my time in Bayhan the horses, once they were
fit, came back into their own.

Still Seager had not come. It was now December and the talks
with Halali were becoming protracted. "I see no chance of getting
up before the new year," he signalled. Again the Sharif shrugged his
shoulders and said nothing. Charles Inge had arrived in the Anson
which collected Thomas, and I decided to cut myself off from political problems as much as I could by taking a few days off against my
allowance of "local leave" (we were entitled to two weeks in a year,
but rarely took it as there was nowhere to spend it), so that I could
conduct him round the archaeological sites with a minimum of
disturbance from Aden.

Inge had just received a letter from an American, Wendell Phillips,
with tentative proposals to bring an archaeological expedition into
South Arabia, and was anxious to see the sites for himself before
replying. His role as Aden's Director of Antiquities was a part-time
one on top of his normal work as an Assistant Secretary in the Aden
Secretariat, but he was an experienced archaeologist well respected
in the profession. The Director administered the Colony's
Antiquities Ordinance and looked after a small museum at the foot
of the "Tanks" in Aden, all for an allowance of £100 a year. Later
on, when I was myself working in the Secretariat, this post came to
me for a period. For some strange reason it always went with two
other part-time jobs – those of the Colony's Registrar of Special
Marriages and Inspector of Brothels; I inherited two large rubber
stamps with which to demonstrate my powers in these two positions,
but was never required to use them.

We set out together on a tour of the relics of Qataban. We climbed
to the sanctuary of Jabal Raydan; we travelled slowly down the wadi
to Hayd Kuhlan, where we spent four nights in Sharif Awadh's house
on the ruin site while we measured and mapped; then we set out on
camels, for Hartley's strictures about the horses were being heeded,
to Najd Marqad and Wadi Ayn. To protect the antique sites in Aden
from vandalism, the Colony employed an Antiquities Guard, a Yafai

called Umbarak, whom Inge had brought with him. Umbarak accompanied us with clothes brushes and enormous rolls of blotting paper and, for the first time, proper "squeezes" were taken of the inscriptions in Hayd Kuhlan and elsewhere. We searched the ancient walls of Najd Marqad for inscriptions, but could find none. Nor was there any trace of the Yemeni garrison and customs post, which I had feared might attempt to block our progress. At the time I thought they had been frightened off by our superior fire-power, for we travelled with a large escort of soldiers and Bal Harith *rafiq*s, but I learned later that Hussain had sent them a warning the night before and they had made a tactful withdrawal. Over two days, while Inge was making squeezes and a ground plan at Hajar Hinnu az-Zurir, I was able to explore more of the neighbouring areas to obtain detail for my map. On the side of Qarn Ubayd, the isolated hill in the centre of the wadi, I found another inscription and several ancient remains. I was told that there were Himyarite rock drawings and a cement-lined water cistern on the top of that mountain, but never had the chance to climb it.

Inge returned to Aden on 23 December. The fact that I was not accompanying him caused some surprise when he got back, for an act so unusual as spending Christmas alone up-country was interpreted as a sure sign that the Political Officer must be going off his head. But there were compelling reasons for the decision to stay.

A few days after Christmas a local treaty which Davey had negotiated with the Amil of Harib was due to lapse. Despite all his pledges during our discussions three months before, Kuhlani had failed to respond to our approaches over its renewal. If it lapsed, then there was a danger that the bitter feud between the Bal Harith and the Ahl Abu Tuhayf, which we had struggled so hard to patch up, would again erupt in bloodshed, and other frontier squabbles would be renewed. Kuhlani had now gone to live in Marib, where a splendid new palace and administrative block, complete with garrison buildings and a prison, had been constructed by him with masonry quarried from the tumbled remains of some of the temples of ancient Sheba. I nurtured the hope that I would be asked there to negotiate the terms and would thereby be enabled to visit what was left of the famous ruins, unseen by any European since Glaser reached them in

1888. But it was not to be. On Christmas Eve a letter arrived from Kuhlani asking for a renewal of the whole treaty with one minor alteration. The wording of the amendment he proposed was liable to such varied interpretation that I rewrote it with Nabih in more legalistic language. We then prepared six copies of the whole revised treaty, which I signed and returned to Kuhlani, asking him to add his own signature and send three copies back. In the Yemen nothing could be done without the consent of the King, and I learned, after a long silence, that because of this tiny amendment all the documents had had to be sent to Ta'izz for Imam Ahmad's approval. They did not come back for three months.

A more important reason for remaining in Bayhan over Christmas was my fear for Shaykh Qassim's safety.

I had hoped to talk over all the affairs of Bayhan with Qassim while I was in Wadi Ayn with Inge, but he was ill and unable to come. Since his return from the pilgrimage he had been keeping to himself, concentrating on his farming and domestic affairs and subsequently getting over an attack of dysentery, so that we had not seen a lot of each other. I had intentionally kept him out of the discussions which followed Hussain's outburst in order to spare him from further recriminations, for Hussain could, if he chose, make Qassim's position very difficult. I had not, however, appreciated the lengths to which Hussain might be prepared to go in order to gag him.

Hartley, during his visit, had asked the Sharif to send somebody to Jawf, the great wadi in the Yemen north of Marib, to buy horses for the Abyan Board. Hussain, with surprising alacrity, had replied that he would send Shaykh Qassim. Next day I was visited by the Qadhi, Sayyid Muhammad Aatiq, with some overt business of no consequence to discuss. As soon as he was certain that Nabih was out of the way and that nobody could see us or hear us, he moved close to me and began to whisper in my ear. "I want you to listen to me very carefully," he said. "It is about Shaykh Qassim. As you know Sharif Hussain plans to send him to Jawf to buy horses for Hartley. You must not let Qassim go. Whatever you do it is most important that the visit be stopped." "Why?" I asked. "Because there is a plot," Sayyid Muhammad continued. "You see, Sharif Hussain wants to get Qassim out of the way to somewhere where you cannot make any enquiries about him. When he gets there something terrible is going to happen. Qassim will not return. It will be made to look like an accident, but it is being planned, *ya* Groom, it is being most carefully planned. Do not trust the Sharif."

Just before I left with Inge for Hayd Kuhlan, Qassim himself came to see me, looking pale and emaciated after his illness, so that his normally thin little frame was almost skeletal. After paying his respects to Inge, the ostensible reason for his call, he took me to one side and whispered: "I am very worried about going to Jawf. I have had a warning. Sharif Hussain blames the two of us for persuading Seager to introduce the new constitution. He has allowed his anger about it to take over his head. I have been told he is planning to have me killed as soon as I get to Jawf." He looked at me pleadingly, as if his life was in my hands. "I beg you," he said. "Ask Hartley to cancel his order for horses, or else arrange with the Sharif for somebody else to go in my place."

"Under no circumstances should you go to Jawf," I told him. "I will see that the order is cancelled, at least for the time being. In any case, you are far too ill to go for the moment. It would be wise if you stay in your house and do not go out until you are better."

The old man looked immensely relieved. "Thank you, thank you very much," he said. "I agree that it would be wisest to stay at home. I will remain there until you come back from Aden after your Id holiday. It would prevent anything being done to me while you are away."

"Do you think the Sharif might harm you even in Bayhan?" I asked.

"I do not know. He might if you are not here to make enquiries. He is very, very angry." Then he added resignedly: "But everything comes from Allah."

I thought of the Ahl Nimran murder, coldly instigated by Hussain. "I shall not be going to Aden for Christmas," I said.

"But you must", Qassim replied. "All *nasranis* like to be in Aden for Christmas. It is your big Id. You cannot miss it."

"I am hoping that Kuhlani may invite me to Marib. If he does you must come with me. But otherwise I shall remain here. I will be quite happy."

"Without gin? Without a Christmas feast?"

"Without any of those things. I will listen to the wireless."

"Thank you," Qassim said. "Thank you a thousand times." Arabs rarely say "thank you".

We shook hands and he took up his rifle to depart.

"*Khayr inshallah* – all will be well if God wills," I said.

"*Inshallah,*" he replied.

I never spoke to Qassim again.

I tried to spend Christmas quietly, listening to my radio and reading, but the word had gone round that this was my Id Kabir, the great festival of the year, and ought to be celebrated. On Christmas Eve Hussain and his whole male household came to visit me unexpectedly in an extraordinarily cheerful mood, as if no tension existed between us whatsoever. He had supplied a number of small boys in the *suq* with a boxful of Chinese crackers, which banged away outside my *dar* until late at night as if it were Guy Fawkes Day. On Christmas morning the notables of Bayhan began to call on me one after the other, each with his own offering of Chinese crackers and rifle salutes, so that the noise outside was sometimes deafening. Throughout the afternoon they continued to call, singly and in small groups. The Festival of Nine Carols, crackling and surging over the ether, was interrupted by the appearance round my doorway of a bearded, brown, beaming face, calling out: "*Salaam alaik! Kaif haalik! Id mubarak!* – Peace be upon you! How are you! A happy Christmas!" In his religion the average South-west Arabian was a tolerant, unbigoted fellow who recognised that we, the *nasrani*s or non-believers, believed in a different Prophet of the same God, for does not the Quran accept Jesus as a Prophet who performed miracles and was born of a Virgin? The expressions of goodwill from my visitors were charmingly genuine. It was a memorable Christmas.

On the morning after Boxing Day, I was working with my typewriter on some report when the wireless operator, Salim Awadh, ran into my room breathlessly: "Sahib! Have you heard? There has been a terrible accident!"

"What has happened?"

"Shaykh Qassim! Shaykh Qassim has had an accident! You must go over at once! The Amir and the Sharif have already left."

I ran down the stairs with him, through the courtyard and past the bemused sentry at the gate, to speak to the boy who had brought this news. But there was no need for words to tell that something dramatic had occurred. From the gateway we could see small knots of men emerging from the houses or downing their tools and hastening off along the pathway which led towards the house of Shaykh Qassim. The rhythmic thumping of the cloth beaters had suddenly ceased.

I shouted for Nabih, ran upstairs to fetch my *kufiyah* – for even in an emergency one never went outside without a head-dress – and set off as fast as I could along the same path. Qassim's house, an isolated farmstead on high ground about a mile from the town and close to the flanking hills of the wadi, was filled and surrounded by a crowd of unspeaking, worried faces – tribesmen, *ryot*, soldiers, townsmen and merchants – and more were converging on it as the news spread. The crowd made way for me in silence as I entered the house and hurried up the stairs.

Qassim lay in the large reception room on the first floor, where I had so often been entertained by him. His elder son, Ahmad, was kneeling over him, hemmed in by silent onlookers.

The small, wizened body of the old man was curled up under a blanket. He was unconscious, choking and gasping with heavy, wheezing, gurgling pants, coughing up blood, fighting grimly to hold on to his life.

Ahmad said: "He fell from the roof. He was doing some repairs and he leaned over and fell." Qassim had dropped down three floors into the courtyard below. It was remarkable that he was still alive.

It seemed very improbable that Qassim would live, but I could sense among those present the feeling that any faint glimmer of hope rested on me. I could not let Qassim down and I knew that Seager would support me.

I breathed a few whispered words to Sharif Hussain, called for Salim Awadh out of the motionless throng, and rushed back with him to the wireless room. It was a holiday in Aden, but this was an emergency. By eleven o'clock we had made radio contact and Salim Awadh was tapping out my "Immediate" signal. I stood behind him at the radio set while we waited for a response.

At two-thirty that afternoon we were on the ar-Rawna landing strip waiting for the plane. At three o'clock an RAF Anson touched down, bringing Dr Walker with a stretcher and medical supplies. I rushed him unceremoniously to the house.

The crowd of spectators still sat motionless and silent around Qassim's limp form. Walker made a brief examination of the heaving body. "His skull has been fractured. Most of his ribs are broken. Those clots of purple blood coming from his mouth show very severe internal injuries."

"Is there any hope?"

"No. None at all. I am astonished that he has clung to life for so long. He cannot live for much longer."

We relayed the news to the impassive onlookers.

Walker injected the old man to try to soften the violence of his breathing, but there was nothing else he could do. We joined the Sharif among the pale-faced spectators listening to the death agony. Incongruously, someone poured out cups of tea.

Qassim's end came with a final rasping cry and a sudden leap of his whole frail body, followed by stillness and silence. Ahmad, strained and tearful, felt for his heart. "My father is dead," he said.

We rose to go. In the next room the women started to wail.

Qassim was buried next day in a graveyard on the edge of al-Wusta. A great crowd was present. My entire contingent of Government Guards attended the funeral, and I ordered them, in recognition of Qassim's long years of service to the *hakuma*, to fire a salvo of three rounds at the graveside. A few days later there was a memorial service over his grave, an honour accorded to great men, when the Quran was read in the customary chanting style, and when sackloads of dates were distributed to the poor.

There was no doubt that Qassim's death was an accident, however suspicious was the timing of it. Suddenly there was no need for me to remain in Bayhan any longer and I felt an urge to leave it for a while. It was the end of the year, almost the end of my first year in the Protectorate, and, as far as Bayhan was concerned, the end of an era. I had been up-country without a break for two months and the time seemed opportune to return to Aden for a few days' rest and change. I left early in January.

When I discussed all that had happened with Seager, he said: "It's hard to believe that Hussain really wanted to see Qassim dead, even though he will be most thankful to have the old man out of the way. But I don't think we have heard the end of the story yet. You had better be standing by for the next *siassa*. I would not expect him to waste any time."

"But he seemed to be extremely relaxed and friendly when I said good-bye."

"Wait and see. He will do everything he can to avoid the constitution, especially if he believes it means accepting financial control. He knows the next stage must be close at hand. As soon as you get back you had better start preparing the ground for my visit. At long last I should be free to come up. I will try to spend a week with you, so that we can have plenty of time to talk him round and can clear up some of the other Bayhan problems at the same time."

On the following day a message arrived for Seager from Hussain. While I was not in Bayhan, the Sharif was permitted to use the Government radio communication system; but there were conventions about what could be said, because radio messages were listened to by the wireless operators of the whole network and soon became public knowledge if they were not encoded. Hussain's message, which was in Arabic and uncoded, stated defiantly and baldly: "Mr Groom has done bad things against me and is seeking to overthrow my power and ruin my *sharaf*."

"I shall have to call him down here to explain himself," Seager said, and sent back a very terse reply summoning Hussain to Aden on the plane which was bringing me back to Bayhan. I met Hussain on the ar-Rawna landing ground and he shook hands without smiling before climbing on board. I was disturbed to see that he was taking Sharif Salih bin Nassir with him, for that suggested that Salih had to provide evidence, even though I knew he would look after my interests. But perhaps it was just to prevent Salih talking to me.

Amir Salih walked back with me from the landing ground. "What has happened that prompted your father to send such a message?" I asked him.

"People have told my father about things you have said to them which show you are hostile to him," he replied.

"Who?"

"That I cannot say. I do not know the details."

In the evening Sharif Awadh called on me, looking extremely concerned. "I am very angry with my brother," he said. "He did not tell me about the signal. He did not consult me at all. He should never have sent it. But please do not be too harsh on him. He has been very upset and he acted without thinking."

"Do you know what was reported about me to him?"

"No. He would not tell me. He has refused to discuss it with me. He thinks I am on your side against him. If you could defer the constitution, he would soon get over his anger. But do not worry. Sharif Salih and I will support you."

A few days later Seager arrived in Bayhan, bringing Hussain with him and accompanied by Abdullah Hassan Jaffer.

"We have placated the Sharif," Seager said as soon as we were able to have a quiet word together, "but it had to be at the cost of a scapegoat. I am posting Nabih elsewhere. He is too talkative and I think he has been very indiscreet with matters he ought to have kept to himself. He seems to have let out to somebody, who reported it to Hussain, that we suspected Hussain was trying to arrange for Qassim's death."

I felt sorry for Nabih, who returned on the next plane, for he had served me with zeal and good humour; but for his part he had few regrets: he was pining for his wife, and the comforts of Aden were beginning to appeal more strongly than the financial benefits of service in the Protectorate.

There was no immediate replacement for Nabih, but some time later I was joined by a young lad who had just been recruited into the political service, initially as a clerk, after leaving the "Protectorate College for the Sons of Chiefs" in Aden. That school, inaugurated by Ingrams, was one of our main hopes for a settled future in the Western Protectorate. It was run much like an English preparatory school and was open to the scions of the ruling families. Not only would the future rulers have a good basic education but they would also make boyhood friends of each other, thereby breaking down some of the great barriers of distrust and tribal antagonism which split the Protectorate. Hussain's son Qaid was a pupil there, together with two of Awadh's younger sons, and I had annoyed Hussain and earned Sharif Salih bin Nassir's undying gratitude by securing admission for Salih's son Haydar. My young clerk was the first member of a ruling family to join the government service after leaving this college. Muhammad Farid was the grandson of the Upper Awlaqi Shaykh. He spent a few weeks with me before going on to Dhala, eventually became a Political Officer and, after a spell at Oxford, entered the new Federal Government as a Minister. Nor did Salih's son Haydar let me down; in due course he became the first Arab to receive a full officer's commission in the Government Guards and later he became a General.

We settled down to a solid week of intense negotiation and discussion. Hussain gave ground reluctantly and bitterly. Finally the shaykhs and *aqils* of the country were summoned to a great public ceremony held in the open space in front of the administrative buildings, where a new constitution was inaugurated and speeches were made. Bayhan had seen nothing like it before. Members of the new *Lujna*, the Executive Council, were sworn in, and there was a huge feast while the school band played and a group of *shahadh* danced.

The *Lujna* was to meet every month, with the Amir as President, Hussain as Secretary, and a membership composed of Sharif Awadh, the Qadhi, the four Wakils, five Musabayn and two Bal Harith shaykhs, a merchant, Shaykh Qassim's son Ahmad, and a blind Bayhani of great eminence and learning who normally lived in Aden – Shaykh Muhammad bin Salim al-Qudadi al-Bayhani. This was a well-balanced Council with powers which were potentially considerable, although we had won Hussain round to it only by agreeing that control of the Bayt al-Mal should remain in his hands "until the *Lujna* has proved its efficiency". External affairs and the appointment and dismissal of state officials were reserved subjects, but over all other matters, except finance, the *Lujna*, voting by secret ballot, was empowered to make decisions which the Amir would promulgate and execute unless he wished to appeal to Aden against them. In addition to the *Lujna* was set up a *Majlis al-Uqal*, an Assembly of Chiefs, of a hundred and forty-four members from the *Lujna* and representatives of the tribes and communities; this was to meet every three months to "discuss matters of interest to the State and its people" and make recommendations to the *Lujna*; it could not legislate or make decisions itself, but it could at least demand that the *Lujna* reconsider any decision with which it disagreed, and could refer a matter to the British Agent if it could not get satisfaction.

We had intended that a formal document should be published setting out this constitution, but Hussain stubbornly refused to accept that, arguing with some cunning that the document be kept secret so that it could if necessary be revised after twelve months in the light of experience. He was shrewd enough to realise that, if nothing appeared in writing, then few of the Council members would really understand what their new powers were or how they should use them. At the end of the day he was looking cockahoop. With his grip on the Treasury as firm as ever and the two Councils confounded and confused, he had successfully drawn the teeth of all the controls we had sought to impose on him. The Sharif's power remained almost unbridled.

We still had to deal with the Salihi shaykh's assassination plot. No court existed in Bayhan competent to try such a case, which in earlier days would probably have been disposed of summarily by the immediate beheading of the culprits. "It is not for me to pass sentence," Hussain said, "for it was against me they were plotting. The *Shayba* will have to do it for me." Seager was often known as the *Shayba* – the Old Man. "I will be the judge," Seager said reluctantly, "but there must be a fair trial. All the evidence must be brought out in full and I shall question the witnesses. You had better arrange for tribal assessors to help me decide whether the accused are guilty." It was agreed that four leading Musabayn shaykhs should sit with Seager and, to ensure a wise counsel, I made certain that Shaykh Naji bin Nassir was one of them.

On 23 January, Shaykh Salih Ahmad Sayf and his three Salihi and Arifi conspirators were arraigned before this *ad hoc* court and, after several witnesses had given their evidence, were found guilty. So much had been expected, but the real issue was the punishment. The sentences had to be heavy enough to deter others but not so severe that the Salihis would be alienated for ever. "I want to think carefully before I make my decision," Seager announced. "We will adjourn for one hour."

Coffee was brought to us in a private room, where the Sharif, the Amir, Sharif Awadh, Abdullah Hassan and I discussed possible sentences with Seager in low tones. There was much debate about the details, with Hussain predictably holding out for strong measures.

Back in the courtroom, Seager eyed the accused severely from his wooden chair. "All four of you," he said, "are to spend three years in the Bayhan prison. In addition you, *ya* Shaykh Salih Ahmad, who was the leader of this group of would-be assassins, will pay a fine of three thousand *riyal*s and your *dar* will be destroyed." The prisoners blenched and were led away by Tribal Guards. Shaykh Salih was pale and trembling; he had been expecting imprisonment, but not for so long, and he had not expected punishment on top of that. By the evening, news of these heavy sentences had reached the far corners of the Amirate.

Early next morning a large delegation gathered outside my *dar* seeking the attention of the British Agent. At its head was Amir Salih, and by his side were his cousins Sharif Abdullah and Sharif Salih bin Nassir, together with the leading Musabayn shaykhs. Several small children, including a babe in arms, were prominent in the front of the crowd. I drew Seager's attention to them as we finished breakfasting, and we donned our *kufiyah*s, called for Abdullah Hassan, and went down to talk to them.

"What is it you seek of me?" Seager called out as we emerged from the gateway.

Amir Salih, speaking loudly so that all could hear, replied: "We have come about the sentence you have passed on Shaykh Salih Ahmad."

"I have given severe punishment for a serious crime," Seager said.

"Yes indeed," the Amir responded. "I have spoken with the shaykhs of the Musabayn, who are all here with me, and with leaders of the Ashraf. We feel it is too severe. We have come to plead for your mercy."

"Why?" said Seager, looking surprised that his decision could be questioned in this way.

"On the grounds that, until this misdeed, Shaykh Salih has always been the most loyal of the Musabayn, both to the Sharif and to the *hakuma*. We have come to request a reduction of the sentence in

recognition of that." Amir Salih pointed to the children and the small
baby, which the oldest girl, aged eleven or twelve, was holding.
"These are the sons and daughters of Shaykh Salih. We throw them
on your mercy."

Seager said: "Let us discuss this matter further in private. If you
will appoint four or five representatives from your delegation to
accompany you, *ya* Amir Salih, we will talk about it inside."

In my room the Amir argued passionately for the cause of the
renegade shaykh, and the Musabayn representatives, bewildered by
these strange procedures, nodded their heads gravely. The outcome
was a substantial reduction in the sentences. Shaykh Salih would be
allowed to move freely, though he must not carry a rifle. No longer
would his *dar* be destroyed. The fine would be reduced from three
thousand to two thousand dollars, which the Amir would guarantee. Firm justice had now been tempered by mercy, and honour was
satisfied all round. The *sharaf* of both Sharif Hussain and the Salihi
Shaykh had been respected, and all parties could feel pleased with
the result.

"You did that very well, *ya* Salih," Seager said to the Amir later,
and the young man smiled proudly; he had performed his part
admirably. Everything had in fact gone exactly as we had planned it
the day before during our adjournment for coffee. Play-acting too
was a part of politics in the Aden Protectorate.

The beneficial effects of Basil Seager's visit went some way beyond
the inauguration of the new state councils and the settlement of the
Salihi shaykh's case. Sharif Hussain, with the keys of the Bayt al-Mal
both figuratively and literally still in his pocket and with the real
significance of the constitution still concealed from public scrutiny,
wore a genial, triumphant expression and became once again friendly
and cheerful. There was even a turn for the better in relations with
the Yemen. The new Yemeni customs posts in Bayhani areas of Wadi
Harib, about which Hussain had been so indignant, were suddenly
withdrawn, prompting a suspicion that Hussain might have connived
with Kuhlani over their establishment in order to distract us. At the
same time, the Yemenis started to allow grain caravans to pass though
Nata into Bayhan once again. Responding to a message which ash-
Shami had sent to Seager during his visit, we even arrested a Yemeni

fugitive hiding with the Ahl Dhurayba, a beduin section who lived in the wild mountains of the Arifis, and handed him over to Kuhlani, following this up with a quite unusual display of international co-operation when Bayhan Tribal Guards combined with a small force of Zaydi troops to root out two other Yemeni fugitives in Arifi territory involved in the same looting incident.

But now there was new cause for concern. The cold weather had killed more than half the growing crops in fields irrigated by wells, and the failure of the rains meant there would be no spring harvest. In all the markets and merchants' stores in Bayhan, stocks of grain were running low, while the grain in the Bayt al-Mal, obtained from the *ushur* tax of one tenth of a crop, had become weevil-infested and had to be sold quickly before it was ruined. The grain the Yemenis were allowing through Nata was a help, but a serious food shortage looked possible, and reports which came to me from Awlaqi and Markha showed that the threat was widespread throughout the North Eastern Area. In the Eastern Protectorate the situation was already very much worse, and within a short time the Royal Air Force was busily employed ferrying sacks of grain to relieve famine conditions in the Hadramawt.

"If we go to Darb al-Ali, we will be able to find grain to buy from the merchants," one of the Bal Harith *aqils* told me deviously.

"I thought Kuhlani had banned the sale of grain for export out of Yemen," I said.

"*Aiwa*. Yes, indeed he has," said the *aqil*, "but the merchants want our money. They charge us a lot. Too much. But we need the grain. We can buy it secretly from them."

"What about the customs duty?"

"You must not ask me about the tax. The merchants charge too much. Let them pay Kuhlani his tax."

"So, why are you still short of grain when you can get it from Darb al-Ali so easily?"

"It is not easy. Indeed, it is very difficult for us. We have to take salt to Darb al-Ali. But there is no fodder left for our camels now and the pasture is being eaten up. Our animals are getting weak. Only half the camels of my people are now strong enough to make the journey to Ayadim for salt. Soon very few of them will be able to

travel. Without salt to sell we cannot buy grain. It is difficult. Very
difficult. We are the children of the *hakuma*. You, *ya* Groom, are our
father. You must help us before it is too late."

Soon I was seeing new faces in the *suq* and elsewhere in the wadi
– the pinched-up faces of hungry *ryot* and impoverished tribesmen
from distant parts of the North Eastern Area, who had come to seek
work in the Amirate. Some of them were living, with their women
and children, in temporary brushwood shelters on the edges of the
villages. Sharif Hussain said: "They are here because of the government agricultural loans. With those loans, the farmers in Bayhan
have money to spend on the repair of their dams and canals. These
people hope to get work from the farmers so that they can buy food.
But so do many Bayhanis. Soon there will be no more work left and
they will be dying of hunger on our dooorstep. What do you advise
me to do, *ya* Groom? Shall I send Tribal Guards to drive the for-
eigners back to their homelands? Or will you feed them for me when
they are starving?"

Not long afterwards, groups of people began to congregate outside my *dar*, some with their veiled womenfolk, squatting silently
and patiently wherever there was shade from the great heat, and
pushing their pot-bellied children forward to attract my attention
whenever I left the building. "We seek help from the *hakuma*," they
cried. "We are hungry. We have no *masub*. Our children have not
eaten for many days. In God's name help us to find food!" Some
among them were angry and threatening.

Hussain said: "I cannot help them. There is no grain left in the
Bayt al-Mal. Dollars would be of no use to them, for there is no
grain to buy. Besides, my customs duties are not coming in, and I
have hardly enough cash to pay the wages of my officials."

I had already sent many signals to Aden reporting our plight, but,
compared with the Eastern Protectorate, our situation had never
been considered desperate. Now I sent a more imperative demand,
seeking a diversion of some of the grain supplies being ferried into
the Hadramawt. This time the response was rapid. Two days later
our smoke signals were going up to show the direction of the wind
at Jaw al-Milah to a heavily laden Dakota. Soon Bal Harith camel
caravans were carrying several tons of grain into Bayhan al-Qasab for

distribution to the needy. It was not a lot, but it was just sufficient to keep us going until the rain, which started to fall early in May, saved us from economic disaster.

10

A Deepening Crisis

If the daylight hours went by fast enough under the constant flow of problems large and small, in the evenings, after the sun had set to the sound of the call to prayer and after Ahmad had brought in my hissing presssure lamp, there was rarely time to feel alone. Then, if there were no visitors or belated petitioners, no evening signals demanding instant decoding, no rolled-up scraps of paper with requests and complaints, written crudely with a pointed stick for a pen and thrust into the hand of the sentry at the gate, then there might at times be a chance to read a book or a two-months-old magazine received on the last mail-boat from England. But more often than not, before sleep became imperative, the evening would be spent typing out reports on the day's affairs, grist for the mills of Aden. At the beginning of each month came the major typing labour of all — the production of the Monthly Intelligence Letter.

The Monthly Intelligence Letter summarised all the events in my Area over the previous month. It was a straightforward, factual account of incidents and affairs, many of which had probably been the topics of more detailed individual reports already. In the WAP Office the highlights of the Monthly Intelligence Letters from all the Areas were compounded into a single report which was sent to the Secretariat. This, together with a similar report from the Eastern Protectorate, and another from the Colony, was then used as the basis of a monthly report which the Secretariat sent to the Colonial Office. There was a further stage still, for in course of time the main features of the reports from all the colonial territories were combined into a Colonial Office Summary, for circulation around government departments in London and also among the more august offices of the colonial territories which had contributed to it. Only rarely did one ever see any portions of one's original report in the final product, and by the time it reached that stage the process of editing and distillation meant that the dramatic edge to the story was removed and it was probably simplified almost beyond recognition.

Our Monthly Intelligence Letters told, in a matter-of-fact way, of our disappointments, and occasionally of our successes. They related deeds of valour and shame. They provided the important gossip and the background to the major political issues. They described intrigues and venalities. There was no better picture of the struggle of the people of the Protectorate to survive against the geographical, economic and climatic odds. The wide range of problems with which a Political Officer was concerned is demonstrated in my own Monthly Intelligence Letters for March and May 1949, which are reproduced in full in the Appendix.

The growing shortage of grain, which meant in effect, among a people who ate little but *masub*, a shortage of food, was a major problem of the time, as my Monthly Intelligence Letter for March makes apparent. But the crises of the Protectorate always arose suddenly, and in February the seriousness of the situation for the North Eastern Area was still not evident, even though the Royal Air Force had already been called upon to start its relief operation in distant Hadramawt. Seager told me that the Governor of Aden had proposed my secondment to the Eastern Protectorate to assist in that operation, but had been persuaded to change his mind because of what was happening in Bayhan.

I was still apprehensive that I might be snatched away without warning to the Hadramawt once the troubles in Wadi Khawra had been overcome. At that time it would not have been a welcome move. I wanted to remain in Bayhan in order to consolidate Hussain's new spirit of co-operation while it lasted, and there was much that had to be done. It therefore seemed an opportune moment to put myself once again at a distance from my radio set by undertaking another flag-march to assert the Sharif's (and the Amir's) authority. For a long time Hussain had spoken of the Jamaliyah plateau, on his most southerly frontier, where the Zaydis frequently endeavoured to collect taxes. I suggested to his delight that the Amir and I should visit this remote area together. Towards the end of February we set off, accompanied by my clerk Muhammad Farid and a small force of Government Guards, Tribal Guards, household retainers and Arifi tribesmen.

The people of Jamaliyah belong to sections of the Arifi tribe, and so, to give point to our journey, we spent the first night as the guest of the Arifi shaykh in al-Haraja. For this preliminary part of the journey Sharif Awadh joined us. In the long period of conversation which followed our goat-meat supper Awadh seemed to be in an unusually ebullient mood, but it was not until next morning that I was told the reason. That evening he had done the honours to the Arifi shaykh by marrying an Arifi girl, thus exercising the rights of a traveller in the way Hussain had done some months before in Wadi Ayn. That a journey of only seven miles counted for such a purpose seemed to be rather stretching the rules, but no one appeared to be very critical of it. The luckless lady had been divorced by the time we set out next morning, Awadh having departed a little earlier because he had pressing business at home. Both Awadh and Hussain had a zestful appetite for female company and their affairs were discussed by my soldiers with a bawdy and envious cynicism.

I had no very clear idea where we were going on this journey. Peter Davey had never reached the area, so there was nothing in his yellow notebook to guide me. The Sharif, pointing South with a dramatic wave of his arms, would insist that his domain extended out into the wild hills almost to Bayda, but neither he nor any other Bayhani was capable of drawing anything remotely resembling a map. On such vague maps as there were in the WAP Office, the frontier was shown to pass through Nata, which we knew was wrong, but how much further south the territory of the Bayhani tribes extended I could not tell. As usual, I carried my prismatic compass with me to take bearings for my own map, now nearing completion.

We left our horses in al-Haraja and walked southwards up Wadi Ghabar al-Aala, a barren tributary of Wadi Bayhan which soon narrowed into a rocky gorge. About five miles on we turned up a water course, climbing steeply into the western hillside to a pass named Aqabat Luwa. The Amir and one or two of his escort had brought donkeys, which struggled gamely up the rough, rocky track with that sureness of foot which makes the donkey a remarkable animal. This was the main access route to Jamaliyah, and even the donkeys found it hazardous.

From the Luwa pass we moved over a crest named Ras Suram, on the far side of which a small watercourse, Wadi Dham Sufa, led down into Wadi Ghabar al-Asfal. Nearby I found, by the side of the pathway, the remains of several ancient circular buildings of stone, different from any of the Himyarite constructions I had seen in Bayhan but clearly, from their patina, very old, and not unlike the circular tombs which Philby had reported in great numbers on the far side of the Ramlat Sabatayn. Were they, I wondered, traces of a people even older than the Himyarites?

We travelled on westwards until we reached a small group of huts, with a central stone *husn*, called Zalaja, and then stumbled onwards to the village of Wahlan. This was the territory of the Ahl Dhurayba, and at Wahlan their shaykh, Ahmad Abdullah al-Dhuraybi, gave us lunch. We had been marching for six hours and, though we had not covered many miles, the journey had been a most exhausting one.

Jamaliyah was a roof-top world, startlingly different from the sandy plains below. We were on a plateau of rocky hills intersected by narrow valleys where cultivation was carried out on terraces. At Wahlan the terraces were imposing, with high earth banks and massive stone walls. In Wadi Ashar, which we reached next day, it was even more substantial, with walls built like dams across the width of the valley. I sensed a Himyarite origin in these constructions, so much more solid than contemporary fieldworks. The narrow strips of soil were mostly watered by rainfall running off the surrounding slopes, and were now cropless, but there were a few patches of well irrigation. *Ilb* trees dotted the fields and there were low bushes and clumps of dried-up grass in cracks and niches on the smooth-worn granite outcrops on the hillsides.

Properly speaking, Jamaliyah was the name of only a part of this plateau, the area to the south-west being called Fadha, after the Wadi Fadha which provided the dividing line. On the edge of the plateau was Jabal Markuza, the highest point in Bayhan. When we reached the crest of Markuza we had probably climbed some 3,000 feet above the plains of Bayhan to a height of about 6,000 feet above sea level. From this vantage point, in the cool, crystal-clear air, we could see to our west the gorge of Wadi Khirr and to our east that of Wadi Bayhan, great clefts dropping out of sight into shadowy depths. On the far side of Wadi Khirr the plateau resumed again and the *dars* of a Yemeni hill tribe, the Awadhis, topped the peaks, deceptively close. Nearer at hand, on the edge of the Bayhan cleft, were the buildings of the Yemeni garrison at al-Ghurayba, whom the Government Guards in Najd al-Mizr, invisible below, delighted to harrass with their bugle calls.

I obtained a list of the Dhuraybi wells as a part of the continuous process of building up detailed information about the Protectorate for our records. Such facts tended to be garnered with difficulty, because the request for them always aroused suspicion that a new tax was about to be imposed, but an assurance from the mouth of the Amir himself soon assuaged the fears of the shaykh of the Ahl Dhurayba. There were forty-two wells in eight valleys, the best watered part of the plateau, but many of them were diminutive and quickly ran dry.

We spent our first night at Ghaylah, some miles south of Wahlan, stretching out on blankets on the mud floors of its single, tiny *dar*. Early next morning we were up and away. For several days we moved around, exploring the different areas of this remote table-land. Besides the Dhuraybi, we visited the narrow valleys of the Ahl Faraj, Ahl Hadi, Ahl Mansur and Ahl Sawdan, all of them sub-sections of the Arifi tribe.

This country had a wild beauty, no doubt enhanced during the green periods after the rains, and the eye-level panorama of distant peaks, like the roof-top view of a great city, was fascinating. It was a land of silence and stillness, where man was diminutive and the echoes of our raucous shoutings were intrusions on nature. In some places the struggle with hostile elements had been lost, and terraces were abandoned and eroding away. There was no wealth in these craggy, granite hills. The tribesmen, who rushed forward eagerly to kiss the hand of their Amir as we approached, obtained only the barest subsistence from their tiny, hard-won terraced fields, their attenuated *ilb* trees, their scrawny goats and emaciated donkeys. They

were themselves small and stocky, gaunt-looking, clothed in little else
but thread-bare loincloths, and covered with indigo. Few of them
lived in anything better than stone huts, and many families had their
homes in caves, or under slabs of overhanging rock. Such people
could ill afford the hospitality they considered due to their visitors,
and their efforts to provide it, made with the proud, unrestrained
generosity of all Arabs, were embarrassing. No one else in our party
seemed concerned, but I felt that when we departed the cupboards
would be absolutely bare. For my part it was therefore with some
relief that we slithered down the alarmingly steep and ill-defined
track which took us back into Wadi Bayhan a few miles south of
Nata. We spent a night being severely bitten by fleas on the mud
floors of stone huts in a small Arifi village, alongside a stretch of the
wadi where the water flowed perennially, and minnow-like fish
darted through the shadows of its pools. Then we were marching
jauntily homewards.

Our journey had provided more place-names and a new area to
insert on my map of Bayhan, and the Sharif's domain, or more properly the Amirate, could now be seen to extend much further to the
south than anyone in Aden would have believed. In a manner of
speaking, I felt I was responsible for the last territorial enlargement
of the British Empire, adding about a hundred square miles to it. But
there was another important outcome of the journey. During our
days together I had at last broken the Amir's reserve, for in front of
his father he was always shy and reluctant to talk. Now that we had
shared an experience involving some hardship and discomfort, for
there was nothing easy about this tour, we had a bond between us,
and from now on we were good friends. Muhammad Farid had
helped bring this about with his disarming bonhomie. I hoped it
would count for much in the future.

The recent rapprochement with Sharif Hussain, which Seager had
engineered by postponing some of his measures over the new
constitution, had produced an air of calm and well-being in Bayhan,
and the Sharif appeared to be imbued with a new spirit of willing
co-operation. I knew him well enough by now to be wary, for the
intention to tighten our control over his administration had not been
abandoned altogether and there were likely to be some further storms

ahead. But Seager had worse troubles on his hands elsewhere in the Protectorate and circumstances persuaded him that for a short period he would have to use me elsewhere. In mid-April I accompanied the Sharif and the Amir to Aden for their annual official visit to the Governor. While I was there I was diverted to Abyan to look into the problem of the Hathat fort.

The Hathat fort was being built on a hillside at a point, some forty miles east of Aden, where Wadi Hathat (pronounced "Hut-hut") left its gorge and flowed into the Abyan plain. The Government was at loggerheads with the Lower Yafai Sultan, who lived in the wild mountains north of Abyan and whose men had taken to raiding into the plain at night. The route for these raiding parties was Wadi Hathat, which led upstream to the Lower Yafai capital, al-Wara, an extraordinary village of ancient origin sited on the flat top of a formidable mountain. The raids were a serious threat to the cotton irrigation scheme being developed in this fertile delta area, and the fort was being constructed for Government Guard occupation to deny the raiders passage. Shortage of staff had meant inadequate supervision and it had become apparent that the enormous cost of the construction indicated serious financial peculation. I was sent to investigate.

I spent nearly a fortnight in Abyan and Hathat, trying to determine what was going wrong. It was a restful change from the pressure of the North Eastern Area. But news began to reach us of further Yemeni threats to Markha, and then, in mid-May, of new trouble with the Bal Harith. I sped back to Aden, handed in a report on the Hathat affair, made a quick purchase of stores and groceries and returned to Bayhan on 19 May. I had been absent for little more than a month.

The rain which had fallen on the southern hills, and encouraged everyone to believe that the days of hunger were nearly over, had not reached the main part of Wadi Bayhan. Neither had any flood-water flowed so far north. The summer heat had now set in, and the wadi looked dry and parched, the more so in contrast with the green fertility of Abyan which I had just left. The little fields of sesame provided dark green patches surrounding the constructions of gnarled branches and squeaking pulleys which marked the wellheads, but elsewhere all vegetation had withered. The heat burned into the rocks and made the sand too hot to walk on. Domestic animals hung their heads listlessly, under-fed, their ribs showing sharply through their coats. The people clung to the shade inside their doors.

Sharif Hussain and his son had stayed behind in Aden, pleading essential business more important than any crisis in Bayhan. "I know very well what is happening there," Hussain said rather crossly when it was suggested he might return with me. "It is just a squabble. There is nothing to worry about. I have everything under control." The bright lights of Aden and Shaykh Uthman fascinated the Sharif and the young Amir. After I had accompanied them to Government House for the formal visit, they had soon shaken me off to immerse themselves in social pleasures, spending, I feared, rather more of the Bayhan revenues than they would care to admit. But Hussain retained a firm grip over the affairs of his state and would not trust Awadh enough to give him a free hand as the Regent in his absence. Through the radio and by hand of anyone travelling up by plane, or even overland, flowed a continual series of messages in response to reports from his trusted secretary, Sayyid Abdullah, whom he had left behind for the very purpose of keeping an ear to the ground.

It was Hussain's greatest fault that he did not understand the virtue of clemency, and was convinced that his authority could best be asserted by a show of force. The mercy shown to the Salihi shaykh was Seager's idea, not his, and he went along with it only because Seager had required it. He believed in the power of armies and air action to heighten his *sharaf*. He could be arrogant and ruthless. When news reached him in Aden that the Bal Harith had, once again, been taking their salt to Harib without first paying customs duty on it due to the Bayhan Treasury, he saw the matter as another rebellion which had to be firmly crushed.

I found Awadh in an angry and dispirited mood. "My brother does not understand the Bal Harith," he complained. "He has never understood them. I will show you the letter he sent me. Look! It is an order. 'I have commanded the Mulazim of the Tribal Guards to arrest all the Bal Harith smugglers and hold them in the prison in Asaylan. You and Sharif Salih should make certain that this is carried out.' What can I say to that? Hussain knows very well what the

risks are. He has not sought my advice. I don't even think all the Bal
Harith on the list are guilty."

Awadh's concern was well-founded. The arrests were more than
a matter of tribal *sharaf*. The prison was a tiny room. The news which
had reached us in Aden was that the prisoners were packed tight
together in it, with no space to lie down, in intense heat and putrid
air. Even the Musabayn had been shocked by this action and tribal
feeling against Hussain was again running high throughout Bayhan.
"The Bal Harith are bedu," Awadh went on. "You have to treat them
like children. You have got to be patient with them and not lose your
temper. My brother is much too headstrong and he has hit them too
hard. It is dangerous to make them angry like this."

Over the months Awadh had revealed himself as an attractive,
kind-hearted, jovial man, a little naive and petulant, perhaps, but a
person of great generosity and simple needs. Hussain enjoyed the
urban bright lights and would be happy in the smart circles of high-
level politics, of which he was later to get a taste. Awadh, given half
a chance, would take a camel into the desert and tell stories, often
bawdy ones, round a camp fire under a roof of stars. I once spent
more than an hour, after lunch in his house at Hayd Kuhlan, trying
to change his belief that the world was flat; it was a good-natured
argument, but he could not be convinced, nor even led to doubt.
For all his obtuseness, Awadh could sense the temper of Bayhan and
had a compassion for its people which Hussain lacked. Yet, in spite
of these differences, he was very loyal to his brother and would not
countermand the instructions he had received. He relied on the
Government, through the Political Officer, to do that.

"How angry do you think the Bal Harith are?" I asked.

"Very angry indeed," Awadh replied. "We shall have to take action
quickly and we must be just, as well as very firm – otherwise there
will be serious trouble. I have tried to explain this to Hussain, but
he is not willing to listen to me."

Seager could have been relied upon to talk Hussain out of his
attitude, but he had just left for England on home leave, and John
Allen, now Acting British Agent, did not have the same pull over
this intransigent personality. Hussain was evidently in no mood for
compassion or compromise, and it looked as if he might even have

chosen this moment quite intentionally to renew his challenge against our efforts to tighten our control over him. I would have to tread carefully, but something drastic had, nevertheless, to be done.

"There has to be punishment for those who smuggle salt out of Bayhan," I said.

"Certainly," Awadh replied. "But do not forget that these people are in a very bad state. Neither flood nor rain has yet reached the lower wadi and their camels are still starving. They have no grain, no food. That is why they smuggled."

"What do you suggest we do?"

"We must give them the stick, of course – the *murr*, the bitter. But at the same time we must give them honey. They need help as well as punishment."

I thought long and hard. "Supposing we were to let the Bal Harith off paying salt tax for a period?" I queried. Hussain would not have contemplated such a measure, but it was hard to see any other satisfactory way of mollifying the Bal Harith.

Awadh became silent while he considered the idea. "I had been thinking about that," he said, "but Hussain would be very angry if I suggested it."

"Naturally it would have to be on my head," I told him. "What other solution can you suggest?"

"None," Awadh replied. "There is no other solution. It is the only honey we have to offer them."

"Very well. I will tell Hussain that it is my order."

"I will support you, of course, but my brother will not be easy to placate."

"We will have to work out what to say to Hussain once the time comes. But we must deal with the Bal Harith urgently. I think I had better leave for Asaylan at once."

Awadh said: "No! Better be patient! Better stay put here for a day or two first!"

I told Awadh I would wait, if that was his wish. Very possibly he was hoping to clear his position with Hussain before our action became irrevocable, for he could get a message to Aden secretly in two or three days by sending a runner through Bayda, who would catch a lorry from Lawdar, at the bottom of the *kawr*. Circumstances

overtook us, however. Early next morning a deputation of four Bal
Harith *aqil*s reached my *dar* and fired a volley of rifle shots.

"We heard you had returned to Bayhan," they said. "We came at
once to see you. This is a disgraceful thing which has been done
against us. We call on the *hakuma* to protect us against the oppression of the Sharif." They spoke quietly, but they were white with
passion and suppressed anger. "You must do something quickly,"
they went on, "or we cannot be responsible for what will happen."

Awadh joined me and together we harangued them about the
wrongs of smuggling and pleaded with them to be patient. "How
can we be patient in the face of this oppression?" they answered, and
we could see that they were in a state of desperation. Without quick
remedial measures the Bal Harith would once again come out in
armed rebellion against the Sharif.

"You had better go to Asaylan tomorrow," Awadh whispered to
me. "I will send Sharif Salih a message at once to expect you. You
will have to give them the honey."

I now had my own horse. Before leaving for Aden, Hussain had
negotiated on my behalf with his cousin Sharif Sayf bin Abud in
Harib, who possessed a stallion said to be of equable temperament
and a comfortable ride. I purchased him for seventy Maria Theresa
dollars, a very favourable price, and named him Tumna, after the
ancient capital of Qataban. He arrived covered with lice and ticks,
his bones protruding under loose skin as with so many of the starving animals of Bayhan, his head drooping to the ground, and I
learned that, since deciding to sell him, Sharif Sayf had fed him on
nothing but straw. Khamis, my self-appointed cook's assistant, immediately changed into a stable lad and made Tumna's restoration to
full fitness a matter of personal pride. For hours on end Khamis
would brush him, and smooth his flanks, and search his knotted black
coat for parasites. When I returned from my spell in Aden and Hathat
my horse was holding his head high and his coat had a bright sheen.

We left for Asaylan in the early hours, my first long journey on
Tumna. I had intended to ride with the Bal Harith shaykhs, but they
had awoken at three o'clock that morning and gone on ahead on
their camels. I travelled with Sayyid Abdullah, the Sharif's secretary,
whom Awadh insisted should accompany me, and Qassim's son

Ahmad, now authorised by the Sharif to use the title "shaykh" himself as a respect to his father. Both carried rifles, so I took no other escort. On horseback one could quickly gallop away from danger. Shaykh Ahmad Qassim meant well. He was a young man, still in his twenties, stocky, round-faced, always smiling amicably, with his father's untiring capacity for work, but he had none of the old man's tact and political acumen, and little in the way of experience. The Sharif had employed him to inspect the administration of the customs posts, and it was in this role that he had become involved in the business leading to our new crisis.

The burned-up state of the wadi became more apparent as we moved northwards. There was no fodder left, no visible greenery anywhere. The *ilb* trees were close-cropped, the clumps of cactus wrinkled and covered with dust, the palm-tree fronds brown and dead-looking; even the *rak* bushes, which gave camels diarrhoea, had been grazed to their stems in the absence of better pasture. There was hardly a leaf in the wadi. Here and there locusts fluttered aimlessly, stragglers from a great swarm which had passed through Bayhan before I got back and had settled somewhere in Rassassi country. There was nothing for these locusts to damage now, and the Bayhanis would catch them, skewer them on a stick, and barbecue them for lunch – a welcome and nutritious variant from their normal and now meagre diet. An ancient Assyrian relief from Sargon II's place at Khorsabad shows locusts being cooked in exactly this way, so the dish was probably known to the Himyarites as well.

It was the hottest day I had experienced in Bayhan. With the great heat, furnace-like soon after dawn, was a dryness which parched one's mouth until the tongue became stiff and leathery. The heat dragged out one's energy, and every movement was an effort. Even the long-tailed, stick-thin rock-lizards, which usually darted from place to place frenetically, changing colour like chameleons to blend into the background, had lost their spirit and moved out of our way reluctantly. Our horses had no liking for such conditions and dragged their hooves over the burning sand, unwilling to exert themselves to more than a walking pace. The heat haze produced quivering mirages, so that distant villages appeared to be on hilltops on the far side of trembling lakes. We drew our *kufiyahs* round our faces against the scorching rays pouring down on us from the empty sky and rebounding upwards fiercely from the ground. We narrowed our eyes to slits against the blinding glare. The sun, "entering", in Doughty's words, "as a tyrant upon the waste landscape and darting upon us as a torment of fiery beams", grew higher and stronger, and the whole shimmering wadi became still and silent around us as we plodded speechlessly onwards.

Sharif Salih met us outside Asaylan and fired his deafening salute. He looked confused and weary, and his normal cheerful affability had gone. As we exchanged greetings and while the attention of my two travelling companions was distracted, he whispered: "I must talk to you secretly before you do anything. Wait until I have found a chance to come and speak to you on your own."

The mood in Asaylan was tense. Awadh had already sent Tribal Guards and a levy of armed Ashraf to fortify the garrison, and their presence recalled the days when I first reached Bayhan and the bombing of the Bal Harith was about to commence. I was anxious to get to grips with the crisis, but could do nothing until I had spoken to Salih. We went through the formalities of lunch, and afterwards, while we sat drinking coffee through the afternoon, waiting for the sun to go down, there were numerous comings and goings by visitors with personal problems of little importance – an exasperating test of patience. The increased military presence had attracted a group of gypsy dancers, who were performing in some shady square, and their distant bagpipe music droned on endlessly in the background.

It was not until after dark, when I had reached the room set aside for me, and Hussain's secretary was safely and unsuspectingly out of the way, that Salih managed to get me alone. He was feeling bitter and upset. Talking, as was so often the case with my conversations in Bayhan, in a conspiratorial whisper, he told me that he was disillusioned by what had now happened. "Power is going to Hussain's head," he said. "I have always served him well, but he has changed so much. He no longer seems to care about us, not as he used to, and he no longer understands."

"You should not be saying such things to me," I replied.

"I have to say them," said Salih. "You must realise, *ya* Groom, that it is you who is most concerned. You must be very careful of him while he continues to behave in this way. He is trying to bring about your downfall. He wants to get you out of Bayhan. He sees you as his enemy now, because you know so much about what is going on. He is frightened that you will persuade the *hakuma* to take over the Bayt al-Mal. That has scared him more than anything."

Although I protested that Salih's fears must be exaggerated, I sensed that they might not be. Hussain aspired to be a powerful Protectorate ruler, and he needed wealth to serve his ambitions.

"I heard you were going to Abyan," Salih went on – an intriguing insight into the way news spread in the Protectorate. "When they told me that, I decided to resign and leave Bayhan with my family. This has become a land of oppression. Hussain is making life unbearable for his subjects, even for us, his close relatives, even for his *wakils*."

"In what way for his *wakils*?" I asked.

Salih drew closer to me. "For the last two months Hussain has refused to pay me my salary," he whispered. "He says it is a fine, a punishment, because I failed to report some of my decisions to him. Now he has taken this terrible action against the Bal Harith. That is *thullum* – oppression – and everyone knows it. He has broken the *sharaf* of the Bal Harith. He has made my position here impossible. I stayed on only because you came back." Salih was tense with emotion and his bitterness was not staged for my benefit. Hussain had never told me about any arbitrary fining of his own *wakils*.

We turned to the events which had led up to the Bal Harith imprisonments. Awadh had given me a summary, but told me that Salih would fill in the details. It had all started when Ahmad Qassim, probing into the administration of the customs posts, found that some of the Bal Harith had declared to the customs clerk in Asaylan that they were on their way to Suq Abdullah, where they would pay the Bayhani tax, but had instead slipped into Wadi Harib through Najd Marqad. "He calculated that about three thousand camel loads of salt had been smuggled into Harib in this way," Salih said, adding: "But in my view there were not nearly so many." Then he went on: "Ahmad Qassim made out a list of the men he suspected, more than a hundred of them, and sent it to Sharif Hussain in Aden. He did not refer it to me, because Hussain had ordered him to report on such things direct without telling any of the *wakils*, or even Sharif Awadh. Hussain didn't consult us. Instead he leapt to the conclusion that it was all going on with my connivance, so he ordered Awadh to dismiss me. Awadh refused to do that. So instead Hussain ordered the arrest of everyone of the Bal Harith named in the list, and said they must be held here, in the prison, until they had paid a fine of ten times the tax they were accused of avoiding. If I refused to accept that, then I would be dismissed at once. What could I do but obey?"

"What would you have done if it had been left to you?" I asked.

"*Wallah*! I would have gone to the shaykhs. We could have worked together. But if they could not help I would have brought in a few of the smugglers at a time. I would have heard their case through, and, if I found them guilty, I would have fined them, but not so much that all their money would be taken from them. Many of them were probably quite innocent. Sending Tribal Guards to arrest them all at once was wrong. That was what made the Bal Harith so angry. They are tribesmen. They have great pride. It was a *kassar sharaf* to arrest them and imprison them altogether. We hoped Hussain would retract when he heard of their reaction, but he refused to listen to us. He would not even come back from Aden to deal with the matter himself. He just repeated his order."

"What is the position now?"

"Most of them have paid their fines, with help from their fellow-tribesmen. But there are about twenty-five still left in prison; some of them have no money, and many of them insist they have not smuggled anything. Some say the only time they have ever been in Harib was with the 'official' salt caravan which Sharif Hussain and you agreed could go there once a month without paying duty. Hussain has now withdrawn that concession. It has all hit the Bal Harith very hard, and they are getting more mutinous with every day that passes. All the dollars they possess have gone into paying these fines. They are all talking of *thullum*, and many of them say they will leave the wadi forever."

We had called for all the Bal Harith leaders to assemble next morning, and they arrived shortly after dawn, shaking off their wide, flapping desert sandals in a pile at the threshold and stacking their rifles in a corner of the room. Soon the room was full of white-robed figures, squatting gravely around us, their faces, behind white and grey beards, looking stern, tense and suspicious. The long greetings were exchanged with formal punctiliousness, but there were few smiles and no further words.

I broke the silence on lines already agreed with Salih. "Oh *shuyukh,*" I said, "You must understand that the Government supports Sharif Hussain when he imposes customs taxes. When your tribesmen avoid paying those taxes they are opposing the Government just as much as they oppose Sharif Hussain. If your people were in difficulties, they should have come to Sharif Salih, or they could have waited for my return and complained to me. But they should not have broken the law. We cannot sympathise with people who have smuggled. They are law-breakers. Anyone who insists he is innocent will have a chance to prove it. But the rest will have to pay the fines which the Sharif has imposed on them."

We had calculated that the Bal Harith would ask for the customs duty to be reduced, but they sat and stared at us, nodding their heads and saying nothing. They may have believed there was nothing to hope for. Salih started to talk about their economic plight – the bare *ilb* trees, the close-cropped *rak* bushes, the skeleton-thin animals – but they seemed to be too angry and too proud to ask for help. "You are our father, *ya* Salih," said one of them, "and Groom here, who has eaten bread and salt with us, understands us. Our case is against the Sharif." "He oppresses us," said another. "He has broken our *sharaf.*" Alawi bin Ghurayba, owner of the only black beard among them, said: "My father has packed his tents and taken his family to Jawf. He can live under the Sharif no longer. Soon I shall follow him with many of our men. It is better to leave our wadi than lose our *sharaf.*"

It was time for what Sharif Awadh had called "the honey". Salih broached the possibility of the salt tax being reduced, and several heads nodded when I asked if this would be much help. Loudly, so that all could hear, I dictated a letter to Sharif Awadh, as the Regent, in words we had already carefully worked out. It suggested that, rather than reducing the tax, he should abolish it altogether for a period of one month. Bal Harith salt caravans could then go freely into Harib.

As I was speaking, the expressions of the shaykhs changed from brooding resentment to bewildered surprise and then to pleased approval. From his impassive, sullen silence, old Ali Munassir's face crinkled into a smile. "*Ya* Groom! That is very just. We came here expecting only the stick." It was as generous an expression of gratitude as a Bal Harith would ever utter and it meant that the crisis was over: they would make the most of their opportunity to earn money quickly; the remaining fines, from those still unable to satisfy Salih of their innocence, would soon be paid; and thoughts of revolt and abandoning the wadi would be put to one side. But I knew that my own crisis was still to come. We had averted a rebellion of Sharif Hussain's making in the only practicable way, but he would regard the settlement as a major challenge to his authority. Seager was no longer available to talk him round. It would not be long before his anger was once more turned against me. Salih knew it too. "Whatever happens," he said quietly as the Bal Harith were leaving, "don't forget that Awadh and I will support you."

At the lunch which followed I remarked on the absence of Sayyid Abdullah, the Sharif's secretary. Salih said: "He has already returned to Suq Abdullah. He has to write a report on what has happened and send it to the Sharif without delay."

Just before I had left Aden, news had come through that the first project for the Protectorate under the British Government's new Colonial Development and Welfare Fund had been approved. New schools were to be built, and they included five for Bayhan. We had already decided that one of these schools should be in Asaylan, to cater for boys from all the villages around, including Bal Harith. To the Bal Harith this would be the first cogent sign of some return for the taxes they paid. If building could be commenced quickly I hoped it might also help to put them off any idea of leaving the wadi for good, and it would certainly provide some much needed employment for labourers who were near to starvation. Two thousand five hundred Maria Theresa dollars, just over four hundred pounds, had been allocated to build the Asaylan school. The cash had not yet reached me, but Salih's money chest was bulging with dollars paid in by the smugglers. In a month's time Ramadhan would be upon us again, and that would mean more delay. I told Salih to take three hundred dollars on loan from his fines and start buying material. The Political Officer had also to be an architect. That evening we drew out plans for the building.

The plan had to follow traditional design, using local materials and labour. The walls would be of *liban* – mud brick baked hard by the sun – for there was no stone available within miles of Asaylan unless we looted it from Hayd Kuhlan. The rafters would be the crooked trunks of *ilb* trees, which limited the width to fifteen feet if we were lucky. The windows would be small, to keep out the heat and glare, and closed with wooden shutters, because there was no glass. We would build a long, single-storeyed school of four adjacent class-rooms, fronted (and here we broke with Bayhan's tradition) by a raised terrace. Mud brick was not expensive to make – just a matter of digging out wadi silt from any convenient site – and by local stan-dards we had enough money for an imposing building. We decided to erect it just to the north of the village walls, overlooking the Bal Harith fields.

Next morning we measured out the building on the ground, and before the sun was fully risen the foundations were being dug and the excavated soil, mixed into mud with water carried over by camels in goatskin buckets, was being kneaded into foot-square bricks and laid out on the ground nearby to bake in the growing heat. By the time I left Asaylan five days later the walls of the first classroom were waist high and I was able to mark out the positions of the windows.

I had intended to return to Bayhan al-Qasab earlier, but Salih pressed me to stay. More discussions were necessary with some of the Bal Harith shaykhs about arrangements to bring in smugglers who had so far eluded arrest. We were unable to persuade all of them to give themselves up and, before I departed, I reluctantly authorised Salih to revert to the time-honoured practice of billeting soldiers in the homes of the miscreants; it was always effective. There was also a complicated dispute over irrigation dykes which threatened more discord among the Bal Harith sections. "I need your help in settling it," Salih said. "One of the disputants, called Rashid Ali, is in prison. He has stated that he will accept any settlement pronounced by the Political Officer. But the other party, Hussain Talaan, is a most difficult person to deal with."

I sent for Hussain Talaan. "I would like you to choose any three of the Bal Harith *aqil*s," I said. "I will then ask them to form a tribunal and give judgement on this case."

"Never," Hussain Talaan replied. "The shaykhs will not give me a fair hearing. I could never agree to that."

"Who would you accept to give judgement?" I asked.

"Only a *harath* would understand a case like this. It is my right to have a *harath*."

In Bayhan a *harath* is a local person, publicly acknowledged as fair-minded, who settles cases of land and water rights for a small fee. In fact one *harath* had already tried to mediate in this case, but the disputants would not accept his judgement.

"I will give you a tribunal of three *harath*s," I said. "But you will have to accept what they say."

Salih called in three well-qualified experts from local villages, sensible-looking elderly men, and we rode over with a crowd of onlookers to inspect the disputed dykes in an area of sandy fields near the village of Zubiban.

Two days later, after the three *harath*s had considered the matter in great detail and come to a unanimous conclusion, I announced their compromise solution, which seemed entirely reasonable both to Salih and to me, in front of the disputants. Rashid Ali, released of his fetters, said: "That is fair. I knew that the Political Officer would make a just decision." Hussain Talaan, however, flew into a violent rage. "Never could I agree to that," he screamed. "It is quite unjust. Rashid Ali has bribed the *harath*s. They would never have made such a decision otherwise."

"You will have to accept it," Salih told him severely. "Nobody could have had a fairer hearing. We made it clear from the beginning that this judgement must be final."

"I shall appeal to the shaykhs. I shall appeal to the Sharif. By Allah! I shall appeal to Aden. I call on you, *ya* Groom, to reverse this wrong." Hussain Talaan was beside himself with rage. "Never could I accept such an injustice."

"There can be no appeal," I said.

He left quite unpacified. Protectorate tribesmen rarely reacted happily to decisions which went against them. I envied Sharif

Hussain his extraordinary ability to give judgements in a way which pleased both sides.

I returned to Bayhan al-Qasab in time to write my reports so that they would catch a Government Guard relief plane due on 2 June. But the wireless schedule on the previous evening brought the Immediate signal I was expecting from Allen, the Acting British Agent. The Sharif of Bayhan had heard of the new settlement with the Bal Harith and taken violent exception to it. I must come straight down to Aden on the morrow's plane to discuss the matter.

Early next morning, before the Anson arrived, Sharif Awadh called on me alone. "I have come to wish you well," he said. "The settlement we reached was a fair one. You must defend it vigorously. We all support the action you have taken, and when Hussain returns I shall tell him so. He has made a serious mistake, and he should be grateful that you have managed to rescue him from trouble. You should try to appease him, but stand up to him and don't let him knock the Bal Harith any more."

Soon afterwards, sharp ears picked up the distant drone of the aeroplane engines and the cry was taken up: "*Tayyara! Tayyara!* The plane is coming!" As I was preparing to walk over to the landing ground, there was another shout, this time from the stables below, where Khamis was giving Tumna his morning groom. Tumna had begun to show a wilder spirit since I rode him to Asaylan. Now he had suddenly kicked out. "Dawar has been hurt," someone called out. Dawar, meaning "hyena", was the nickname by which Khamis, because of his loud voice, was always known. Two *askaris* carried the little fellow up to my room, limp and in great pain, with blood all over his arms, face and clothes. Fortunately the wound was less serious than it looked and the bleeding soon stopped, but he had had a nasty knock and seemed to be concussed. We put him on my camp bed and left him to sleep it off. It was the first time he had ever slept on a bed.

McIntosh met me at Khormaksar and we drove straight to the British Agency, where the Sharif was already in discussion with John Allen.

I had expected Hussain to voice disapproval of the settlement we had made. However, I was quite unprepared for the torrent of angry recrimination which followed my explanation of it. He had not, he expostulated, been consulted, and we must have known that the decision would be most objectionable to him. I could not tell him of the full part that Awadh and Salih had played, though he must have guessed that they had at least connived with me, and so I had to take all the blame. So intense was his rage that there was no point in arguing with him, and only occasionally did we interject to make a point. His face grew red. His eyes were fiery. "Awadh concurred with my decision," I said at one point. "As the Regent it is right that he should make decisions in your absence." "Never," Hussain replied. "I have signed nothing which gives him power as a Regent while I am away. Awadh has no more powers than at any other time. He is just the *Hakim Urfi,* the Common Law Judge. Even when I am in Aden I am the ruler of Bayhan – I and no one else!"

The meeting ended with no satisfactory conclusion. Our efforts at placation had been quite unsuccessful. "There can be no question of cancelling the settlement," the Sharif was told. Hussain, glaring at Allen wildly, retorted: "It will have to be cancelled. No other solution is possible."

Early next morning, making my way back to Bayhan, I found an unexpected visitor waiting to see me off at Khormaksar airport. It was Amir Salih.

"My father does not know I have come here to see you," he said, speaking in a low voice and glancing round to make sure nobody could overhear. "I am sorry he got so worked up yesterday. He has not been his normal self for some time. I came to tell you that his anger has cooled down today, and he does not feel nearly so bitter. I will work on him on your behalf. Do not worry! I will do my best. *Inshallah* things will get better by the time we return to Bayhan."

"*Inshallah,*" I repeated, shaking his hand.

It was the first time I had seen Salih break away from his father, and I knew it had been a very big decision to come out secretly like this to see me off. Our days together in Jamaliyah had borne fruit.

11

The Storm Breaks

To a male visitor Arabia is a world of men. Apart from the *shahadh* gipsies and a few beduin, I rarely saw a woman's face in Bayhan, for, if not veiled, and often even when they were, women would turn their backs to me as I passed, or dart into hiding behind a wall or tree. Sometimes one noticed bright, black eyes, heavily ringed with *kohl*, staring at one through a crack in the doorway; quite often there was excited giggling in a nearby room as the *harim* discussed the *nasrani* visitor and his strange appearance – for I was the only person in all Bayhan who wore spectacles; but women were never normally admitted into my company, they had no part in my life, and they were never discussed. One does not, in Arabia, even ask after the health of a man's wife; one asks how is his *bayt*, his house, a term signifying his whole household and embracing both his wives and his children. It would be considered quite improper to mention his womenfolk by name.

My acceptance of the celibate bachelor's existence occasioned much surprise. Marriage was often suggested as quite essential, either to a well-rounded lady from England, or perhaps even to a Bayhani girl. Davey had married a Bayhani, incidentally gaining thereby a valuable new source of information, for the Arab ladies love to gossip. Hints were occasionally thrown at me by Sharif Hussain, no doubt with half an eye to improving his own intelligence service, that I should follow Davey's example. Such a step would have required my first becoming a Muslim, for a Muslim woman cannot marry a non-believer. I had no disposition to such an arrangement. Sometimes there were direct offers from persons who saw enormous advantage to themselves if they could contrive to become related to me. On one journey I was accosted by a wretched fellow with wrinkled black skin and spindly legs, a rag of a loin-cloth wrapped round his bony middle. "*Ya* Groom! You must need *zig-zig*," he called out, voicing the local word for the sexual act and illustrating it by thrusting the pointed finger of one hand piston-like into the closed fist of the other. "You should marry my daughter. She is very beautiful. The most beautiful girl in all Bayhan. You can have her for fifty dollars." I thanked him and said I was quite happy as I was, urging my horse into a trot to escape him. Behind me I could hear the voice of an incurable optimist: "Well! Forty-five dollars, perhaps!"

Yet despite their unenviable position as chattels, the women of South-west Arabia often exercised considerable influence behind the scene. We who saw only the Arab male could never acquire a true picture of the Arab in his domestic scene. Men like Sharif Salih were blissfully married and revelled in their children and their homes. The Arab woman was pampered with silver trinkets, much of her husband's wealth going round her neck and wrists and ankles in the form of jewellery made from Maria Theresa dollars. Under their concealing robes the wives of the wealthy wore rich silks, and sometimes, in Aden, Paris fashions. There were women among them fully capable of advising their husbands on their business affairs, and the nagging wife was not unknown.

Although Islam permits a man to have four wives, few men in Bayhan married more than two and most were monogamous as much through choice as through economic circumstances. It is a tenet of Islam that each wife must be accorded equal favour, though by custom the first wife usually retains a senior position of control over the household. The domestic stresses of such an arrangement were recognised, and when a man married more than once the ideal arrangement was for him to keep each wife in a separate household, well divided by distance. But this was only possible if he were wealthy. Awadh had picked up a story in Aden, which he related with glee, about an Adeni who had ignored this simple precept. Buying a four-storey terrace house in Crater, he had installed his four wives in it, one on each floor. The senior wife insisted on having the ground floor, while the young and beautiful girl he had only just married was on the top. "You can imagine the state he was in," Awadh chuck-led. "He would take his shoes off and try to tip-toe up the stairs past the first three doors in order to reach the fourth. *Wallah*! One of the first three wives always heard him and pulled him in by the hair. She's probably a virgin still, that young one!"

The purdah system was so rigid that the vast majority of Protectorate women had no hope of avoiding it. Yet there were a very few, like the *shahadh* girls, who spurned the veil, and very occa-sionally one heard of a woman of exceptionally strong personality, who had broken into the world of men and competed with them on almost equal terms. Such a person was Bint Issa.

Bint Issa had a Protectorate origin but she lived in Aden, where she made much money as a procuress, and had used it, together with an acute business acumen, to become a wealthy merchant. She was a formidable, middle-aged lady with a penetrating voice, and it was inadvisable to fall foul of her. Unfortunately a Hammami named Mubarak bin Salih had succeeded in doing this. He had arranged some deal which left him owing her four thousand dollars – a sub-stantial sum by local standards – and had then produced excuses for refusing to pay it. Bint Issa began to pester the WAP Office demand-ing satisfaction, and eventually started to present her shrill complaints to Seager. The right appeared to be on her side, and when the Hammami still refused to pay, Seager took the only action open to him and imposed an order to repay on the Hammami tribe as a whole. When this was rejected, he had to take steps to enforce it, but action was difficult, because the Hammamis were not in terri-tory under administrative control. "Until the money is handed over," he wrote to the Hammami shaykhs, "Hammamis are banned from entering the *suqs* of Bayhan and Dathina." There was still no repay-ment, and Seager then had to ban the Hammamis from entering Bayhan at all.

I was deeply saddened by this development. Of all the tribes in the uncontrolled parts of the North Eastern Area, the Hammamis had for long been our greatest friends. Only a few months before, Seager had been talking of my taking a military force across the desert to link up with them as the first stage of an operation to bring peace and order into Upper Awlaqi. Hammami caravans conveyed much of the merchandise of the area, for it was as carriers that they earned their living, and in this time of economic hardship, when their wadi was as parched as Bayhan, the ban might easily turn them into desperate men. Nor could they understand the reason for the order, which they interpreted as an inexplicable attempt to shame them. Within the tribe the affair was regarded as one for Mubarak bin Salih's section, the Ahl Hussain, to resolve on its own; the other main sections, Shamlan, Misfar and Dhiyab, began to blame the Hussainis for the ban, and rising tempers led to the danger of blood being spilled; this would have been a tragedy, for the Hammamis were at that time unique in having no blood-feuds between any of their sections. Bayhanis, too, thought the ban was unreasonable. "Why," I was asked many times, "do you choose to sacrifice your friends for the sake of an Aden prostitute?" It was difficult to know what to reply. When I ordered patrols out at the end of May to round up a Hammami caravan reported to be passing through the desert from the Yemen, I was secretly relieved that it could not be found. The Hammamis knew all the desert tracks, and they could rely on the complete connivance of the Bal Harith when travelling clandestinely through the northern reaches of Bayhan.

Nobody was more anxious to reverse Seager's order against the Hammamis than Sharif Awadh, still, despite Hussain's outburst, actively doing his duty as Regent in his brother's absence. Awadh consistently exhorted me to intercede. Together and separately we wrote letters to the Hammami Shaykh and to my Hammami friend, Shaykh Abdullah bin Ali, urging payment of the debt. We even enlisted the aid of an important member of the offending family, who had been trapped in Bayhan, when the full ban was imposed, and arrested. "He too," Awadh said, "must write." "Will they pay?" I asked, when all our letters had gone. "The Hammamis are not proud like many other tribes," Awadh said, "and they do not want blood to be spilled. I think they will pay." He was right and serious trouble was avoided, but it was a near thing.

If there were unusually strong-minded women like Bint Issa, there were also women who could be as violent and dangerous as their menfolk. Early in 1949 a lady of the Dhaifallah tribe quarrelled with her two brothers and settled the matter by cutting their throats with a *jambya* while they were asleep, escaping immediately afterwards into the territory of the Bani Yub, a Yemeni tribe. The Ahl Dhaifallah were a small beduin section, of some forty fighting men, who lived in the area of Bir ad-Dimna, just south of a pass through which ran the main trade route between Bayhan and Markha. Their territory was thus of some importance to Bayhan, especially as we were looking to the day when it might carry a motor road, and the Sharif had for long insisted they were Bayhani subjects, though for their part they had preferred to claim they were independent in order to avoid his taxation. The murder coincided with the occupation of Rassassi and Bani Yub country by Yemeni forces, and not long afterwards ash-Shami sent soldiers to collect taxes from the Ahl Dhaifallah. One morning, after I had heard much firing of rifles outside the Sharif's *dar*, Sharif Awadh called on me. "The Dhaifallah have come to see us. They say they are subjects of the *hakuma* and the Sharif, and they want protection."

"I thought they always claimed to have no masters," I said.

"Not now. The *nidham*, the Yemeni soldiers, will take everything they possess. It's cheaper to be a Bayhani."

"What will ash-Shami say if we accept them?"

"They will have documents to prove that they are Bayhanis."

"What documents?"

"My clerks are preparing them now. They recognise that the Dhaifallah have been Bayhani citizens since 1946."

"But ash-Shami might dispute that!"

"We won't challenge him directly, *ya* Groom. That way he would be bound to oppose us. But if you show him you recognise that the Zaydis control the Bani Yub, which we don't dispute anyway, it will please him and he might forget the Dhaifallah. That is the way ash-Shami thinks. You won't need to mention the Dhaifallah at all, just the name of the murderess."

I took his point and together we composed a letter which I would send to ash-Shami. It simply asked him, very politely, now that the Bani Yub were under his control, to persuade them to hand the Dhaifallah woman over to us. Awadh's ruse was successful and we heard that ash-Shami had sent soldiers to arrest her. She made good her escape to a more inaccessible area, but the *nidham* made no further attempts to extort taxes from the hapless Dhaifallah.

The Dhaifallah were not the only tribe in that area of the Protectorate to be threatened by the *nidham* at that time. Their next-door neighbours, a tiny clan called Ahl Kushr, who roamed a tract named Jibah, in the hills north-west of the ar-Riba pass, also called for protection. They too lived astride the main trading route between Bayhan and Markha, and, until reports reached us that ash-Shami intended to subjugate them, it had never been questioned that their territory was in the Protectorate. But the frontier was not mapped, let alone demarcated, and they had a traditional, loose tribal affinity with the Bani Yub. I assured the two Kushri shaykhs who visited me that the *hakuma* would resist any Yemeni attempt to take them over. They looked relieved, and one of them then confessed that a rival delegation was at that moment in Bayda offering the tribe's loyalty to ash-Shami and the Imam. The Kuhayl, for long regarded as peaceful if impecunious citizens of Bayhan, were even more concerned, for they had in earlier days paid a small tribute to the Rassassi Sultan, in consequence of which the Zaydis still held a hostage from them in Nata. Fortunately ash-Shami heeded the news that we were resolved to resist him; with other preoccupations engaging his attention, he decided that his expansionist plans had best be deferred. They were not renewed.

It was surprising how many little tribes there were like the Kushris, the Kuhaylis and the Dhaifallahis. Living in isolated *shaabs* and tiny valleys amidst the mountains, they were so remote that they would be unheard of until some incident brought them suddenly to the forefront. For a few days most of my attention would be focused on them while we wrestled with their problem. As soon as we had overcome it, their deputation of *aqils*, pacified or sometimes still indignant, would return home to their black tents and herds of goats, wealthier by a few *riyals* from my money bag, and the tribe would vanish from our ken as if it no longer existed.

A few days after my stormy meeting with the Sharif in Aden, I rode back to Asaylan with the newly arrived G.G. Rais, Mubarak Abdullah Tawsali, to see that all was well with the construction of the new school. We travelled without luggage in the grilling heat of the afternoon, and by the time we reached the village my mouth was so dried up that I was literally unable to utter the words of greeting until water had been brought.

Sharif Salih had put Shaykh Ahmad Qassim in charge of the work on the school, so I knew that the accounts would be honestly kept. The walls were gaining height at an impressive speed. *Asha* – supper – was with Salih and was followed by an evening of chat with a score of visitors in the half-light of Hurricane lanterns. The conversation carried on until long past midnight. I spent the night on a roof-top under the stars, and the Asaylan flies and donkeys combined to provide an alarm on the stroke of dawn. Ahmad Qassim and his builders were back at the site as soon as it was light, and I joined them to measure out the last of the classrooms, on which work had yet to begin: this piecemeal method of construction suited our circumstances. Breakfast, with Mubarak and Salih, was a cup of ginger tea, a flat loaf of unleavened bread, and some fried mutton. By eight o'clock our horses were saddled and we were on our way back to the capital.

There had been no opportunity for private discussion with Salih the previous evening, but he clearly hoped to talk to me and said he would come part of the way with us. When we were out of sight of the village, Mubarak, a man of tact and discretion, moved ahead of us, and Salih asked anxiously about my Aden visit. I gave him a brief account of what had happened, and told him I hoped Hussain would soon get over his anger and become more conciliatory. "I don't think he is very likely to do that," Salih said. "He does not forget things easily and he is very ambitious. He does not like to have anybody standing in his way. You are in his way now." Salih paused, and then added earnestly: "You must be very careful."

When we got back to Bayhan al-Qasab, Sharif Awadh came hurrying over with news from another quarter. For some time there had been rumours that the Imam was preparing a punitive expedition against the Dahm tribe, who lived north of Bayhan in Wadi Jawf and had been resisting him ever since he wrested back his throne. Jawf was a great wadi, once the centre of the ancient kingdom of Ma'in and said to contain many ancient ruins, which led out into a vast area of desert where the Dahm could vanish whenever the *nidham* came to seek them. Awadh said: "I have just heard that Shaykh

Mabkut al-Iraqi was arrested by the Zaydis. He was one of the most important Dahmi shaykhs. They wanted to take him to Sanaa. He knew the Imam would have him beheaded, so he tried to escape. He was shot dead by his guards." "What will happen now?" I asked. "*Wallah*! Most of the Dahm have already fled into the desert, and the *nidham* have taken over their *dars* in the wadi. Now the Abida are frightened it will be their turn next; they are the allies of the Dahm." The tribal territory of the Abida was near Marib, on the far side of the Ramlat Sabatayn, and they were the northern neighbours of the Bal Harith. We knew that the trouble could easily spill over into Bayhan.

Shortly after this news reached us, I was warned that a prominent Abida shaykh who had persistently refused to answer a summons to the Imam's presence in Ta'izz was likely to seek political asylum in Bayhan. When Awadh came to discuss this development, I had to follow instructions from Aden and tell him: "You must discourage this and try to put him off." Awadh was taken aback, as I knew he would be, and expostulated: "But he is an important man, and he is seeking refuge from execution by the Imam!" "I know that, and I, like you, would wish to help him. But it would put the *hakuma* in a difficult position. We have signed an agreement with the Imam about the extradition of criminals. The Imam will call the Abida Shaykh a criminal, because that is how he regards any political opponent, and if he needs to he will make out false accusations against him." "That is true." "So then the *hakuma* will be asked to hand him over under the treaty." Awadh said: "Yes. But we will let him escape to another sanctuary if that happens." I left it at that. In the event the Abida Shaykh did not come to Bayhan, but whether Awadh had put him off I never knew.

With trouble and disturbance all around us, the land was rife with rumours at that time. The first action of any beduin when he meets another, after the formal exchange of the peace greeting, is to ask: "What is your news?" In such manner information quickly spreads over vast distances. One day Sharif Abdullah, the Wakil in Wadi Ayn, sent me a letter with some most extraordinary news. "There is a great army out in the Empty Quarter, and it is heading west through the sand dunes towards us. Several people have come to tell me about it, so there must be truth in what they say. It is an army of all races and creeds, clad in armour; it moves forward a mile a day, and has a pipe to bring water; the leader is a one-eyed man; he has said they are going to drive the Imam of Yemen into the Bab al-Mandab, and the Imam has despatched a large army into Jawf to meet the attack. Without a doubt the size of the Imam's force is thirty thousand men. *Wallah!* This is what they all say, and it must surely be true." In the days of ancient Ma'in, nearly twenty-five centuries before, there seems to have been a similar tendency to exaggerate: "Kariba-Ilu," records one monumental inscription in Marib, "killed 4,000 men in a war against Qataban, then turned on Ma'in and killed 45,000 while taking 63,000 prisoners and 31,000 head of cattle." But there was indeed a basis of truth in Abdullah's report, which soon reached me from other sources as well. We knew already that the Imam had sent several hundred men into Jawf to punish the Dahm and Abida. In addition, hundreds of miles away, on the eastern side of Arabia, men with metal hoods over their heads, like armour, were welding together a new oil pipeline from Dhahran, moving steadily westwards with an army of foreign engineers and Arab and Indian labourers at the rate of about one mile a day.

We expected Sharif Hussain and Amir Salih to return to Bayhan on 10 June after their long holiday, and due pomp and ceremony was provided on the ar-Rawna landing ground to greet them. At ten o'clock two RAF Ansons touched down, one close behind the other. The Amir clambered out with a number of retainers, but there was no sign of his father. "Abdul Karim, the Sultan of Lahej, is in Zara with the Awdhali Sultan," the Amir said. "My father has gone to join them to discuss a union of the Protectorate states." This was important news – the first tentative step towards federation; but it was to be some years before this seed, which Seager had planted, began to germinate.

With the Amir came an officer who had recently taken up a new post in the WAP Office. His name was Rigby-Jones and he was the Finance Officer. He had come, with an Adeni interpreter, to follow up my cursory inspection of the Bayt al-Mal. Nobody had warned me that such a visit was being planned. "I shall be glad of your company," I told him, "but the last thing I want here at the moment is an efficient new accounting system, however bad the present one may be. It will drive Hussain into a frenzy. Our relations are bad enough already. You could not have arrived at a worse time." There were occasions when the WAP Office seemed unable to understand the realities of our difficulties in the field. Rigby-Jones looked taken aback. "I am sorry" he said. "I had no idea it was like that. I will play my cards very gently." "I don't think you should suggest any changes whatsoever for the time being," I said. He agreed reluctantly, adding: "But I shall have to do something. Now that I'm here I can hardly call off my examination of the books altogether. Besides, Sharif Hussain knows I have been sent here to look at them." We agreed that he should stress from the outset that he was only in Bayhan to find out how the present accounting system worked. "We will have to assure Hussain that there is no intention of introducing anything new," I said. It seemed very doubtful whether Hussain would be content with such an assurance. We decided to make a quick start, before Hussain returned and made difficulties, and for much of that day and the next I helped Rigby-Jones to inspect the confused and much amended ledgers which I had been through during Ramadhan. It did not take him long to draw the same conclusion. "The accounting is abominable," he commented. "Those books conceal a great deal more than they reveal."

Sharif Awadh, as if sensing our thoughts, came over unexpectedly in the afternoon to talk to us in the privacy of my room. He was tense and worked up, no longer able to contain himself. I was prepared for a complaint that our examination of the accounts was a serious *kassar sharaf* for the Sharif, but instead he launched into a virulent condemnation of Hussain's handling of the state finances. I had never heard him speak so openly before against his brother. When I sought to play down one of his complaints with a bantering remark he took me to task. "You must not think lightly of this matter, *ya* Groom. I have hidden my feelings until this day, but now I trust you, and I can tell you what is in my heart. Hussain is milking the people of Bayhan. *Wallah!* He takes their taxes and spends the money on himself."

I had found that when the Ashraf criticised their chief it was usually because they had some personal grievance which upset them.

Awadh's quickly came tumbling out. "While my brother has been in Aden this time," Awadh continued, "he has spent no less than four thousand rupees on new clothing for himself, and God knows how much more on other things. Yet, when my two sons left the Protectorate College last month at the end of term and asked Hussain for a little money on loan to replace their worn-out clothes before they came back to Bayhan, do you know how he treated their request? He refused to give them one single anna. That is the truth! Four thousand rupees on clothes for himself and not a single anna for my sons. That is what is happening to the Bayhan revenues. You have got to stop it." Four thousand rupees, or about three hundred pounds, was not a lot by other standards, but in Bayhan it was a fortune, compared with which the salaries of even the senior officials like Awadh and Salih were mere pittances. Their disgruntlement was understandable.

Hussain returned on the following day. A mounted messenger had galloped ahead down Wadi Bayhan to herald him, and there were rifle shots and Chinese crackers to salute him when he arrived on horseback with an escort of soldiers. He inspected his guard-of-honour, greeted us hastily and disappeared into his *dar*, not to be seen again that day. It was not unreasonable that he should be tired after his journey, but on Bayhan standards his abruptness was a deliberate act of bad manners. Awadh came round that afternoon to apologise. "Hussain has insulted Mr Rigby-Jones," he said. "It is against our custom to behave like that. But you should know that he has shown an ill face towards Salih and me as well. He is in a very bad mood." I said: "When you have placated him I hope you will try to patch up his quarrel with Sharif Salih." "Salih has every cause to be angry," Awadh replied. "My brother has never given Salih the respect which is his due."

We waited another day, and then I took Rigby-Jones over to talk to Hussain about his work on the accounts. Awadh, Salih and Salih's elder brother Ahmad were there. We had worked out very carefully how to explain the inspection. "I only wish to see and understand," Rigby-Jones said, and I translated his words into Arabic. "I am not here to make changes, and I do not have time for very detailed enquiries. As far as I can gather, the system you are using is good, but there may be improvements I can suggest later to make it more efficient." While he was speaking the tension on Hussain's face relaxed and gave way to a smile of relief as he realised that there was no immediate threat. The smile remained as we moved on to other matters. It seemed an opportune moment to raise the question of the new schools.

During Hussain's absence, Awadh and I had selected a site for the big new school to be built in Bayhan al-Qasab, for which five thousand Maria Theresa dollars, some eight hundred pounds, had been allocated in the Colonial Development and Welfare Scheme. This was to be an impressive school, in a good position and of sound design. But Hussain, directing from Aden, had rejected the site chosen on the grounds that it was too near his *husn* and intended already for other administrative buildings. I asked in all innocence: "Have you decided where you would like the new school to be?"

I had misjudged Hussain's mood. The smile changed into a frown, he started to tug at his beard, and then he said sullenly: "I do not want it anywhere. I cannot accept any responsibility for these schools, *ya* Groom, and I am not prepared to have anything to do with them. I wanted the Asaylan school to be built of stone, but you are disregarding my wishes and building it of *liban*." I saw Awadh and Salih exchange glances. They knew, as did I, that the cost of carrying stone from the hillside to Asaylan would have been prohibitive, and that Hussain had said nothing about the matter until now. Clearly I was not forgiven for relieving the Bal Harith of their salt tax and now I was going to face Hussain's opposition in other fields. Salih was right and I would have to be careful, for Hussain could be quite unscrupulous. Planning for the other schools had better wait for a while, although the construction work at Asaylan could go forward to completion, for Sharif Salih and Shaykh Ahmad Qassim would not let me down over that.

Once again Awadh called in the afternoon to apologise: "I am angry indeed over my brother's behaviour," he said, "but I am glad it happened in front of another officer of the *hakuma*. Now Rigby-Jones can give evidence of my brother's attitude when he gets back to Aden."

It was a windy, dusty day, when the mountains flanking the wadi

appeared only in hazy outline, towering and distant. I took Rigby-
Jones for a short walk that evening through the *suq* and round the
edge of the town, and decided on the spur of the moment to call on
the Qadhi. He greeted us with enthusiasm and gave us tea and unripe
dates. Over the months I had got to know him well and visited him
frequently, for his conversational charm made his home a place of
respite from the tensions of the day.

Later that evening the Sharif did the honours to his visitor and
invited us to supper. The angry, sullen man we had last seen had
changed into a genial host, and as we reclined on cushions in his
upstairs room after the meal, he showed no signs of wrath and made
no reference to matters of contention. But Amir Salih, kept firmly
under his father's domination, looked embarrassed and stared at the
floor, while Sharif Salih remained in one corner in a state of utter
dejection, and Sharif Awadh was conspicuously absent.

When I mentioned the schools to Hussain next day, all his hostility had returned. Now there was a new reason for refusing to accept
any responsibility for them. "I was told in Aden," he said, but he
would not say by whom, "that you have written to the British Agent
accusing me of stealing money from the Bayt al-Mal." "What you
heard is quite untrue," I replied firmly, for I had been very careful
about what I committed to paper. But the secret files of the WAP
Office certainly contained much more than we would care him to
know about, and it was quite possible that people in the office had
gossiped.

The same afternoon I rode over to Asaylan again with Sharif Salih,
for I could not afford to let anything go wrong with the building
work there and that meant giving it constant attention. On the way
Salih became more indignant about the Sharif's behaviour than ever
before. "You should not say such things to me," I protested. "Hussain
may make mistakes, but he will change and he is still the ruler of this
country. A Political Officer can go, but the ruler remains."
"Certainly Hussain is our ruler," Salih replied, "but he must rule
properly."

After we had ridden a little further, Salih drew his horse up close
alongside mine and said: "Hussain has now ordered me and the other
wakils to withhold all assistance from you over the building of the

schools. He has even ordered me to take away my son Abdullah, who has been helping to supervise. He has told me to put difficulties in your way so that the building will never be completed."

We were growing increasingly conspirational in our conversations. We rode our horses at walking pace while we conversed, but as soon as anyone came into view Salih veered off at a sharp canter. In this manner we agreed that Abdullah had better keep out of the way, for Salih could not openly disobey so specific an instruction. "But you need have no doubt," Salih said reassuringly. "The building will go on just the same."

When we reached Asaylan the dark was closing in, for there was no long twilight in these latitudes. Through the gloom I could see that impressive progress had been made on the building. We supped in Salih's dining-room and retreated afterwards to an upper room for the inevitable long evening conversation with local visitors, to a background of gurgling water pipes. I had hoped to satisfy myself that all was well with the building accounts, but when at last Ahmad Qassim proudly presented them to me I could make neither head nor tail of them. There were innumerable scraps of paper with lists of names and thumbprints, the normal form of receipt for wages from men who could not write. But nothing had been added up and I could not make Ahmad Qassim's balances tally. At midnight I gave up the struggle, told Ahmad Qassim how I wanted the details set out, and retired to bed. That night I dreamed about falling buildings. As always at that time my dreams were in Arabic, for it was only when visitors were around that I heard English spoken.

We were up at four o'clock next morning, in order to get back to Bayhan al-Qasab before the heat became unbearable. Salih insisted on accompanying me personally, evidently having decided that, when I moved without Government Guards, he could no longer trust anybody else to protect me.

We reached Bayhan shortly before the RAF Anson which would take Rigby-Jones back to Aden was due. "I was worried you might not get here in time," Rigby-Jones said. "There has been a new development."

Even the Finance Officer was now caught up in political intrigue. "Shortly after you left for Asaylan," Rigby-Jones went on, "Sharif

Hussain sent for my young clerk and asked him to translate into English some letters he had written personally to the British Agent. One was a report about his journey through Yemen and of no consequence to us. But the other letter was a very bitter complaint against you."

We sent for the clerk, a lively young Adeni who on this his first trip up-country had been finding Bayhan primitive beyond belief. "Yes," he told us. "It was a very angry letter. It said you had been asking people in Bayhan for information about the Sharif's misuse of money from the Bayt al-Mal. There were some other accusations in it too."

As he spoke the drone of the Anson forced us to hurry over to ar-Rawna. There was just time to arrange for Rigby-Jones to explain to Allen what was happening. Soon he and his clerk, together with the Sharif's accusatory letter were on their way to Aden.

I was now very worried about the situation. The new accusation, which was quite without foundation, showed that Hussain had decided to work towards my removal from Bayhan. My lead in an act of clemency to the Bal Harith, meeting a challenge from Hussain which he was probably not expecting us to take up, had had the effect of increasing the stock of the *hakuma*, the Government, at the cost of the *dawla*, the State, and had damaged his reputation. Among the tribesmen, both Bal Harith and Musabayn, my personal stock was now high, and this had the undesirable effect of encouraging them to come in with complaints which they would not previously have dared to express and which were not always justified. For some weeks I had been hearing the word *thullum*, meaning "oppression", often uttered for no valid reason. The Sharif knew of all this and resented it, particularly because he did not know what grievances were being voiced to me, nor how I was reacting. Moreover, he had other fears. He had always regarded the new constitution as an assault on his authority, and he knew that its enforcement would be taken a stage further if I remained. Nor was he deceived by our protestations of innocent intention towards his Bayt al-Mal; he could well appreciate that once we put his State finances on a proper footing he would no longer be able to use them as a personal fund. He probably saw me as the instrument of this reform; if it went through he would no longer be able to hold his own in the hierarchy of Protectorate chiefs, where wealth counted, and his high ambitions would be stifled. I could even see why he was irritated over the new grants for five schools, because the *hakuma* was publicly displayed as the benefactor, enhancing my prestige at the expense of his own. In short, Hussain now regarded my position in Bayhan as a threat to his own influence.

There had been an inevitability about these developments and I felt almost powerless to stem the tide of events. Hussain was a Treaty Chief and I was only a young Political Officer and therefore sacrificeable. Only Seager could control Hussain in this mood, and he was still in England on leave. Hussain, the master of the *siassa*, was bound to win in the end. If he chose to, he would do so without scruples. I reflected on old Shaykh Qassim's impassioned appeal against going to Jawf to buy horses, and on Sharif Salih's earnest plea to me to take great care.

Although we were in the vortex of a crisis of gathering momentum, there was little spare time in which to worry about it. The aeroplane which collected Rigby-Jones had brought up a new party of visitors who had to be organised and cared for. Tring, the Commandant of the Government Guards, had come up with James, his second-in-command, to inspect the G.G. garrisons. With them was an American, Bob Ferris, the Assistant Consul in Aden.

I had invited Ferris to come and see the archaeological sites, because Inge and I were hoping that, by stimulating the American Consulate, and through it the State Department, we would smooth the pathway for the expedition Wendell Phillips had proposed to bring over. Phillips had been silent since Inge's first, encouraging reply. Ferris would be the first American to step foot in Bayhan, and his visit should demonstrate that it was a place where Americans could survive.

I could not take my guests on the main tour I had planned for them until after the Lujna had met, its first full meeting for some months. It was now a larger body than when we had first set it up. Hussain tolerated it only under duress, doing nothing to foster its discussions and offering it no ideas, and its members spoke with embarrassment, frightened of incurring his displeasure. At this meeting some of the Musabayn shaykhs suggested, very sheepishly, that a fortnightly market should be started up in Bayhan al-Qasab; the proposal quickly received a majority vote and in due course the market was established and became a huge success. One of the Musabayn then asked if a religious teacher could be provided for the main school now that al-Alimi was having nothing more to do with it. "We cannot," he said, "expect the Holy Quran to be taught properly by a layman." Hussain replied: "Certainly that is so and a religious teacher is needed. But the new school is being built by the *hakuma*, so it is up to the *hakuma* to provide all the teachers." I did not respond, but I saw several faces cloud over, and Awadh told me later: "We were all made angry by that remark."

Hussain had now launched his campaign against me in earnest. Shortly after the Lujna meeting ended, the Musabayn members returned to the council room in a deputation, with a serious look on their faces, to speak to me in front of Hussain and Awadh. "It is about the announcement in the mosque," they said. "What announcement?" I asked. "Your notice about our visits to Aden." It took me some while to find out what they were referring to, and I did not learn the full background until I spoke to Ahmad Qassim later. It all began when the Sharif went to Aden for his official visit. On each of these annual visits he had been bringing down with him an increasingly large number of hangers-on, mostly minor Musabayn *aqils*, who would call on the British Agent in the WAP Office with the sole object of collecting a few Maria Theresa dollars. There was an item in the Protectorate budget called "Subsistence to Indigent Tribesmen" from which this time-honoured method of petty extortion was funded, but the growing abuse of the system had sucked it dry. This year Seager had asked me to spread the information around that in future visitors to the British Agent should seek an appointment through their Political Officer. I was not sure how to go about this, but wrote out a draft notice which could be promulgated by the town crier, and took it round to discuss with Sharif Awadh. Awadh said: "No. Not that way. It may annoy people. It would be better if we tell each shaykh personally in a tactful manner. Leave it to me. I will speak with them." I thanked him and left, leaving my draft with him as a reminder of what we wanted said. Awadh had

kept the paper and on his return Hussain had found it. On the Friday
prior to the Lujna meeting, Hussain had arranged for my draft notice
to be read out in the mosque during the noon-day prayers. He had
then convened a secret meeting of the Musabayn shaykhs to discuss
what action should be taken about it. The deputation now before us
was the outcome of that discussion.

It was difficult to remain calm and diplomatic in such circumstances. "Surely," I said to Hussain, "you must have seen that the
words there would cause difficulties. When you found my draft in
your papers, could you not have consulted me before having it read
out in the mosque?" Hussain, not expecting anger from me, hastily
dismissed the Musabayn, saying: "Come back tomorrow for an
answer, *ya shuyukh*"; and they left, murmuring among themselves.
As soon as they had gone, Awadh turned on his brother: "That was
a most shameful thing which you have done! You knew quite well
that we had decided the notice would not be made public in that
way. I had told you what we were doing about it. How could you
have it read out in the mosque? You did it deliberately to embarrass
us. You have shamed Groom and you have shamed me in front of
the Musabayn." Hussain, taken aback by this outburst of fury, turned
pale. Awadh stumped out, leaving us alone. Suddenly Hussain stood
up, looking down on me from his full height with an ice-cold smile.
"How could I foresee that there would be trouble over your notice?"
he said. "I fully agreed with every word which was written in it."
Then he, too, departed.

That evening, Hussain applied another pin-prick. Ahmad, my
cook, who by now must have had some inkling of what was going
on, came up to my room looking very concerned. "I went round to
the garden to get some tomatoes for you," he said. "But the Sharif's
gardener would not let me have any. He said the Sharif has ordered
him not to supply you with any more."

When the Musabayn shaykhs returned in the morning to renew
their complaint, they produced an additional one. It was remarkably
vague. "We have been told," one of them protested in an embarrassed manner, "that you are planning new things for Bayhan which
will destroy our *sharaf*."

"What things are these, *ya* Shaykh?" I asked.

"We do not know the details," he said awkwardly, "but we are told they will have serious consequences for us. *Wallah*! Our *sharaf* is important to us. Do not break it!"

"If you have real complaints you must tell me the facts, so that if necessary I can pass them on to Aden," I said. "But don't listen to rumours! Only the stupid believe stories brought by the wind."

They smiled wryly. They would not tell me who they had been speaking to, but I had a shrewd suspicion. At least my old friend Naji bin Nassir had kept himself out of their number. A few days later Ahmad Qassim told me: "The Salihi Shaykh has been to see me. He wanted you to know that the shaykhs were ordered to say those things by Sharif Hussain. They did not wish to say them, and they felt no concern about the matters they were told to raise. The Salihi Shaykh is angry about it, and says that if this *siassa* goes too far he will make their views public."

Not long after the Musabayn delegation had left me, a letter was delivered signed by the four Wakils. It was a request for me to intercede with Sharif Hussain over a bid they were making for their salaries to be increased. They had been trying to enlist my support over this for some weeks, but it was a delicate matter and, although I felt sympathy for them, I had refused to get involved. These four men, all senior members of the Ashraf and cousins of Hussain, were among the State's most important officials, yet their salary was only thirty-five dollars a month, and they could exist only by supplementing it from the fees and taxes they collected. Now their bitterness over Hussain's meanness had welled up. "We have spoken to the Sharif," the letter said, "and he has told us that he cannot consider our case without knowing the views of the *hakuma*. So now we ask you to intercede on our behalf."

I sent a brief note to Hussain saying I had a matter to discuss which had been raised by his Wakils. In earlier days he would have answered promptly, inviting me to call or very likely coming round to my *dar* straight away, but now there was no answer until he strode into my room angrily some three hours later. "The Wakils have sent me this," I said, handing him the letter.

He read it quickly and asked: "Do you think they have a good case?"

"Yes," I replied. "Their salaries are very low."

"If you think that, *ya* Groom, then write to me and tell me how much you think they ought to be paid." With that, he turned and walked out.

I composed a letter in the normal polite and formal style of Arabian correspondence, suggesting that he might consider paying his Wakils an extra twenty dollars a month. One of the Wakils, Sharif Salih bin Abdullah, had called on other business, and I asked him to take it to Hussain, which he did with alacrity. Two hours later a short note arrived, addressed jointly to me and to Sharif Awadh, bearing the names of all four Wakils as signatories. "In the past we have been receiving orders from you both as well as from Sharif Hussain," it said. "This is confusing to us. We therefore now request you in future to address any order to us through Sharif Hussain and not to send it to us directly." The names of the four Wakils at the bottom were all in the same handwriting.

The web of intrigue was becoming increasingly complicated and confused. It was a *siassa* which I could not hope to win.

For some weeks I had been thinking about my leave. Our "tour" was normally for eighteen months and I had been preparing to return to England in August, hoping that the storm in Bayhan would have abated before then. But Hussain had now clearly decided to secure my more rapid departure, and there seemed little point in prolonging my own agony. I had been informed that a new Political Officer, James Watson, had arrived in Aden on a posting from the Arab Legion and was scheduled to succeed me. That evening, with mixed feelings of remorse, failure and relief, I sent a signal to Allen: "The situation is becoming impossible. I think it will be best for everybody if Watson takes over here as soon as you can make him available."

12

Departure and Aftermath

In the rush of events I had been able to give but scant attention to my guests. Fortunately the two Government Guard officers were able to take the American Vice-Consul in hand and show him something of the town. My *dar* was their dormitory, and it was difficult in our crowded conditions to conceal the fact that relations between the ruler and the Political Officer were at breaking point. Ferris came from Texas, but he had never ridden a horse and needed to get used to a saddle before we set out on our main trip. For this purpose I took him to see the ruins at al-Haraja, while Tring and James went on with Amir Salih to inspect the post at Najd al-Mizr.

Near al-Haraja, floodwaters from the mountain-side had eroded deep channels in the high silt deposit of ancient Himyarite fields, exposing the walls of houses which had been inundated and buried twenty feet under the mud. These buildings may well have been flooded intentionally by later Himyarites undertaking some major irrigation scheme, and in such case they would date from the earliest days of the civilisation, perhaps before 500 BC, when all belonged to Sheba. It was a tantalising place where one longed to grab a spade and dig deeper into the embankments in order to discover what lay inside those buried boxes of stone.

In my frequent journeys up and down Wadi Bayhan I had examined many of the tumbled heaps of masonry which marked the remains of Himyarite constructions. Slowly the significance of some of these ancient piles had dawned on me. They were what was left of the embankments and sluices of an elaborate system of irrigation canals, which the people of Qataban had constructed to tame and control the wild flood waters. Along the eastern side of most of the lower wadi were traces of the main canal, together with remnants of ancient fields, which were often eroded into a pattern of squares following the lines of the old water channels, and now stood high above the modern level of the wadi. I handed my notes about this in due course to Wendell Phillips, and a member of his expedition, Dr Richard Bowen, was able to develop them into a detailed study a year later.*

As soon as Allen had replied to my signal and confirmed that Watson would be despatched in the near future, I left with Ferris and Rais Mubarak to tour the main archaeological sites. We headed north to the area of Jabal Khadra, and climbed a spur where stood the ruins of a fine building in a commanding position; there were graffiti, drawings and writing on the rocks, together with a small inscription (Jamme 405). In the evening we cantered on further towards Mablaqa and joined up with the main party – Amir Salih, Tring and James, with a contingent of Government and Tribal Guards. Away from his father's watching eye, the young Amir went out of his way to be friendly, but never again did he dare to criticise his father's behaviour to me.

We spent the night encamped round Bir Hajira, the only well in the vicinity. It was difficult to sleep, even had we been able to feel comfortable on the stony ground: the donkeys on which many of the party had ridden brayed incessantly throughout the night; the Amir's black pony, Nijm, broke away and attacked Tumna; the mosquitoes and sand-flies were drawn towards our Hurricane lamps and crackling fire from miles around.

With the dawn we were up and away, moving over the Mablaqa pass into Wadi Ayn. On the road we encountered the private body-guard of Seager's secret agent, the Qadhi of Marib; I suspected he was on his way with an intelligence report for Sharif Hussain, for the Qadhi had long ago given up reporting to me. "What is the news?" we asked him after the formal greetings were over. "I have news of the Dahm," he said. "Twenty of their shaykhs have been

---

* See "Irrigation in Ancient Qataban" by Richard Le Baron Bowen Jr., published in Bowen: *Archaeological Discoveries in South Arabia*, Johns Hopkins Press, Baltimore, 1958.

captured by the *nidham* and are being sent to Ta'izz to confront the Imam. Without any doubt they will all lose their heads."

We reached al-Hajb early, but could not shake off the obligations of the guest to receive entertainment, which took up the rest of the day. There was coffee to be drunk in Sharif Abdullah's *dar* while lunch was being prepared, and, having digested that, we learned that the Government Guards were boiling another sheep for supper in their fort. Next morning I took Ferris away early, before further hosts could assert themselves, for a quick visit to Hajar Hinnu az-Zurir and the necropolis in the hills north-east of it. Then we headed back towards the Mablaqa pass, lunching at Bir Jawaynah and idling through the heat of the early afternoon under tamarisk trees at the foot of the climb.

We had planned to spend the night at Bir Hajira again, and Sharif Hussain had said he would meet us there, as a way of giving *sharaf* to our guests. He reached the well with a small party just after we did, bringing with him sheep and goats for our supper, together with the pots to cook them in, but forgetting to bring any fodder for our animals. Once again Hussain became an attentive host, full of open charm, and showing no sign at all of the tense situation which existed privately between us.

We sat on Bayhan carpets under the strong light of a pressure lamp – for the Sharif believed in camping in luxury – while our supper was slaughtered, skinned, and boiled in cauldrons over a brushwood fire. There was a hazy starlight, but no moon. After the meal we conversed idly, while the mosquitoes and sand-flies resumed their assault. Hussain was in a rare good humour.

I had almost forgotten the crisis, when a series of flashes pricked the darkness to our north. Simultaneously, two thin red rods of flame suddenly shot over our heads with a sharp clap. Tracer bullets! We were under fire! Crack – thump! The bullet whipping past and then the explosion from the rifle. Crack – thump! Crack – thump!

"*Yallah!*" Rais Mubarak shouted, assuming instant command. "Put out the light! Throw water on the fire! Quickly! Quickly!"

Someone leapt to the pressure lamp and extinguished it. Our camp fire was torn asunder and its crackling flames died with a hissing protest.

Soldiers grabbed their rifles and dashed away to make a defensive ring round us. Rifle bolts clicked.

We peered outwards into the gloom, looking for more flashes.

I could only think of moving closer to Hussain, lest to stay apart might be interpreted as willingness to see him as the target of our assailants. "You should lie down," I whispered, "then they cannot see you so easily." His white clothing would make him discernible even in near darkness.

"*Asma*! Listen!" the Rais commanded. We waited tensely, straining for sounds in the surrounding blackness. Nothing moved. The sniping was not repeated.

"Anybody hurt?"

"No. They were firing too high."

"*Al-hamd l'Illah*! Praise be to God!"

"They were quite a distance away."

"*Al-hamd l'Illah*!"

"Maybe their rifles are no good."

"*Al-hamd l'Illah*!"

"Better send out a patrol to see what's there," James called out to Mubarak. Six men went off in the direction of the firing, but returned to say they could find no traces. Nothing was seen. Nothing was heard. Our attackers must have scampered away after their first volley. We relit the lamp.

Hussain seemed quite unperturbed by the incident. "Wandering Awlaqis, perhaps," he said jokingly. Mubarak was an Awlaqi. "Or maybe Yemenis making a stab in the dark out of sheer devilment."

I feared the matter was more serious than that, for there were many people in Bayhan with grievances against the Sharif. Whoever it was must have known we would be there.

Sleep was not easy that night.

At dawn, Hussain returned home with the Amir and I took Ferris northwards to visit Hayd Kuhlan. I chose a route I had not traversed before, along a track running between a line of hills on the western edge of Wadi Bayhan and the main massif from which we had emerged. Here was a wide wilderness, a stony plain with stunted thorn bushes growing among the boulders. A few miles from Bir Hajira an ancient wall spanned the plain between rock outcrops. This

19. Wadi Bayhan, looking east from the walls of Hayd Kuhlan, ancient Tumna: a camel-draw well irrigates fields overlooked by the ruins of a Qatabanian temple. In the background the sands of the Ramlat Sabatayn can just be seen encroaching into the Wadi.

20. Remains of the main temple of Tumma (Hayd Kuhlan).

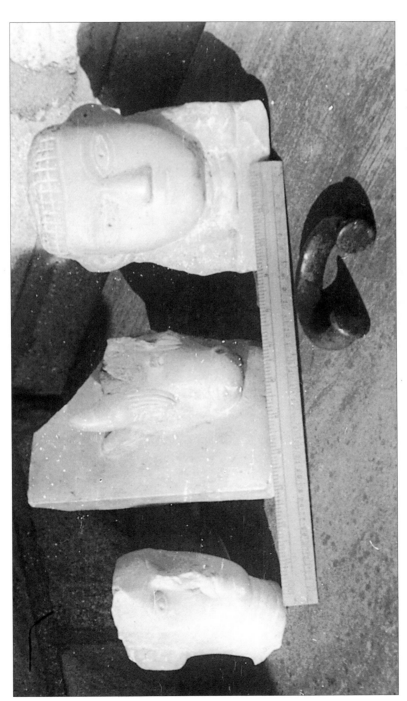

21. Alabaster carvings and an iron anklet from Qatabanian tombs near Tumna (Hayd Kuhlan). (Now in the Cambridge Museum of Archaeology.)

22. This inscription (R 3688) of c.160 BC in Shaab Labakh records rights given to the Labakh people by the Qatabanian king to collect rents in Dathina. A corner of inscription R 3689 can be seen at top right.

23. The paved Qatabanian camel road, an impressive feat of civil engineering, winds up and down the Mablaqa pass between Bayhan and Ayn. It was constructed c.210 BC to take the frankincense caravans from Shabwa and Tumna on to Marib, the capital of Sheba.

24. This giant "pebble" performs its puzzling balancing act near the summit of Jabal Raydan, the lone peak which dominates Bayhan al-Qasab and its surrounding area. Unsurprisingly, it seems to have been a sacred high place in Qatabanian times.

25. Ruins of the main temple at Hajar Hinnu az-Zurir, ancient Haribat, in Wadi Harib.

26. Shaykh Qassim bin Ahmad stands by a section of the imposing masonry of Hajar Hinnu az-Zurir, Wadi Harib.

27. Part of an ancient necropolis on the slope of Jabal Dhahat Shaqir, in the Ayn district.

28. Husn al-Aatabar, in Wadi Ayn, belonging to the Amr tribe: an interesting example of local defensive architecture.

29. A *husn* or stronghold in Wadi Bayhan.

30. A *ghayl* (spring-fed perennial running water) in the upper reaches of Wadi Bayhan.

31. Oxen were used, as elsewhere in Yemen, to amass simple but sometimes very long earth dams. These were designed to impound flood-water flowing down the wadi after rain and divert it for irrigating the fields. They required continual maintenance after floods.

32. The fort at Najd al-Mizr, the Government Guard outpost in upper Wadi Bayhan, in Arifi territory.

33. The Arifi tribe lived in upper Wadi Bayhan, many of them in the mountains but some also in the village of al-Haraja. These tribesmen are painted with indigo.

34. Gipsy dancing girls, or *shahadh*, with their troupe of musicians.

35. Indigo vats and cloth hanging up to dry in Suq Abdullah, Bayhan al-Qasab.

36. Jews in al-Haraja, upper Wadi Bayhan, weaving one of the typical Bayhan rugs. In the late 1940s, weaving was still the preserve of a small number of Jewish families in the wadi settlements, notably Bayhan al-Qasab.

37. The village of al-Haraja, in upper Wadi Bayhan, nestles among acres of eroded ancient Qatabanian fields, extending from the foreground of this picture. The flood channels cutting down through the silt reveal many traces of ancient habitation.

wall, now denoting the boundary between the territories of the Hudaybi and the Mutahiri tribes, was too low to have been a defensive work. I deduced it may have been erected to help the kings of Qataban collect their customs duties, for a camel could not get over it, so that caravans would have been forced to use the main wadi; if so, its construction was probably contemporaneous with the building of the Mablaqa pass.

We rode for three-and-a-half hours before we reached the great ruin-field of Tumna, and, after a cursory preview, entered the cool of Sharif Awadh's house on the mound for another mutton lunch. Awadh himself was elsewhere. Late in the afternoon, as soon as we could decently excuse ourselves, I took Ferris over the site. A strong northerly wind was blowing, whipping the sand into our faces in stinging gusts, blotting out all but the nearest landmarks. It was quite impossible to take photographs, and very little could be seen of the ruins. He did not seem to be very impressed.

Next morning an RAF plane was due to collect my three guests from Jaw al-Milah, but a dense haze had settled over the land. We loaded their baggage on to camels and rode over to the landing ground in case the RAF got through, but it soon became obvious that they would not. I remembered with some unease, having in mind the strain which a prolonged delay would impose on my rations, how this haze had persisted for days when I was ill with jaundice a year before. While the others returned to rest in Awadh's house, I took the opportunity for another visit, unaccompanied, to Asaylan to examine progress on the school building.

Salih and Ahmad Qassim were certainly not going to let me down, and, despite the Sharif's orders, work was clearly forging ahead. Construction techniques did not have the precision of western architecture. Here a window was placed too low. There a door was too high. One room was even five feet longer than the plan intended. But in the Protectorate one learned not to be dismayed by such minor points. Significant errors could always be corrected. The encouraging fact was that the work was still in hand and was proceeding with enthusiasm. On local standards it was turning out to be a fine building.

Sharif Salih insisted on escorting me back to Hayd Kuhlan, which gave him an opportunity to talk to me again in confidence. "Hussain continues to be angry with me," he said. "Things are worse now than ever. When you left for Ayn, he told me to remain in Bayhan al-Qasab. He would not let me accompany you. Instead he castigated me over my friendship with you. He wants the Wakils to have nothing more to do with you."

"I read that meaning in the letter you all sent me," I said.

"We did not send that letter," Salih replied. "All four of us refused to sign it. The Sharif insisted that it must be sent to you, and when we refused to put our names on it he wrote them in himself. There was nothing more we could do to stop the letter being delivered to you. We are all ashamed of what happened. Awadh is so angry about it that he refuses to see anyone."

"I was expecting to go on leave in August," I confided, "but now I have asked the British Agent if I can leave Bayhan before then."

"Oh no! You can't do that. We would not wish you to go." Salih seemed very taken aback.

"It is quite clear that Hussain does not want me here any longer," I went on. "In such case it is better for Bayhan if I depart. Then the quarrel will cease."

"We will all be very sorry." Salih was silent for a while and then he added: "It would avoid more *rabsha*, more trouble, but it would not be best for Bayhan. We all know you now. Awadh and I and the other Wakils have learned to trust you. We know your intentions are good and you understand our difficulties. Much better for Bayhan if you stay with us and help us to make Hussain a more benevolent ruler. You have discovered more about Hussain than he wants you to know and he is frightened of you; that is the basic problem. If he really cared for the people of Bayhan he would have no need to be frightened."

Cloud was still blanketing the wadi next morning, and, after an exchange of radio messages with Aden, we decided to return to the greater comforts of Bayhan al-Qasab. Amir Salih had rejoined us, and my visitors moved on ahead with him while I sorted out some last-minute difficulties over the baggage camels. There was always much bargaining to be done when camels were hired for these journeys, for every cameleer saw a government officer's luggage as a golden opportunity to make his fortune.

While I was still haggling, one of the more patriarchal Bal Harith shaykhs appeared. Shaykh Fuhayd bin Hussain's white robes, white beard, chubby round face and benign expression would have guaranteed him the role of one of the magi in any Christmas nativity play. We exchanged the long Bal Harith greeting formula in solemn tones. Then he said, in his deep, resonant voice: "*Ya* Groom! I have come for your help."

"What is it you wish, *ya* Shaykh Fuhayd?"

"I have been cheated by an Awlaqi in Aden."

"How were you cheated, *ya* Shaykh?"

"I took two of my sons down to Aden to see a doctor. They were in need of strong medicines."

"Were you cheated over the medicine?"

"No. It was not the medicines."

"What happened, then?"

"I met this Awlaqi in Shaykh Uthman. He offered me some ammunition."

"And he cheated you over it?"

"Yes indeed. He sold me one hundred and fifty rounds. It was a good price and I paid him on the spot with good silver dollars."

"It is not lawful to buy ammunition in Aden."

"Yes. I know that. But it was a very good price."

"But he cheated you?"

"Yes."

"How did he do that?"

"It was night-time. I could not see the ammunition properly."

"There was something wrong with it?"

"Yes. It was bad ammunition. Look! I have one to show you."

He produced a .303 cartridge from his belt and handed it to me. "Pull at the bullet, *ya* Groom."

I pulled and the bullet came out of the cartridge case. The case was full of sand, plugged with a wadding of paper, and the cap in it had already been fired. The bullet, no doubt dug out of the sand butt of some Aden rifle range, had been beaten roughly back into shape and crudely reinserted with glue. It must have been a very dark night.

"Were they all like that?"

"Yes. Every one. All except the one he showed me when I agreed to buy them. I know that was all right."

I felt sorry for the old man. In Aden a beduin was rapidly relieved of his money, and Fuhayd, who, like most of the Bal Harith, looked and felt out of place even in Suq Abdullah, must have been an easy prey.

"What did you do about it?"

"I went to the police."

"That was the right thing to do. But I suppose they could not find the Awlaqi?"

"Oh! They found him all right. When I told them what he had done they arrested him and put him in prison."

"So all is well then! Justice was done."

"No. That was not justice. How can you call that justice? Only the Awlaqi was given justice. I have been cheated. I paid him good dollars and all I am left with now is dud ammunition. That is why I want your help."

"What is it you expect me to do?"

"I was hoping you could arrange for the *hakuma* to replace these bad rounds with real ones. After all, that is what I paid for!"

"You were caught by your own stupidity," I said. "You should have seen that the cartridges were fakes."

"When I came to Aden," the old shaykh replied with quiet dignity, "I had to hand in my rifle and my *jambya* at the customs post. So I was relying on the *hakuma* for protection. How could I look after myself without my arms? If the *hakuma* takes away my arms then it must protect me."

"I will see what I can do," I told him, adding: "But it will be difficult and I may not be able to help you at all." I had in mind, rather vaguely, that Dick Tring might have a soft heart for the Bal Harith after his visit to their territory. An expression of hopeful happiness spread over Fuhayd's face and he turned away without another word and departed. It was not in the nature of the Bal Harith to express gratitude.

There was a further day of delay before the cloud lifted and it was possible for planes to land. That day was the eve of Ramadhan, which meant more feasting, and we were asked to lunch by Sharif Hussain and to supper by Sharif Awadh. Both saw to it that their guests were properly honoured and made sure that they ate their fill, Awadh following the custom of the country by proffering with his own hand the more succulent pieces of the carcass, laying them before his guests with beaming pleasure in little piles which seemed to increase in height the more one ate. It was difficult to reject delicacies so offered, and we much envied the Arabs their distendible stomachs. On such occasions I greatly missed Nabih.

We heard aircraft engines early next morning, and, as we stepped outside to hurry over to the landing ground, two Ansons appeared overhead. We expected them to turn, but instead they flew on down the wadi. Word that we were in Bayhan al-Qasab had not reached the RAF and the pilots had been briefed to land at Jaw al-Milah. Fortunately Sharif Salih realised what had happened as soon as he heard the aircraft over Asaylan. He saddled his horse and galloped across to Jaw al-Milah at once to divert them. The pilots were able to take off just before a sand-storm, advancing suddenly out of the desert like an enormous yellow cliff, blotted out all visibility. But we had not finished with trouble that day. At ar-Rawna, Ferris boarded one of the aircraft with a few Government Guards, but, as it was gaining speed to take off, the port engine cut out. It was halted with seconds to spare. Tring and James made good their departure in the second aircraft while the first was taxi-ing back down the side of the runway to start again. When it swung round at the end of the strip one of its wheels dug deeply into the soft sand. I mustered all the men I could lay eyes on to heave it out of the rut and push it into position. The engines were then started once more, but the port engine was spluttering wildly. The misbehaviour of an engine was always alarming, because on take-off the aircraft had to gain height rapidly in order to climb over the mountains to the south. The young pilot, a Flight-Sergeant, revved and slowed the engine for nearly half an hour trying to clear the blockage. As the plane at last soared up into the sky, there was a fervent murmuring among the onlookers. "*Bism Illah! Bism Illah! Bism Illah!*" they kept repeating. "*Bism Illah ar-Rahman ar-Raheem!* In the name of God, the Merciful, the Compassionate." They did not cease their prayers until the drone of the engines had died in the distance.

With them in the first Anson, the two Government Guard officers carried a *saluki* puppy and a baby oryx. The *saluki* is the only dog acceptable to Muslims, for the Prophet himself approved of them. The miserable curs which hung round the outskirts of the villages were pariahs beloved of no man, though their barking when anybody approached made them useful sentries at night. They scavenged for food and were kicked rather than handled, even the puppies being regarded as outcasts. Rabies and its consequences were widely feared. Normally, an Arab would touch a dog only on the top of its head, and then reluctantly: if it tried to lick him he would shrink away appalled. But the *saluki* was quite different and would be stroked and cosseted without inhibitions. This particular puppy did not come from Bayhan, which had no *saluki*s, but on hearing that James wished to acquire one, Hussain had sent a messenger over to the turbulent Abida, on the far side of the Ramlat Sabatayn, to locate one and purchase it. The young oryx, however, was of Bayhani origin, having been brought in by a Bal Harith who had, I suspected, shot and eaten the mother.

I never saw an oryx (the only Arabian antelope) in Bayhan except on this one occasion, though gazelle still abounded despite the depredations of modern rifles. There were said to be hill leopards (later, in Dhala, I was given a leopard skin and saw the low, stone huts with a trap door entrance used to catch them). Wolves and hyenas were referred to in Bayhan, but again I neither saw nor heard one, though the nickname Dawar given to my small houseboy Khamis indicated that the Bayhanis were familiar with their call. Alfred Marsack, who joined the Protectorate staff as a Political Officer later, found a rare sand-cat in the Bal Harith dunes which he presented to the London Zoo, but this too was an animal I did not come across. In earlier days there had been ostrich in the desert edges; these are featured in many Himyarite graffiti and were still hunted, according to Wyman Bury, early in this century. The ibex, too, was sought then; and in the days of the Himyarites it was hunted as part of the religious ritual. A well-known Himyarite inscription (Philby 84) on a sacred rock called al-Uqla, near Shabwa, records the sacrificing by the King of Hadramawt at one ceremony, probably in the second century AD, of 35 ibex, 82 oryx, 25 gazelle and 8 lynx, suggesting that the animal population in those early days was very much greater than in the twentieth century, even before the firearm replaced the spear as the weapon for hunting.

While the two Government Guard officers left Bayhan with their animal souvenirs, Ferris was clutching a memento which I coveted rather more. This was a fine, chalice-shaped alabaster cup, dug up, despite my objections to such despoliation, from one of the Tumna graves, and presented to him by Sharif Hussain. I hoped it would consolidate an enthusiasm for ancient South Arabia engendered by our tour round the sites, and this would in its turn expedite the arrival of Wendell Phillips.

In the event, Phillips reached Bayhan in August. I had left by then, but Inge accompanied him on his reconnaissance of Tumna, and at meetings in Aden we were able to convince him that a "dig" would be worthwhile. Phillips was not an archaeologist, but he had a flair for organising, for persuading the right experts to join him, and for extracting financial support from millionaires and large companies. Once he had decided to go ahead, there was no holding him back. Forming "The American Foundation for the Study of Man" for the purpose, he began to assemble one of the largest and best-equipped archaeological expeditions ever known.

The Foundation spent two short sessions in Bayhan: nearly two months in 1950 and a few weeks in 1951, before it went on to Marib. The main excavation was at the south gate of Tumna, where there were major inscriptions visible above the sand surface; besides discovering, among much else, two magnificent statues of bronze lions surmounted by cherubs, lying where they had fallen in the ashes of the conflagration which destroyed the city, the expedition exposed some impressive buildings of very fine masonry; these buildings were later quarried by Sharif Hussain in order to create a new palace for himself, so that nothing of them is now left. Further south, at Hajar bin Humayd, the eminent biblical archaeologist, Professor W.F. Albright, undertook a carefully controlled excavation of a small segment of the mound in order to establish a pottery sequence, vital for dating purposes. Bowen moved up and down the northern end of the wadi making his detailed analysis of the ancient irrigation works, and the expedition's geologist and surveyor, Friso Heybroek, traversed the same area making a map which was combined with my own when published. Dr Albert Jamme, an epigraphist, dealt with many of the new inscriptions which had come to light, while others, which still await publication, were taken over by Professor Honeyman of Aberdeen University, who also excavated some of the graves at Hayd bin Aqil.

The expedition owed their most intriguing discovery of all to Sharif Salih bin Nassir. One day when I was discussing what was afoot with him, Salih said: "I know a secret place where statues can be found. I have never said anything about it to anyone, because everybody will go digging there if I do. Now you have put me in an awkward position. You have asked me to help the Americans. But I feel I ought to hide this secret from them, so that you can come back yourself one day and together we will dig up what is there." I said: "No, *ya* Salih. Let them have the secret. It is for the sake of *ilm*, of science and learning, that the Americans are coming and they will share their knowledge with everybody." In due course Salih took the archaeologists to a spot on the hillside of Hayd bin Aqil. When they dug they found a deep hole hacked out of the rock, with many inscribed stones and alabaster statues buried in its sand and rubble filling. Hoping it might lead into concealed vaults, the excavators dug down the shaft for no less than sixty feet, until they reached the bed-rock bottom. This shaft could not have been a well; as it was situated in the middle of the necropolis, it had probably had a religious significance, but its real purpose has never been deduced.

The faulty Anson which took Ferris away to the sound of our prayers had brought with it James Watson, my replacement. Suddenly the end of my eighteen months in Bayhan was a reality with a date. The two rooms, one above the other, in the tower in the corner of the *hakuma* building were very much my home, and it was a strange feeling to be surrendering them to somebody else. Yet for much of the time I had not lived in them, for over the whole period of my tour I had never stayed in the same place for longer than three weeks on end. To the extent that a beduin is a nomad I had been as much a beduin as any of the Sharif's subjects. I had grown to love this unsettled life, where excitement and the unexpected lay round every corner and in which one never knew for sure where one would be next day. Despite the intractability and resentments of Sharif Hussain's behaviour over the last few weeks, I was leaving Bayhan with sadness.

The silent days of Ramadhan increased the gloom. Outside in the glare of the sunshine all was still. A group of children played; distant donkeys brayed; an occasional Bal Harith tribesman plodded slowly by leading a string of salt camels, skeleton-thin through lack of pasture; the cloth-beaters still pounded away with their mallets; but most of the population remained indoors, sleeping until the evening.

In this period of abnormal peace, I was able to talk to Watson until my throat dried up. He was a tall, angular Scot, speaking an Arabic which would sound strange to the citizens of Bayhan. He had only just joined the Colonial Service, so he was quite new to the odd complexities of our position in the Aden Protectorate, and he had much to learn.

I had intended to return to Asaylan once more in order to have another look at the school building, but when Salih bin Nassir called to say that all was well and there would be enough money to finish the job, I cancelled the arrangements. I had imposed myself enough on Salih already and a visit during Ramadhan was best avoided.

A more surprising day-time caller during this period of fasting was the Qadhi, who in latter weeks had taken to confiding his thoughts to me with an alarming frankness. Having arranged a secret meeting through Khamis at a time when Watson was not there, he entered my room furtively, checked that there was nobody within earshot, and then asked if it was true that I was leaving for good. "I cannot say," I told him. "I am just a servant of the *hakuma*, and if I am posted back here after my leave I will come here." "I would like to know," he went on, "because if what they say is true, that you are not coming back here, then I am going to leave Bayhan too. Hussain has become an oppressor. If you do not come back, there will be nobody who can stop him." It was a dramatic gesture, probably made to flatter and please me rather than because he seriously meant what he said. I was fond of the Qadhi, but I could not see him leaving Bayhan.

With Watson's arrival new policies had to be introduced. Our attempts to impose a tight control on Hussain had failed, and whatever was done next would have to be something which did not antagonise him. It had been my misfortune to have to put through measures to which he was totally opposed. He had managed to force a compromise over the new constitution at the time it was introduced which nullified much of what had been intended, although we could still claim, but only just, that it had introduced the elements of a representative government into this little Protectorate state. Control of the Bayt al-Mal was really the key issue and here, although Hussain did not yet know it, he had already won his battle. In future the British Agency would concern itself only with those books which he chose to present as the accounts of his Treasury; despite increasing subsidies, the Government would no longer be able to check that all the State revenue was included in them. From now on, the Political Officer would have little direct contact with the Wakils and other officers of the State except through the Sharif. Hussain would in fact be allowed to run his country as he chose, provided there was an outward appearance of efficiency and justice. Within a short time the Political Officer, North Eastern Area, would extend his parish to include the territories of Awdhali and Dathina and would move his office to the Dathina capital of Mudia, south of the mountain range. There was never a resident Political Officer in Bayhan again.

I was anxious to leave Bayhan with some action which might, despite his ruffled feelings, convince Hussain that we wished to further his interests. An opportunity presented itself over the question of the frontier with the Yemen. For a long time, I had concurred with Hussain's assertion that the frontier in Wadi Harib lay along the route down which I had staged my flag march the year before – from Najd Marqad past Bir Aqil and Manawa to Husn Shaqir – though it seemed unwise to support his contention that some of the houses in Darb al-Ali itself were within Bayhan territory. In Aden it had never been possible to obtain support for any of these claims, principally because nobody understood the geography of the area and no maps existed on which they could be demonsrated. Despite Hussain's bitterness about Yemeni encroachments, nobody in Aden was prepared to express firm views in case he was wrong. Now I had my map and enough facts and first-hand knowledge at my finger tips to be able to argue the case forcefully. Seager was about to return. I told

Hussain: "When I get back to Aden I am going to raise your case for building a fort and customs post at Najd Marqad." Hussain looked surprised and said: "Nobody understands the matter in Aden. I am tired of hearing the word 'No'." "This time," I said, "I think the answer may be different. I will wait until Seager gets back. Then I will explain everything to him and together we will take it up with the *hakuma* in the Secretariat. My map will help them to understand." "*Inshallah!*" Hussain said, with every sign of pessimism, but there was a new light in his eye which I had not seen for months. In due course I discussed the matter with Seager and it was agreed to give Hussain the "go-ahead". The fort was constructed while I was in England and I learned the outcome from reports in the newspapers. The Imam had reacted with unexpected vigour, sending troops to build a rival fort nearby, and attempting to blockade the pass. Warnings and ultimatums were ignored, and the RAF were called in to bomb the Yemeni positions. The whole frontier situation changed, and, while the Sharif gained his territorial rights, his Yemeni neighbours were now openly hostile. The episode did the economy of Bayhan no good at all, but it had the effect of rallying Bayhanis to the flag. Hussain was delighted with this enhancement of his *sharaf* – particularly when the Arab League took the matter to the Security Council – and was convinced by the air action that the British Government would support him to greater extremes than he had ever previously expected.

I had held reservations about the new policy of allowing the Sharif to run his country with minimal interference, for I had seen the makings of a tyrant and feared the population might rise up against him. In the event they did not, partly because of the unifying effect of the trouble on the frontier, but partly, also, because Hussain had gained in wisdom from the experiences of 1948 and 1949. Henceforward he was to become more tolerant and very much more temperate in the handling of his tribal affairs. Ultimately, economic developments assisted as well. Bayhan was connected with Aden by a road through Awlaqi, and Hussain, with a commercial acumen as sharp as his political instincts, added to the perquisites of high office in the Federal Government, where he became Minister of Defence, the substantial wealth to be derived from owning a fleet of trading lorries.

A few years after I left Bayhan, when I had finished my service in the Protectorate altogether and was working in the Aden Secretariat, my wife and I invited Hussain, with Awadh and the young Amir Salih, to supper in our Aden flat. By then they had plenty of new troubles to worry about. Suddenly changing the subject of our conversation and putting on a serious expression, Hussain said: "There is something I have been wanting to tell you for a long while. I have not had a chance to say it until now. It is about the quarrel we had when you were the Political Officer. It has been on my conscience ever since." He pulled at his beard, but this time it was an intentional movement designed to display it. "Do you see the grey hairs I have now, how many of them there are? In those days there were very few. You will understand what I mean by that. I need say no more to you than this – you were right, *ya* Groom, and I was wrong. I wish I had known it at the time. The new constitution has not destroyed my *sharaf* as I expected, and I can see now that, if I had opened the Bayt al-Mal for you, the *hakuma* would have given me more money to spend on Bayhan, not less. I wanted you to be taken away from Bayhan. I thought you were trying to turn the tribes against me. I know now that your intentions were good. I made a great mistake." His eyes, which had been staring at me intently as he spoke, looked away and he became silent. Awadh touched me on the shoulder and brought his face close to mine, saying slowly and earnestly: "What my brother has just said to you was spoken from the heart, *ya* Groom, from the heart."

I left Bayhan a week after Watson arrived. I rather envied him the detailed hand-over I was able to give him, compared with the untutored initiation I had received into the affairs of the North Eastern Area a year-and-a-half before. We had talked until we were hoarse, and there were now orderly files to which he could refer in addition to Davey's precious notebook. I had shown him around the nearby places and introduced him to a large number of people, although Ramadhan prevented our going far afield. I had booked passage on a P&O liner, the *Stratheden*, due to call at Aden in about a month's time on her voyage from Australia to London, and was prepared for an office desk until then.

Hussain had been remarkably happier and more friendly from the moment I promised to argue his case for a customs post at Najd Marqad, and accompanied us to the landing ground in a cheerful mood. I had expected a quiet send-off, for the day was now a time for fasting and sleeping, but as we crossed the wadi bed I could see a crowd assembling. "There are always a lot of people to greet the planes," I explained to Watson. "Half of them are hoping to scrounge a free flight to Aden; the other half just come to stare. Even Ramadhan won't deter them, so it seems." But this crowd was different. I realised what was happening as we emerged from the fringe of palm trees on to the open plain where the Anson was now halted. Almost everybody of consequence in Bayhan and many others besides had come to see me off. Many of them must have set out the day before, ignoring the discomforts of their fast, for this sole purpose of saying good-bye at the airfield. They were gathering in a long line, down which I shuffled to shake everybody by the hand. "*Fi aman Illah* – God be with you," they muttered as we looked into each other's eyes for the last time. Awadh and Amir Salih headed the line; the Qadhi stood next to the schoolmaster; Naji Nassir and several of the Musabayn shaykhs were there; Sharif Salih had ridden down from Asaylan with old Ali bin Munassir, his son al-Bahri and most of the Bal Harith *aqils*; the other three Wakils were in the line-up; so was Ahmad Qassim; every man in the Government Guards had turned out, and the Mulazim of the Tribal Guards had brought a contingent of his soldiers, now dressed in the beginnings of a khaki uniform provided from Tring's budget. Most astonishing of all, the young Sayyid Nassir bin Ahmad from Markha had somehow learned of my departure and trekked over from that unhappy wadi with some of his henchmen to pay his respects. "When you come back," he said, "I hope they will make you Political Officer of Markha. We are all longing for the *hakuma* to bring peace to our wadi." "*Inshallah*," I replied, thinking also of the many Himyarite sites he had promised to show me there. "*Inshallah*," he said with fervour.

Ahmad, who had for so long cooked and cared for my needs without complaint, was heaving my baggage on to the aircraft. He would come back with me, and from Aden he would take a lorry back to the Yemen to visit his family near Ta'izz before returning to the Colony to seek another employer, for I could not afford to pay him a retaining fee during my leave. Khamis, he of the hyena's voice, would stay in Bayhan and safeguard Tumna during my absence under the watchful eye of the Government Guard Rais. When I returned six months later and was posted to Dhala, Khamis led my pony over the Yemeni plateau to rejoin me in those angry mountains.

The aircraft taxied to the end of the runway, turned without mishap, gained speed with a tremendous roar and suddenly lurched upwards. Flashing past upturned faces, we flew north into the wind, so that, as we circled, still climbing, to veer south, I could see the delta of the Bal Harith and the distant, endless golden-yellow of the Ramlat Sabatayn. Below us were vast stretches of pale sand and silt in the wadi, to our west the stony entrance into Wadi Mablaqa, and ahead of us the sun glinted on the rocky pinnacle of the ancient sanctuary of Raydan. We dipped our wings in salute as we flew back over Bayhan al-Qasab, and the great crowd which had come to say farewell was now a scattering of minuscule specks crossing the wide ribbon of the *sayl* bed. The mud-brick houses and Hussain's shining white tower became smaller behind us. Then, as we gained altitude into air which was deliciously cool, the green squares of sesame around the well-heads and the darker patches of date-palm groves, which flanked the dry watercourse, began to fade, until they could no longer be distinguished in the wide expanse of the wadi. Soon I could see nothing but the sand colour of the plain, shimmering in the growing heat, and the wild brown hills converging on either side as the valley narrowed. Then there was only mountain-top and the gashes of deep gorges, sinking below us as we climbed and merging into a thickening blue haze, until at last the land of Sheba and Qataban had vanished from view, and we were alone in the dazzling white glare of a cloudless Arabian sky.

Retrospect

This is no place for a history lesson and the tangled skein of events which has engulfed South-west Arabia during the fifty years since my time in Bayhan cannot be chronicled here. For the people of all the land of Sheba the events have been momentous. Federal government, with Sharif Hussain in a leading role and with a huge increase in staff and expenditure, was developed alongside civil war in the Yemen of the Imams. For a short time Aden became a vast military base and British troops fought wars in the Protectorate which in earlier days might have been handled by a Political Officer with a few Government Guards and perhaps a bomb or two from the RAF. In 1967, in the face of revolution nurtured from outside, the British Government abandoned its distant territory, together with its promises and moral obligations, leaving both the Colony and the Protectorate to a Marxist regime. Rulers and officials who had stayed loyal to Britain were obliged to flee and many of them sought asylum in Saudi Arabia, finding refuge, like Sharif Hussain and his family, in Taif, near Makkah. For a long while there were two Yemens, North and South, and various attempts to unite them foundered. In 1991 unification was followed by parliamentary elections, but continuing tension brought the 1994 civil war, when Aden itself was besieged and captured by northern troops. A wise amnesty after that victory of the North seems finally to have created a single Yemen state acceptable to Yemenis of all persuasions, although by no means free of dissension and tribal dispute.

All the old North Eastern Area, including Bayhan, is now a part of the administrative province of Shabwa. Tarmac roads run through it and in the sand–dunes of the Ramlat Sabatayn the rusting hulks of old trucks have symbolically replaced the skeletons of dead camels. Light now comes from electricity and water from pumps and pipes. Schools and hospitals have been built. Oil has been discovered. Tourists, security permitting, can now reach places in a few hours which in my time, if it were possible to go there at all, would have taken days. Back-packers have even been seen in Bayhan, having arrived from Aden by bus.

Visitors who go there now will encounter a people who are unquestionably more prosperous and better provided for. They can visit many of the relics of ancient Qataban and Sheba, Himyar and Hadramawt, now explored and exposed by archaeologists, and find their artefacts displayed and protected in a number of museums. They will also discover that much which I have described is still as it was. But almost all of the individuals who play a part in this book are now dead. I hope that my writing will help to preserve their memory.

Appendix

Monthly Intelligence Letters
North Eastern Area

Secret

Intelligence Letter March 1949

Habili Amirate

1.   Following strong complaints by Bal Harith concerning under-representation in the Lujna, a substantial alteration has been made in that council. Five Shaykhs from the Bal Harith are now members of the Lujna and will be replaced by five others at the end of every six months. To balance the additional tribal representation, three Ashraf have also been admitted as members, so that the total membership is now twenty-two. This adjustment has satisfied all the Bal Harith except the two original members, but has induced other Bayhan shaykhs to seek membership on the grounds that their tribes and areas should be represented.

2.   Continuing lack of rain is beginning to have a noticeable effect in Bayhan, as pasture becomes more and more meagre. Small *sayl*s in the upper reaches of Wadi Dhuba and Wadi Ayn have averted hardship for bedu in those areas, but elsewhere many bedu are being compelled to bring their flocks down from the mountains to seek pasture in the wadis. Bal Harith camels are weakening from lack of pasture and this may soon seriously affect the salt trade.

3.   Hardship from lack of grain, which might have become serious, has temporarily been averted by the ineffectiveness of the Yemeni ban on grain export. There was never any shortage of grain in Yemeni areas adjacent to Bayhan and the eagerness of the Yemeni merchants to sell their stocks has led to smuggling on a large scale, to which Zaydi officials, to help their own merchants, have in many cases been prepared to turn a blind eye. This

was particularly the case in Harib, where the people of Manawa have for some weeks been subsisting on smuggled grain. Ahl Shurayf have now, however, obtained official permission from the Imam to purchase grain freely in Darb al-Ali, an order which, when it can be put into effect, should be welcome to the Darb al-Ali officials, who have been unable to collect customs duty on the grain being smuggled out. Grain imports from the Yemen, both official and unofficial, should be effective in staving off threatening famine conditions, but the situation now depends entirely on the long-delayed summer *sayls*.

4.   A serious blow was struck at Bayhan prosperity when it was learned that an order from the Imam had reached Bayda banning the import into Yemen of indigo-dyed cloth. Cloth dyeing is Bayhan's biggest industry and an essential of the country's economy, since it provides, in normal times, the means with which to purchase Yemeni grain. The dyed cloth is traded solely with Yemen and if continued the ban will consequently mean the cessation of the industry, affecting several hundred people whom it employs. Attempts are being made to induce the Imam to lift the ban, but in case these are without avail consideration is being given to finding other employment for those affected. The matter was discussed at the monthly meeting of the Lujna and recommendations were put forward by that body for the Government's consideration. These asked for assistance in the development of other industries and in placing some of the unemployed in agriculture, but no further action is being taken until the intentions of the Imam are clear and until the Sharif of Bayhan has been able to discuss the matter in Aden. Meanwhile the industry continues to function while hope and stocks of cloth remain.

5.   The long-delayed renewal of the tribal truce between Bayhan on the one hand and Harib, Marib and Juba on the other came into effect on 3 March when the necessary documents were received from the Amil of Harib and signed. The truce is to last a further year.

6.   The Yemeni grain and cloth bans and greatly increased customs duties, by seriously hampering Bayhani-Yemeni trade, have led to a considerable reduction in Bayhan customs receipts, the State's most important source of income. Measures to counter this have included the raising of the salt export tax by 5 buqash to 15 buqash[*] per camel load and a stringent watchfulness over minor Bayhan customs officials to stamp out increasing petty corruption. It is later hoped to revise certain customs duties

---

[*] The *buqsha* (plural *buqash*) was a Yemeni coin, forty of which equalled one Maria Theresa dollar. They were minted, very crudely, in the Yemen and used in adjacent areas of the Protectorate.

and instal further customs points at points as yet unguarded.

7.   On 13 March a small raiding party of Dahm and Abida looted thirteen camels belonging to a combined Sulaymani, Sahaqi and Hammami caravan from a point in the desert a few miles east of Asaylan. The raiders had previously watered at Bir Aqil, in Wadi Harib. Shaykh Muhammad bin Muhsin Aydrus al-Sulaymani, with a deputation of Bal Harith and Ashraf, has been sent to Marib to seek the assistance of the Amil of Harib (who has more control over the sections of Dahm concerned than the Amil of Jawf) in securing the restoration of the camels.

8.   On 26 March it was reported that Dahm in Wadi Abida had killed a Bayhani of Ahl Abdul Qadir and looted his camel. Details are awaited.

9.   Owing to the widespread grain shortage in areas east of Bayhan, large numbers of tribesmen entered Bayhan during the month with their families to seek grain in exchange for labour, mainly preparing dykes and canals for the floods. It is estimated that over four hundred persons thus arrived in Wadi Bal Harith alone, drawn from Nisiyin, Kurab, Sahaqi, Qaramish, Awlaqi, Fashr and many other tribes. With the end of flood preparation work they are now beginning to leave.

10.   An attempt is being made to cope with the widespread eye diseases endemic amongst Bal Harith. No trained dispensers are now available in Bayhan, but an intelligent Bayhani has been trained in the elementary knowledge necessary for him to apply simple medicines for the eyes and he is now practising among the Bal Harith under the auspices of the local Wakil. The experiment will last for a month and if successful will be renewed.

11.   Work proceeds apace on the new mosque being built in Suq Abdullah, which it is intended shall be the largest and finest in the Protectorate. A new technique of baking bricks in a kiln has been introduced by artisans from Bayda and its employment has allowed Bayhan builders, for the first time, to break away from the limitations of the traditional mud and stone design.

12.   The property of the Ashraf of Marib looted by a Rajihi (see last month's Intelligence Letter) was returned through the assistance of the Rajihi Shaykh, but the thief is still at large.

Markha

13.   With attention rivetted on Government's political action in Wadi Khawra, on the result of which many tepid loyalties will be decided one way or the other, Markha has remained comparatively quiet throughout

the month. A certain amount of underhand Yemeni intrigue continues, however, probably as a political adjunct to the military moves against the Rassassi Sultan.

14.   Shaykh Ad-Dawshal of Ahl Khamis Nisiyin visited PONEA to ask for further Government assistance in securing the release of his hostages held in Yashbum. Measures were first taken at Ahl Khamis request (see the January Intelligence Letter) but the effect of the threats then applied was to induce Ruways bin Muhsin to shackle the boy's legs and keep him permanently in prison. Release was adamantly refused as a retaliation, it was claimed, to the Ahl Khamis breach of good faith in resorting to Government for assistance.

Upper Awlaqi

15.   Attempts to persuade certain members of the Ahl Dayyan to cease sheltering the families, property and money of the Rassassi Sultan continued throughout the month with no result. Letters sent by PONEA produced only rude retorts and all accounts agreed that the Dayyanis were becoming increasingly swollen-headed, a fact which owes much to the machinations of the Rassassi Sultan. On 17 March an ultimatum from the British Agent was dropped on Wadi Khawra by an RAF plane ordering Dayyanis to expel the Sultan's relatives and followers and to return his property, grain and money to the Yemen by 24 March. No attempt to obey this was made by the Dayyanis, who were in fact reported to have responded by forming a closer alliance with the Rassassis, but the threatened air action was delayed for a period to allow a delegation of Awlaqi Shaykhs then in Aden to make their own efforts to persuade their fellow tribesmen to comply. Meanwhile the Rassassi Sultan remains in Shaab Nimar, from where he frequently visits Khawra Suq, and his relatives have been more widely distributed throughout the wadi. Both Dayyanis and Rassassis are reported to have been purchasing incendiary ammunition with which to oppose air action. Yemeni action against the Rassassi Sultan appears to have ceased entirely and no reply was received to the Rassassi proposal for peace terms to be mediated in Bayhan.

Secret

Intelligence Letter May 1949

Habili Amirate

1.   The Amir and Sharif of Bayhan remained in Aden throughout the month on business following their official visit to His Excellency the Acting Governor. Sharif Awadh bin Ahmad continued to act as Regent in their absence.

2.   There has been a slight improvement in the economic position of the country during the month. Small *sayls* watered about a quarter of the fields under flood irrigation while scattered rain in southern and eastern districts has restored pasturage to a sufficient abundance in those areas. In the Ashraf and Bal Harith areas to the north, however, there has been no *sayl* and only occasional showers. Harithi camels are weak and only about half the usual number are working on the salt trade. Unless rain in the next few weeks restores desert pasturage it is likely that the Bal Harith will be compelled to kill off a substantial proportion of their stock. The grain situation has eased owing to the gradual relaxation of Yemeni restrictions. The Yemeni grain ban is still officially in force, but grain is nevertheless being exported into the Protectorate with the full knowledge and assistance of local Yemeni officials, who collect customs duties on it.

3.   A locust swarm entered Bayhan from the north on 14 May, but moved south-west into Yemeni territory without settling. A few stragglers remain in the Nuqub-Asaylan area, where the damage they are doing is outweighed by their value as food. It is reported that the main swarm is now breeding in Rassassi territory and measures are in hand to combat them should they return.

4.   The economic situation among the Bal Harith induced a considerable number of that tribe to avoid paying customs duties on salt. It is likely that this large-scale smuggling was secretly encouraged by the Shaykhs. The matter could have been dealt with quietly and firmly, but high-handed action by the Sharif of Bayhan (directing from Aden) unfortunately inflamed the Bal Harith to a point where trouble was dangerously close. Against the advice of his Wakil in Asaylan, eighty-five Harithi smugglers were arrested on the Sharif's orders and incarcerated in the tiny prison at Asaylan. Among these were many guiltless persons. Such action angered the Bal Harith understandably, and it was found necessary to reinforce the Asaylan garrison with extra Tribal Guards and a party of Ashraf to guard

against likely disorder. PONEA proceeded to Asaylan on 22 May and after talks with the Harithi shaykhs the temper of the Bal Harith eased. The smugglers are being fined the maximum fine of ten times the customs duty they have avoided paying and about half the 150 Harithis involved have now paid. Steps are being taken to bring in those of the remainder who have fled, while those who protest their innocence are being given a fair trial in Bayhan al-Qasab before the Regent. To counter the ill-feeling this matter has caused and in order to assist the Bal Harith in their very real economic difficulties, it has been decided to relieve them from paying all customs duty on salt for the duration of Shaaban.

5.   Relationship with the Yemen was satisfactory during most of the month, although latterly Yemeni movements in the Markha border area caused considerable concern. The Governor of Bayda, having occupied and taxed Bani Yub country, proceeded to try and round up those tribes which he considered pendants of the Bani Yub for the same purpose. Among these were the Ahl Dhayfallah, a small bedu tribe lying round Bir ad-Dimna below the Aqaba of ar-Riba. This tribe, which has little or no connection with the Bani Yub and has admitted the authority of the Sharif of Bayhan and paid taxes to him, was visited by *nidham* (Yemeni soldiers) with orders to secure the payment of taxes to the Imam. The tribesmen promptly fled into the heart of Bayhan and protested to the Regent and the Political Officer. The matter is being taken up through official channels. Apart from this no serious frontier incidents were reported during the month.

6.   The monthly meeting of the Lujna took place on 14 May, but, owing to the absence of the Amir, the Sharif and the Political Officer, no business of importance was discussed.

Wadi Markha

7.   The inhabitants of Markha were seriously alarmed towards the end of the month by Yemeni troop movements in the Rassassi–Bani Yub border area. Most of those living adjacent to the border fled down the Wadi in expectation of an imminent invasion and not until a reassuring letter was dropped by plane did they return to their homes. The prime objective of the Yemeni movements appears to have been to take a grip on Bani Yub country and areas of Rassassi country not yet controlled and for this purpose large numbers of troops were quartered in Nuqaq, Halhal, Am Haydar and Am Aajar. Having done this and collected taxes (the essence of Zaydi administration) ash-Shami directed his attention to certain tribes which he falsely believed to be Bani Yub. These included the Ahl

Dhayfallah (see para 5 above) and the Ahl Kushr, a tribe living within the Protectorate in hills to the north of Wadi Markha. This action has exaggerated fears in Markha itself. It is not believed that the Zaydis intend to occupy Wadi Markha, but at the same time there are reasons for suspecting that their action may be followed by intensive political intrigue in the Wadi. The intention behind the attempted occupation of Kushri country is probably to cut decisively the important trade route between Markha and Bayhan, which passes through the ar-Riba pass, and it seems likely that a customs post will later be installed there. The pass itself is admittedly in Bani Yub country.

8.   Small *sayls* were reported in the upper reaches of Wadi Markha and eastern parts of the Wadi have received light rain.

Hammami

9.   The ban on Hammamis entering Bayhan, imposed as a result of the Mubarak Salih–bint Issa dispute, has caused concern in Bayhan, where trade has been hit, and in Upper Awlaqi, where our action is interpreted as a sign that Government intend later to establish the Sharif of Bayhan as their ruler there. The Hammami themselves have complained bitterly against the order, avowing that this matter is purely the concern of the Ahl Hussain section. Hammamis generally are hard hit as they badly need grain from Yemen, which they can only reach by passing through Bayhan. There have consequently been several Hammami attempts at smuggling grain through the north of Wadi Bal Harith and two Hammamis have been arrested. There is some fear that grain shortage and resultant hunger might make the Hammami smugglers desperate, when there could be a serious risk of clashes between Hammamis and Bayhani anti-smuggling patrols.

10.   Rain is reported to have fallen lightly in Hammami country.

Upper Awlaqi

11.   Some rain reported from most districts, but the grain situation is said to be serious.

12.   The incident in March, when Ahl Jebah kidnapped two women of Ahl Umm Salab, is still a major topic of conversation throughout Upper Awlaqi and serious trouble sooner or later is said to be regarded as inevitable. It is reported that the Awlaqi Sultan is biding his time in order to study Government's attitude towards the matter. There is little question of the matter being dropped without retaliation.

Khawra

13.   No reports have been received of Khawra reaction to our message informing them that the bombing of their Wadi would not take place.
14.   A small *sayl* is said to have watered the majority of the fields in Wadi Khawra.

Sulaymani

15.   A letter was submitted to the Amil of Bayda requesting his assistance in the matter of the looting of thirteen Sulaymani camels by Dahm (as reported in March). No reply has yet been received.

Glossary

ahlan wa sahlan	Welcome.
amīl	Governor.
aqāl	Double rope ring used to hold the *kufiyah* on the head (and to hobble a camel).
aqīl (pl. *uqāl*)	Wise man. The shaykh of a tribal section.
aqira	(Bal Harith) Money given as a token payment when seeking a favour.
askari	Soldier.
asad	Lion.
asha	Supper.
ath-thābat as-siāssi	Political Officer.
ayb	Shame, stigma.
ayn	Spring (of water).
aysh wa milh	Bread and salt. To eat bread and salt with someone is to become that person's guest and hence to receive his protection.
aywa	Yes. Yes indeed.
batūl	Ploughman. Labourer. Serf.
bishār	(Bal Harith) Trial by ordeal. The tongue of the accused is touched with a piece of red hot iron; if it blisters he is guilty.
bir	Well.
bism Illah	In the name of God.
buqsha (pl. *buqāsh*)	Yemeni bronze coin (40 to 1 Maria Theresa dollar).

dār	A fortified tower house.
dawar	Hyena.
dawla	The State (as opposed to the *Hakūma*).
dawm	An edible fruit like a very small dried up cherry produced by the *ilb* tree.
dhakhr	Treasure.
dīra	Tribal grazing area.
diwān	Assembly and entertaining room.
diya	Blood money paid to the family of a murdered man.
dustūr	Constitution.
fūtah	A length of cotton cloth worn round the waist like a kilt. A loincloth.
ghayl	Spring-fed perennial water.
gilgil	Sesame oil.
hajj	Pilgrimage.
hākim	Wise man. Judge.
hākim urfi	Common law judge.
al-hamd l'Illah	Praise be to God.
hammal	A desert shrub.
harath	(To plough). A person appointed to decide a dispute over land or water rights.
hasham	Blood money paid to the protector of a murdered man.
hakūma	Government. The British administration based in Aden.
husn	Fortified tower house (see also *dār*).
ilb	Syrian thorn, *Zizyphus spina-christi*, a common tree of the wadis, also known elsewhere in Arabia as *sidr*. Its branches and trunk are used for timber, its leaves as fodder and its berries for food.

jambya	Arab dagger with a curved blade.
kassar sharaf	Something which breaks a person's respect or dignity. A shaming action or remark seen as an insult.
kawr	Literally a plateau. The name used for the spectacular, high cliff in the Awdhali area at the top of which is the Yemeni plateau.
kufiyah	Beduin head cloth.
libān	Sun-dried mud brick.
Lujna	(In Bayhan) Executive Council.
Majlis	Council.
Majlis al-Uqāl	(In Bayhan) The Council of Chiefs.
al-Majlis al-Tanfidhi	Executive Council.
masūb	A staple dish in Bayhan made out of wheat dough and soused with sesame oil (*simsim*).
māshallah	Heavens above!
mātamad	(In the Protectorate) The British Agent.
Mishqas	(In Bayhan) Desert tribes east of Bayhan.
muezzin	Official in a mosque who calls the faithful to prayer.
mulazim	Lieutenant (Military rank used in the Government and Tribal Guards).
mushadda	Turban cloth.
nasrāni	Non-believer. British officers in the Protectorate.
nayb	Sergeant (in Government and Tribal Guards). Deputy. Local governor.
nidhām	Yemeni soldiers.
qadhi	Religious judge; judge of *Sharīa* law.
qāt	Narcotic leaves from the *qat* tree (*Catha edulis*) which are chewed as a stimulant.

rabsha	Trouble.
rafīq	Literally companion. An escort providing safe conduct.
rak	*Salvadora persica*, a common desert shrub.
riyal	Maria Theresa silver dollar (the main coin in circulation).
ryot	Non-tribesmen. Peasants.
sayyar	A guide giving safe conduct through hostile territory.
sayyid (pl. *sāda*)	A descendant of the Prophet, through his younger grandson Hussain. Influential as mediators in South-west Arabia.
sayl	Flash flood. The torrent bed of a wadi.
shaab	A narrow valley or ravine. A valley without a watercourse.
shahadh	Literally beggars. Gipsy dancers and entertainers.
sharab	Drink.
sharaf	Respect. Prestige. Self-respect.
Sharīa	Islamic law based on the Qur'an and Hadith.
sharīf (pl. *ashrāf*)	A descendant of the Prophet, through his elder grandson Hassan. Ashrāf were in wide demand as mediators and peacemakers and, as a result, have produced many ruling families in Arabia.
shayba	Old man. Arab nickname for Seager.
shaykh (pl. *shuyūkh*)	Tribal chief. Title given to an eminent person. *Shaykh min shuyukh* – head shaykh of a tribe with sections.
shaytān	Devil.
siassa	Politics. Political intrigue.
simsim	Sesame oil.
sūq	Market. Bazaar area.
tayyāra	Aeroplane.

thābat	Officer.
thābat as-siassa	Political Officer.
thullum	Oppression.
uhda	Contract. Mortgage. In Bayhan this specifically relates to land mortgaged by a peasant–landowner to a merchant for a loan of money or in payment of a debt.
urf	Common law; customary law as opposed to Sharīa law.
ushur	Crop tax (one tenth of total crop).
wajh	A pledge (usually written) given to someone as a guarantee of safety.
wakīl	(In Bayhan) Provincial governor.
wallah!	By God!
ya ayba	A formal admission of shame and guilt used in settling feuds (Bal Harith).
Zaydi	The religious sect of the Imams. Used loosely from earliest days to describe any of the Imam's officials and adherents, including his troops.

Bibliography

Arnaud, T.J. and Mohl, J., "Relation d'un voyage à Marib (Saba) entrepris en 1843", *Journal asiatique*, Vol. 4, 1845.

Beeston, A.F.L., *Epigraphic South Arabian Calendars and Dating*, London, Luzac, 1956.
– *Qahtan – Studies in Old South Arabian Epigraphy*, Fascicule 2, London, Luzac, 1971.

Belhaven, Lord (Hon. R.A.B. Hamilton), *The Kingdom of Melchior*, London, John Murray, 1949.

Bidwell, Robin, *The Two Yemens*, London, Longman, and Colorado, Westview, 1983.

Bowen, Richard and Albright, Frank P. (eds.) *Archaeological Discoveries in South Arabia*, Baltimore, Johns Hopkins Press, 1958.

Bury, G. Wyman ("Abdulla Mansur"), *The Land of Uz*, London, Macmillan, 1911.

Cleveland, Ray L., *An Ancient Arabian Necropolis: Objects from the Second Campaign in the Timna' Cemetery*, Baltimore, Johns Hopkins Press, 1965.

Crouch, Michael, *An Element of Luck*, London, Ratcliffe Press, 1993.

Doe, Brian, *Southern Arabia*, London, Thames and Hudson, 1971.
– *Monuments of South Arabia*, Cambridge, Falcon/Oleander, 1983.

Fakhri, Ahmad, *An Archaeological Journey to Yemen (March–May 1947)*, Cairo, 1952.

Glaser, Edouard, *Reise nach Marib*, ed. D.H. Müller and N. Rhodokanakis, Vienna, 1913.

Grohmann, Adolf, *Kulturgeschichte des Altes Orients – Arabien*, Munich, Beck'sche Verlagsbuchhandlung, 1968.

Groom, Nigel, "A New Map of 'Pre-Islamic South-west Arabia'", *Proceedings of the 8th Seminar, Oxford, 1974*, London, Seminar for Arabian Studies, 1975.
– "The Northern Passes of Qataban", *Proceedings of the 9th Seminar, London, 1975*, London, Seminar for Arabian Studies, 1976.
– "The Frankincense Region", *Proceedings of the 10th Seminar, Cambridge, 1976*, London, Seminar for Arabian Studies, 1977.
– *Frankincense and Myrrh – A Study of the Arabian Incense Trade*, London, Longman, and Beirut, Librairie du Liban, 1981.
– "The *Periplus*, Pliny and Arabia", *Arabian Archaeology and Epigraphy*, Vol. 6, Copenhagen, Munksgaard, 1995.
– "The Roman Expedition into South Arabia", *Bulletin of the Society for Arabian Studies*, No. 1, London, 1996.
– "Les parfums de l'Arabie", in exhibition catalogue *Yémen au pays de la reine de Saba'*, Paris, Institut du Monde Arabe/Flammarion, 1997.
– "The Secrets of Jabal Raydan", *Bulletin of the Society for Arabian Studies*, No. 6, London, 2001.
– "Trade, Incense and Perfume", in exhibition catalogue *The Queen of Sheba: Treasures from Ancient Yemen*, London, British Museum, 2002.
– "Maymar's Ring", *Bulletin of the Society for Arabian Studies*, No. 7, London, 2002.

Halévy, Joseph, "Rapport sur une mission archéologique dans le Yémen", *Journal asiatique*, 6th series, XIX, Jan.–June 1872, pp.5–98, 129–266 and 489–547, Paris, 1872.

Harding, G. Lankester, *Archaeology in the Aden Protectorate*, London, HM Stationery Office, 1964.

Helfritz, Hans, *Land Without Shade*, London, Hurst and Blackett, 1935.

Hickinbotham, Sir Tom, *Aden*, London, Constable, 1958.

Ingrams, Doreen, *A Survey of Social and Economic Conditions in the Aden Protectorate*, Aden, Government of Aden, 1949.

Jamme, Albert, *Sabaean Inscriptions from Mahram Bilqis (Marib)*, Baltimore, Johns Hopkins Press, 1962.

Johnstone, Sir Charles, *The View from Steamer Point*, London, Collins, 1964.

Kitchen, K.A., *Documentation for Ancient Arabia, Part I: Chronological Framework and Historical Sources*, Liverpool, Liverpool University Press, 1994.
– *Documentation for Ancient Arabia, Part II: Bibliographical Catalogue of Texts*, Liverpool, Liverpool University Press, 2000.

Landberg, le Comte de, *Arabica V*, Leiden, Brill, 1898.

Meulen, D. van der, *Aden to the Hadramaut*, London, John Murray, 1947.

Naval Intelligence Division, *Western Arabia and the Red Sea*, London, Admiralty, 1946.

Philby, H.St J.B., *Sheba's Daughters*, London, Methuen, 1939.

Phillips, Wendell, *Qataban and Sheba*, London, Gollancz, 1955.

Pirenne, Jacqueline, *Le royaume sud-arabe de Qataban et sa datation*, Louvain, Publications Universitaires, Bibliothèque du *Muséon*, Vol. 48, 1961.

Robin, Christian, "Sheba dans les inscriptions d'Arabie du Sud", *Supplément au Dictionnaire de la Bible*, Paris, Letouzey et Ané, 1996.

Ryckmans, Gonzague, "Inscriptions sud-arabes", Louvain, *Le Muséon*, 62, 1–2, 1949.

Trevaskis, Kennedy, *Shades of Amber*, London, Hutchinson, 1968.

Van Beek, Gus W. et al., *Hajar bin Humeid. Investigations at a Pre-Islamic Site in South Arabia*, Baltimore, Johns Hopkins Press, 1969.

Wissmann, Hermann von, and Höfner, Maria, *Beiträge zur historischen Geographie des vorislamischen Südarabischen*, Akademie der Wissenschaften und der Literatur, 1952.

Wissmann, Hermann von, "Himyar Ancient History", *Le Muséon*, Vol. 77, 3–4, pp.429–97, Louvain, 1964.

Index

For reasons of space the word *bin* ("son of"), normally used in South-west Arabia in personal names, is omitted in this Index. Similarly the word *Ahl*, frequently used in front of a tribal name and signifying "people of", is also generally omitted. In alphabetising, *Ahl* where retained, and the Arabic definite article (*al-* and variants), are ignored.